HIGH-FLYING WOMEN

A WORLD HISTORY OF FEMALE PILOTS

ALAIN PELLETIER

© Alain Pelletier 2012

All rights reserved. No part of this publication may be reproduced, stored in a retrieval system
or transmitted, in any form or by any means, electronic, mechanical, photocopying, recording
or otherwise, without prior permission in writing from the publisher.

First published in the French language in October 2011 by E-T-A-I as *Les Filles D'Icare*.
This English-language edition published in July 2012.

Translated by Ken Smith

A catalogue record for this book is available from the British Library.

ISBN 978 0 85733 257 8

Library of Congress control card no 2012933487

Published by Haynes Publishing,
Sparkford, Yeovil, Somerset BA22 7JJ, UK
Tel: 01963 442030 Fax: 01963 440001
Int. tel: +44 1963 442030 Int. fax: +44 1963 440001
E-mail: sales@haynes.co.uk
Website: www.haynes.co.uk

Haynes North America Inc.,
861 Lawrence Drive, Newbury Park, California 91320, USA

Printed and bound in the USA by Odcombe Press LP,
1299 Bridgestone Parkway, La Vergne, TN 37086

At a meeting, sometime in 1910...
A man and a woman...
...sharing in the same lure of the skies. (LoC)

Contents

Aviation is many things to different people; a sport, a hobby, a profession; but it knows no gender and is an equal playing field for any person who dreams of a freedom that those bound to the ground do not comprehend. In fact, the very same year in which the first female was awarded a pilot's licence, another five women added their name to that exclusive list – an incredible statistic when you consider the traditional role played by women in society in 1910.

However, in those early days it took true courage and bravery to fly those wood and fabric machines. So much about aviation was learned through experience rather than theory, and the consequences of failing to understand or learn quickly were dire. The number of aviation pioneers, male and female, who died pursuing their dream indicates the dangers.

But the lessons they highlighted have been learned by pilots ever since, and it is right that we should look back through the last century and remember those individuals who stepped outside their comfort zone and entered the world of flying. Their reasons for doing so are unfortunately often now lost, but the evidence of their tenacity, bravery and, ultimately their achievements, should be celebrated by all.

This book does exactly that. It records and honours the names of the women who have achieved something great or something small, but always something significant, in the world of aviation. It is important to remember that for every named aviatrix in this book there is another unnamed one who achieved something great that has now sadly been forgotten.

I take my hat off to each and every one of them, for they have carved the way ahead of me – and in doing so they have made my path all the easier to travel along.

Flt Lt Kirsty Stewart
April 2012
Red Arrows 2010-11

Foreword

Our memories can be selective, but this is often because the sources of our information are themselves highly selective. The media make choices about what to tell us and only a tiny fraction of what we've been told remains imprinted on our collective memory. The years pass, memories fade, pictures blur and things disappear. Today, the man in the street would be hard pressed to name just three aviatrixes who have influenced the history of flying. Yet 70 or 80 years ago, names such as Maryse Hilsz, Maryse Bastié, Amelia Earhart, Jean Batten, Amy Johnson, Hélène Boucher and Jacqueline Cochran were at the front of everyone's minds and on the front pages of many newspapers. In this book I have attempted to retrieve these women from the obscurity into which the passage of time has threatened to cast them. I have also taken the opportunity to invoke the memory of other female flyers who were known in their time, but whose fame has been even more ephemeral – perhaps making the headlines for no more than a few days, or barely known outside their own country. And what about all those other anonymous aviatrixes – and there were thousands of them – who have left not a single trace in the archives? Of course, it would have been an impossible task to include them all; there are simply too many. Despite this obvious constraint, the book attempts to go beyond the celebrities and celebrate the flying careers of numerous aviatrixes who, while less well known, have nonetheless made their contribution to the history of aviation.

So let us take a moment to examine, one by one, all those faces from days gone by. They all play a full part in the heritage on which aviation, as we know it today, has been built.

Who would have believed it a few decades ago: an entirely female aircrew? These 12 women make up the crew of one of the C-17A Globemaster IIIs of no. 36 Squadron, the Royal Australian Air Force. (RAAF)

Introduction

On 2 September 1910, Hélène Dutrieu, flying a Farman biplane like this, made the 50km flight from Blankenberge, Ostend, to Bruges. (Library of Congress)

Dutrieu, Harriet Quimby, Katherine Stinson, Blanche Scott, Ruth Law, Bessie Coleman, Adrienne Bolland, Florence Klingensmith, Laura Ingalls, Liesel Bach, Lady Heath, Lady Mary Bailey, Louise Thaden, Thea Rasche, Ruth Rowland Nichols, Elinor Smith, Ruth Elder, Carina Negrone, Paulina Denisovna Ossipenko, Hanna Reitsch, Marcelle Choisnet, Maryse Bastié, Léna Bernstein, Amy Johnson-Mollison, Anne Morrow-Lindbergh, Marga Von Etzdorf, Maryse Hilsz, Beryl Markham, Elly Beinhorn, Jean Batten, Elisabeth Lion, Helen Richey, Eugénie M. Shakhovskaya, Cecil W. "Teddy" Kenyon, Pauline Gower, Nancy Harkness Love, Maria Ivanovna Dolina, Amélia Earhart, Hélène Boucher, Jacqueline Cochran, Jacqueline Auriol, Eileen Marie Collins, Anna Walker, Ellen Church, Clara Adams, Harriet Quimby, Marjorie Stinson, Mrs Eyman, Fay Gillis, Virginia Waibel, Eleanor Blevins, Aniwegi Boudinot, Helen Clifford, Janett Moffett, Bernetta Miller, Ruth Fontes, Jeanne Pallier, Blossom Miles, Emily Schaeffer, Raymonde de Laroche, Amelie Beese, Hélène Dutrieu, Harriet Quimby, Katherine Stinson, Blanche Scott, Ruth Law, Bessie Coleman, Adrienne Bolland, Florence Klingensmith, Laura Ingalls, Liesel Bach, Lady Heath, Lady Mary Bailey, Louise Thaden, Thea Rasche, Ruth Rowland Nichols, Elinor Smith, Ruth Elder, Carina Negrone, Paulina Denisovna Ossipenko, Hanna Reitsch, Marcelle Choisnet, Maryse Bastié, Léna Bernstein, Amy Johnson-Mollison, Anne Morrow-Lindbergh, Marga Von Etzdorf, Maryse Hilsz, Beryl Markham, Elly Beinhorn, Jean Batten, Elisabeth Lion, Helen Richey, Eugénie M. Shakhovskaya, Cecil W. "Teddy" Kenyon, Pauline Gower, Nancy Harkness Love, Maria Ivanovna Dolina, Amélia Earhart, Hélène Boucher, Jacqueline Cochran, Jacqueline Auriol, Eileen Marie Collins, Anna

The Pioneers

On Christmas Day, Saturday 25 December 1909, *Flight* magazine published a photograph of a group of aviators on a training session at Châlons airfield, in France. Among the 20 or so pictured were four women, a fact that could easily have encouraged the false belief that it was not unusual for women to experience the joys of flying. As it happens, these four represented almost the total number of those involved in aviation at the time. In the middle of the group, wrapped up in a thick, black, knitted coat, her hands thrust into her pockets, was Elise de Roche, better known as Baroness Raymonde de Laroche, the first woman to receive a pilot's licence, on 8 March 1910. Her maiden flight – the first ever by a woman – had been on 22 October of the previous year, on this very airfield. By the end of 1910, five further names had been added to the shortlist of qualified female pilots: three Frenchwomen, Marthe Niel, Marie Marvingt and Jeanne Herveu; one Belgian, Hélène Dutrieu, and a Russian, Lydia Zvereva. Others soon followed (see p. 22), but the list of qualified male pilots grew a great deal faster.

The first woman to take to the air, at Turin on 8 July 1908, was Thérèse Peltier, a French sculptor who flew aboard a Voisin biplane piloted by her companion, Léon Delagrange. She was soon followed by other women, such as Edith Berg, the first American woman to go aloft as a passenger, and Mabel Cody, the wife of Samuel Franklin Cody, who was the first British female passenger. Thérèse Peltier's flying career was cut short, however, when Léon Delagrange was killed while flying a Blériot monoplane at Bordeaux on 4 January 1910. Overcome by fear, Thérèse vowed never to go in an aeroplane again. These flights, of course, proved very little. What was true, though, was that a small group of women were keen to show that they could take the controls of an aeroplane and fly it just as well as any man.

So what was it about flying that attracted these intrepid women? There was undoubtedly the thrill of powered flight, but also the opportunity to challenge a certain masculine view that seized any pretext to denigrate women, who, it was believed, 'lacked coolness and judgment'[1]. In fact, some women had already built themselves a reputation in cycle, motorbike and car racing. Raymonde de Laroche, who held pretensions to being both a sculptor

The third Frenchwoman to become a qualified pilot, Marie Marvingt (1875-1963) was described as 'wedded to danger' because of the number of crashes in which she was involved. (Library of Congress)

A period postcard showing Marie Marvingt at the controls of her monoplane, Antoinette, at the St-Etienne Air Meeting, in August 1911. (Champiroc and La Bertraudière)

and an actress, was just 23 years old when Charles Voisin, who was not entirely indifferent to her charms, offered to teach her to fly. By 8 March 1910, she had her pilot's licence. Although the first female, she was only the 36th French person to gain a pilot's licence. The Belgian, Hélène Dutrieu, was the second woman to be granted a licence, on 23 August.

While some women could count on their families for financial support, most of these would-be pilots had to finance themselves by working, finding a patron or organising their own PR, as did many actresses of the period. Harriet Quimby, the first qualified female pilot in the US, was a case in point, using the women's magazine she worked for as a platform (see p. 22). Others indulged in what were perhaps less high-profile activities, but more profitable in the long term. The American, Bernetta A. Miller, for example, was hired by Alfred J. Moisant to demonstrate the planes he built, and Hélène Dutrieu did the same for Henry Farman. In December 1911, Jeanne (Jane) Herveu opened the first flying school exclusively reserved for women.

Across the Atlantic, too, women were getting involved in the adventure, although who was first off the ground is not entirely clear. Arguing that Blanche Scott's 2 September flight at Curtiss was just a fluke, Bessica Medlar Raiche laid claim to the title. The next year, two other Americans, Harriet Quimby and Matilde Moisant, followed in England by Hilda Beatrice Hewlett and Cherida de Beauvoir Stocks, received their pilot's licences, as did the Russian, Lydia Zvereva. Germany was not to be outdone: despite a constant battle against prejudice, Melli Beese became the first licensed German female pilot (see p. 13).

In July 1910, Hilda B. Hewlett and Gustave Blondeau opened the Hewlett-Blondeau School from which three quarters of the British pilots were to emerge. Such schools multiplied. Early in 1912, Melli Beese opened her own school at Johannisthal, near Berlin. Shortly afterwards, Bessica Raiche founded a school in Chicago which, like Jeanne Herveu's, was exclusively for women, although it had but a brief existence.

The first 'death-defying' female pilot made her emergence in the form of Edith Maud Cook. According to her whim, she was known publicly as

Mathilde Franck was a French aviatrix who never gained a pilot's licence. She is seen here in a Farman biplane. (Library of Congress)

Spencer-Kavanagh, Elsa Spencer, Viola Fleet, Viola Spencer-Kavanagh or Viola Kavanagh. The first British woman to fly solo, she died on 10 July 1910 after parachuting from a balloon. Other female pilots appeared at air shows. One of these was Blanche Stuart Scott who, risking her life, raked in around $5,000 a week.

American female pilots learned to fly at the San Diego Curtiss School, or at Hempstead Plains (Long Island), which was run by Matilde Moisant's brother, John B. Moisant who, just a year after Louis Blériot, had crossed the Channel carrying two passengers: his mechanic and a cat. It was thanks to him that Harriet Quimby and her friend Matilde Moisant had learned to fly. Not even John's death in an accident in October 1910 deterred the two young women: 'No, I'm not afraid; when I am, I'll give up flying' declared

Born on 13 September, Matilde Moisant claimed to have been born under a lucky star. Though frail in appearance, she showed courage on many occasions. This photograph is one of a series she and her friend Harriet Quimby had taken. (Library of Congress)

Under her real name of Edith Maud Cook, Spencer-Kavanagh was the first British woman to fly. She was to die in hospital on 14 July 1910 after a failed parachute jump. She is seen here in a Blériot XI while learning to fly at Pau. (Editions Jacques)

The third American woman to be a qualified pilot, and nicknamed 'the winged suffragette', Julia Clark (1880–1912) learned to fly at the Curtiss School in San Diego. Her career was cut short by a fatal accident on 17 June 1912, at Springfield. She thus became the first American woman to die in an air crash. (Curtiss Museum)

Flying too close to the sun

From a purely statistical perspective, the early years of flying were no more risky for women than for men. Between July 1911 and the outbreak of the First World War, four aviatrixes were killed in crashes:

- Denise Moore (real name E. Jane Wright), on 21 July 1911, at Etampes. She fell from her plane when it flipped over at a height of 50m;
- Suzanne Bernard, on 10 March 1912, at Etampes, during her third attempt at her flying licence test;
- Julia Clark, on 17 June 1912, at Springfield (Illinois), after hitting a tree on take-off;
- Harriet Quimby, on 1 July 1912, at Boston. The accident is described in this chapter (see p. 17)

Matilde. She began flying lessons on 1 July 1911 and gained her licence the following 14 August.

Having received her licence on 2 August 1911, Harriet Quimby became the darling of the media. On 16 April 1912, following in the footsteps of Louis Blériot, she crossed the Channel between Dean and Cap Gris-Nez then, in July, took part in the Harvard-Boston Aviation Meet at Squantum aerodrome. On the final day, 7 July 1912, Harriet was killed, along with her passenger William Willard the event's organiser, when they were thrown out of the Blériot they were flying in. They died on the spot, while the unmanned Blériot managed to land a little further on without suffering too much damage. The cause of the accident was never really established, but her friend's sudden death shook Matilde Moisant. With the number of fatal accidents on the rise, her entourage strongly urged her to give up before it was too late[2]. Succumbing to their entreaties, she made a final flight, which almost became one too many as she miraculously emerged unhurt from a crash.

During the years before the First World War, women began to become involved in the design and construction of aircraft. One of the first was the American, E. Lillian Todd, who designed and built a biplane, although it is not known if it ever flew. Another was Lilian E. Bland, from Ireland, who constructed an aeroplane of her own design that, perhaps tongue-in-cheek,

she named *Mayfly*, later writing an article describing its construction for *Flight* magazine[3].

In August 1914, war broke out in Europe and the small, but enthusiastic, rise of women into the skies was brought to a halt. No more aerial frolics; it was back into the home, or work, while the men went to the front. Despite all the publicity that had been generated around their exploits, women fliers couldn't manage to convince the military authorities of their value. Not one of them was permitted to join the ranks of those fighting the war.

In the United States, these early women aviatrixes had the advantage of three extra years of peace in which a few new names appeared on the aeronautical scene. One was Ruth Law who broke various cross-country and altitude records (see p. 36) and became the first woman to be hired by the postmaster general to carry the mails by air. The Stinson sisters, Katherine and Marjorie, were authorised to train Canadian pilots who were then sent to strengthen British squadrons fighting in Europe. In November 1915, there were five Canadians training in preparation for joining the Royal Navy Air Service. By the end of March 1916, the Stinson flying school had 24 trainee pilots on its books. With the entry of the United States into the war, the government would ban all civil aviation, forcing the Stinson sisters to close their doors. As in Europe, American women aviators were forbidden to fly military planes.

1. Arnold Kruckman, in the New York American, 14 May 1911, quoted by E. F. Lebow in Before Amelia.
2. By the beginning of 1912, out of 82 aviators certificated by the ACA, eight had been killed in accidents. Including unqualified pilots, this figure rose to 29.
3. In Flight, 17 December 1910: The Mayfly – The first Irish biplane and how it was built.

The American E. Lilian Todd designed this plane, but she never learned to fly. (Library of Congress)

The Baroness: Raymonde de Laroche

(1886-1919)

'Yet another bastion that men may have thought they could hold for themselves – for a little longer at any rate – has fallen to the weaker sex. Baroness de Laroche has successfully flown a Voisin biplane and in so doing has won the right to be recognised as the first female pilot, or aviatrix,' thus reported the editor of the British weekly magazine *Flight*[1], following the Frenchwoman's historic flight.

A baroness in name only, in reality Elise Deroche was an attractive young woman whose ambition was matched only by her enthusiasm for motor sports, reasoning that if motorbikes and cars were fun, why not flying, too? Her flights with Santos-Dumont and Henry Farman had fired her interest and the woman who called herself Raymonde de Laroche began to frequent aviation circles, where she first met Charles Voisin. It was he who gave her the opportunity to go up in one of the biplanes that he and his brother Gabriel had built. She flew increasingly often and by 10 February 1910 she had gained her pilot's certificate from the Aero-Club of France, which opened the door for her to take part in aviation meetings, both in France and abroad. It was during one of these, on 9 May 1910, that she found herself in St Petersburg performing before Tsar Nicholas II, who conferred on her the title of 'baroness'.

Between 19 and 26 June 1910, during the Rouen Aviation Week, Raymonde de Laroche came 15th in the distance competition, covering 21km in a 50hp ENV-powered Voisin. A month later, she took part in the Champagne Aviation Week. Everything appeared to be going well for 'the baroness' until 8 July when, competing for the ladies' prize, she was the victim of a serious accident, causing multiple fractures as well as giving free rein to her detractors who seized any opportunity to express their misogynistic views.

Endowed with an iron will, she gradually recovered from the 18 fractures that had left her body broken. Charles Voisin's presence at her side was not approved of by everyone, especially by Gabriel Voisin who, half a century

Elise Deroche did not make a career in the music hall as she had intended.
(Underwood/CORBIS)

Raymonde de Laroche in August 1909, posing in front of the Voisin biplane in which she made her historic flight.
(Library of Congress)

'Baroness' de Laroche was an enthusiast for motorised sports of all kinds, and loved driving powerful, fast cars. (Getty Images)

later, wrote in his memoirs: 'Charles, who lived with "Baroness de Laroche", made it impossible for us to sustain a shared existence. Hard though I tried, I could not bring myself to put up with that woman, who was to cause a split between us shortly afterwards.'[2]

She had not long been back on her feet when, on 11 February 1912, she got back into a Henry Farman biplane and started to fly again at air meetings. During one of these, she and Charles were the victims of yet another crash, from which she escaped unhurt, but which cost the life of her companion. To overcome her grief, she threw herself body and soul into aviation meetings and a frenetic pursuit of the Prix Femina (see p. 22) that she won in 1913, receiving it in January 1914 at the Aéro-Club de France premises.

After a four-year break because of the war, Raymonde de Laroche was back in the pilot's seat. On 7 June 1919, she took the altitude record from Ruth Law, reaching 4270m at Issy-les-Moulineaux at the controls of a Caudron G.3. Sadly she was killed instantly in a crash on 18 July 1919, when the pilot of a plane in which she was the passenger executed a loop at too low an altitude.

1. In Flight *30 October 1909, p.695.*
2. In Mes 10000 Cerfs-volants *by Gabriel Voisin (La Table Ronde, 1960) p. 201-202.*

Shielding herself against the early-morning sun as it rises over the Chaumont airfield, Baroness de Laroche waits for the signal to take off. (Roll, M. Bénichou collection)

The Voisin biplane no. 22, with Raymonde de Laroche at the controls, at Chaumont. (Rapid, Bénichou collection)

Raymonde de Laroche after the First World War, posing in front of a Caudron G.3. (Roll, H. Hazewinkel collection)

Melli Beese at her drawing board during the period she was running her aeronautical manufacturing company in Johannisthal. (V. Koos collection)

The second daughter of the architect Friedrich Karl Richard Beese, Amelie Hedwig Beese lived in the suburbs of Dresden. A precocious child, Melli, as she was familiarly known, was gifted in languages and the arts. Deciding she wanted to be a sculptor, she set off in the autumn of 1906 to pursue her studies in Sweden. The flying exploits of the Wright brothers that she saw in the papers captured her attention, but it was Louis Blériot's Channel crossing that prompted her to learn to fly. In 1910, she went to Johannisthal. However, she did not have the money to pay for flying lessons, still less to buy an aeroplane.[1] Furthermore, it did not take her long to find out that being a woman she was far from welcome. She encountered one rejection after another, but fortunately was able to join the aeronautical manufacturer

A career full of pitfalls: Amelie Beese

(1886-1925)

Page from a 1911 meeting programme, lauding the merits of Rumpler aircraft. (DR)

Melli Beese and her husband, Charles Boutard, in front of a Rumpler Taube at Johannisthal, near Berlin. (V. Koos collection)

Ad Astra, and by the beginning of December she had had been lucky enough to fly as a passenger. Unfortunately, her first training flight, on 12 December, ended in a crash in which she broke a number of bones. Tired of waiting for promised flying lessons that didn't materialise, she left Ad Astra and went to Weimar where, for several months, she was the pupil of Robert von Mossner.

On her return to Berlin, she discovered that Ad Astra had gone. She was taken on by Edmund Rumpler who saw in her a way to convince the authorities how easy it was to fly his new plane – der Taube (the Dove). However, Rumpler's chief pilot, Hellmuth Hirth, was adamant in his belief that women were not made to fly. After a first flight with Hirth aboard the Taube, Melli asked when she could fly the plane herself. Hirth replied instantly 'but you're a woman'.[2] Melli bore these stings patiently, and made her first solo flight on 27 July. The Berlin press reported the event.[3] On 13 September, she got her licence, though not without first checking that Hirth would not be present on the day.

An 'Aeronautical Week' was held at Johannisthal from 26 September, with the organisers expecting a big turnout. Melli, who had been left with an old 75hp Taube, had some difficulty in finding a passenger so she could get through the qualification stages. The Frenchman, Charles Boutard, formerly of Ad Astra, was the only one to volunteer. Rumpler's pilots were ill-inclined to compete beside Melli, but this didn't prevent her from taking part in the competition and beating the female altitude record with a passenger by climbing to 825m, on the second day. This was reported in the press as 'The sensation of the week'. However, towards the end of the week, the weather deteriorated and Hirth seized the occasion to bar Melli from flying. Overall, the event's results were unexceptional. Melli came in fifth and pocketed 2,498.56 Marks.

The following year, Melli decided to set up a flying school in partnership with Charles Boutard and Hermann Reichelt, where they would also build their own planes. In January, the school opened with three aeroplanes on its books and, in the course of the same month, Melli married Charles Boutard. The first plane to emerge from the workshops was the Melli Beese-Taube. It

Melli Beese in discussion with Charles Boutard before a flight. (DR)

Melli Beese and her flying school at Johannisthal, in March 1913. (DR)

was a Rumpler machine to which Melli had added a few French improvements and some modifications of her own invention. Whatever the merits of her plane, Melli didn't manage to attract the government investment needed to build a production run. She realised that her marriage to a Frenchman had turned her into a foreigner, which was just one more reason to exclude her from any competitive tenders. She was therefore very happy to lend one of her planes to Hermann Dorner and participate with him on the construction of a seaplane, which was completed by the autumn of 1913. The German military came along to look at the plane with a degree of suspicion towards this French creation, finding it inconceivable that a woman could have had a hand in the project.

At the beginning of 1914, as the rumours of war were spreading, the couple settled at Warnemünde for tests on the seaplane. They were arrested as enemy agents. Melli was quickly released, but Charles was imprisoned and the authorities seized all their property. Melli returned to Johannisthal where she found no-one ready to help her out in her trials, and when Charles was freed, the pair of them were put under house arrest in Prignitz. Charles contracted tuberculosis. The end of the war saw the couple freed and they went back to Berlin, where Melli started proceedings to regain possession of their confiscated property. The news of Alcock and Brown's crossing of the Atlantic gave Melli a new impetus and she conceived the idea of flying around the world, but was unable to raise the necessary capital. She then abandoned aviation and turned to selling motorbikes. In 1921, Melli Beese wrote her memoirs. Only then was any government compensation forthcoming, but the amount was insufficient to set up a business. Suffering from depression, Melli Beese shot herself on 22 December 1925.

1. At the time, a Wright cost 30,000 Marks and an Albatross 25,000 Marks.
2. Quoted by E.F. Lebow in Before Amelia, p. 68.
3. Calling her Böse instead of Beese.

The professional daredevil: Hélène Dutrieu

(1877–1961)

Hélène Dutrieu at Issy-les-Moulineaux, at the controls of a Demoiselle biplane built by Auguste Clément in his Levallois workshops. (Library of Congress)

Hélène Dutrieu and her instructor at the time the Demoiselle was being tested. (Library of Congress)

Having made a bit of a name for herself in cycling, with several women's world records on her C.V.,[1] Hélène Dutrieu, a native of Tournai in Belgium, tried her hand at motor racing, followed by a spot of music hall. Living in Paris, she derived most of her income from evocatively named stunts such as 'the death leap' and other daredevilry. Unquestionably, her stunts were far from being risk free, as a lengthy hospitalisation in Berlin testified. In 1909, Auguste Clément offered her a 2,000F-a-month contract to help promote the little Demoiselle monoplane designed by Alberto Santos-Dumont, of which he had initiated a small production run. The collaboration started badly when Hélène Dutrieu crashed on 21 January, fortunately escaping unhurt. After a few more flights, however, she decided to pull out of the collaboration with the manufacturer, Levallois.

In the spring of 1910, she was at Mouzon (Ardennes) where she was practising on a biplane designed by Roger Sommer, becoming in the process the first female pilot to take a passenger on board. Having mastered the aircraft, she set off for Odessa to do some demonstration flights. However, her collaboration with Roger Sommer proved to be short-lived. By July, Hélène Dutrieu had linked up with Louis Dufour and it was in his Farman biplane that she took her flying test, which she failed to pass. This setback in no way prevented her from taking part in a number of meetings and making

preparations for the Femina Cup (see table, p. 22), as well as retaking her pilot's test, which this time she passed. Her tenacity was rewarded when she won the cup for 1910, with a non-stop flight of 167km, an achievement she surpassed in 1911 with 254km. In the meantime, she had participated in numerous air shows, both in France and abroad, although with mixed fortune, being the victim of several serious crashes. Yet nothing seemed able to stop her – with the exception of the war, during which she switched from flying planes to driving ambulances at the Messini hospital, before taking over the running of the field hospital at Val-de-Grâce.

With the return of peace, she took charge of the periodicals that her husband had launched, including *Le Miroir du Monde* and *L'Agriculture Nouvelle*.[2] With his death, Hélène Dutrieu went back to flying, notably establishing the Hélène Dutrieu-Mortier Cup, awarded to the female pilot flying the greatest distance, solo, in a straight line and without a stop, recalling the conditions of the Femina Cup of her early flying days.

1. World speed champion in 1897 and 1898 at Ostend. Her brother, Eugène Dutrieu, was the sporting director of the Excelsior cycling team.
2. Hélène Dutrieu married Pierre Mortier in 1922.

The innocent smile hid an intrepid character. (Library of Congress)

Hélène Dutrieu at the controls of a Farman biplane. (Library of Congress)

Hélène Dutrieu on the promenade deck of the liner bringing her back from New York in October 1911, where she had broken speed and altitude records. (Library of Congress)

It is ironic that someone with such a keen sense of PR and the presentation of events to gain maximum effect should miss out on her own date with history. A date that will long remain engraved in the memory is 15 April; the day the *Titanic* sank. Against such a momentous event, how could the first crossing of the Channel by a woman be expected to register? Not that Harriet Quimby had neglected to polish her image.

This talented and ambitious American was born in May 1875 at Arroyo Grande, in California. The turn of the century saw her working as an actress in San Francisco and making her first tentative steps in a more lucrative career as a freelance journalist, writing articles for periodicals such as the *San Francisco Bulletin*. Doubtless encouraged by the success of these early articles, Harriet moved to New York in 1903 to further her career. With a great deal of determination, she approached various editors, catching the editorial eye of *Leslie's Illustrated Weekly*[1], a magazine in which she became increasingly involved, soon joining the editorial committee. Turning out a huge amount of material, Harriet Quimby wrote – under her own name as well as different pseudonyms – articles and reports on a very wide range of subjects (domestic advice, theatre criticism, photo-reports from around the world etc.).[2]

Towards the end of October 1910, while reporting on the aviation meeting at Belmont Park, she met Matilde and John Moisant, and the latter agreed that she and Matilde could take flying lessons at the school in Mineola run by his brother, Alfred. Despite having her hands full with journalism and now flying, Harriet Quimby found the time to get in contact with a couple of San Francisco friends, David and Linda Griffith, who were making a career for themselves in the movies, and for whom she wrote the screenplays for seven films during 1911.

Over the two days of 31 July and 1 August 1911, and after five weeks of training, Harriet Quimby passed the Aero Club of America's flying test and became the first American woman to gain a pilot's licence, followed shortly

Harriet Quimby turns the propeller over on the Blériot XI that she flew at Fred Moisant's flying school. (Library of Congress)

Missing a date with history: Harriet Quimby

(1875-1912)

Harriet Quimby was possessed of a natural elegance. (NASM)

According to Matilde Moisant, Harriet Quimby made it a point of honour to qualify before her. (Library of Congress)

Harriet at the controls of a Blériot XI. Ever cautious, she insisted that every part of her plane be checked before each flight. (Library of Congress)

afterwards by Matilde Moisant. On 4 September, she participated in the Richmond County Fair, making a great impression on the public by accomplishing a night flight. In November, the two women became part of the Moisant International Aviators Exhibition Team, putting on a show in Mexico.

Naturally, Harriet did not miss out on the opportunity to publish numerous articles in *Leslie's*, but her desire for fame was not satisfied. She therefore took on an agent – A. Leo Stevens – who was charged with organising her promotion and the details of her career. In the utmost secrecy, she laid down her plans to become the first woman to fly across the Channel. Arriving in Europe in March 1912, she borrowed a 50hp Anzani-engined monoplane from Louis Blériot and had it brought to England. The persistently bad weather at Dover prevented her from taking off for several days. Eventually, on Tuesday 16 April, at 5.30 in the morning, she was able to take off, landing 59 minutes later on the beach near Hardelot, about 50km from the intended destination. Regardless of the significance of her achievement, it received little coverage in the press, being dwarfed by the story of the loss of the *Titanic*.

On her return to New York, Harriet asked Stevens to arrange her participation in the third Boston air meet[3] in which she was to use her new Blériot XI two-seater that she had brought from France. When she arrived there on

It was at the Belmont Park meeting that Harriet Quimby persuaded John B. Moisant to teach her to fly. (Library of Congress)

1 July, William Willard – the meeting's organiser – and his son Charles tossed up to see who would be the first to fly with Harriet. William won and, in front of thousands of spectators, Harriet took off with her passenger. At 500m altitude, the Blériot suddenly went into a dive. A few seconds later, Willard and Harriet Quimby were thrown out of the plane, their bodies landing on the shore of Dorchester bay. Harriet Quimby's meteoric career had lasted just 11 months.

1. *Literary and news magazine started in 1852 by Frank Leslie under the title of Frank Leslie's Illustrated, and lasting until 1922.*
2. *It is estimated that she published 250 articles under her name in Leslie's Illustrated Weekly.*
3. *The Third Annual Boston Air Meet took place at Squantum, near Quincy, Massachusetts. Some sources report a $100,000 contract.*

During her short career, Harriet Quimby had an agent to run her affairs. This advertisement for Vin Fiz, a popular drink at the time, was one of a number that made use of her image. (DR)

'The flying schoolgirl': Katherine Stinson
(1891–1977)

Katherine Stinson's adolescent looks gave her considerable appeal with the public. (Curtiss Museum)

One of Katherine Stinson's specialities was racing planes against cars. Here she is seen competing against the racing driver Dario Resta, on 13 May 1916. (Library of Congress)

Looking mischievous, Katherine Stinson poses with her 80hp-engined Partridge-Keller biplane. (Library of Congress)

In the years before the United States entered the war, Katherine Stinson's name had, for a variety of reasons, become very well known. Firstly, there was the very fact of being a woman, but her teenage looks and her sense of showmanship never failed to amaze her growing public following, and with good reason. At 1.5m tall, with her hair in long brown curls, a youthful appearance, Cherokee ancestry and ever-present cap, this 22-year-old looked at least five years younger, a characteristic that brought her the nickname of 'the flying schoolgirl'.

Yet this flying devil had come to aviation, not so much out of passion, but more by careful calculation. Her initial idea was to become a piano teacher. After winning a piano in a young talent competition, Katherine would not rest until she was able to leave for Europe to take up her musical studies. Not having a penny to her name, it didn't take her long to discover from the press that flying was an excellent way to make money quickly, and she decided that this would be a perfect way to finance her studies. However, she first had to learn to fly, which in 1911 was a particularly expensive business. She sold her piano for $200 and convinced her father to lend her an additional $300. She then set out for New Orleans, where John Moisant's school was situated, then for Chicago, where Max Lillie[1] taught her to fly in a Wright B biplane.

Katherine Stinson made her first solo flight on 13 July 1912 (the same day that Harriet Quimby was killed in Boston – see p. 18) and, on 24 July, she gained pilot's licence number 148 (the fourth awarded to a woman). Shortly after this, she acquired the Wright aeroplane on which she had learned to fly. A number of 'firsts' now began to get her noticed. It was thus in July 1913 that she made the first night flight by a woman, and started to appear at aviation fairs, such as the one held at Helena, Montana, where she managed to win $1,000 over four days (becoming at the same time the first woman to be authorised to carry the mail). At Brandon, Manitoba, she

Katherine Stinson waves at the photographer while surrounded by admiring crowds in the streets of Tokyo. (Library of Congress)

that war was marching inexorably onwards, the Stinson family set up a flying school in San Antonio (which remained in operation until the United States entered the war) to train Canadian pilots. Meanwhile, in December 1916, Katherine had left on a six-month trip to Japan and China to promote aviation in Asia. There, her displays drew considerable crowds, inspiring both men and women to take up the career. At one of these events, on 15 December 1916, no fewer than 25,000 people gathered to watch her trace a luminous 'S' in the sky over Tokyo.

However, the entry of the United States into the war cut her journey short. On her return, she was impatient to do something to serve her country. She decided to undertake fund-raising flights on behalf of the Red Cross[4], piloting a Curtiss JN-4, dropping thousands of leaflets over the country's big cities. During this period, Katherine Stinson also had the opportunity to break two cross-country records: the first on 11 December 1917 between San Diego and San Francisco, a distance of 980km covered in 9hr 10min; the second on 23 May 1918 from Chicago to Binghamton (New York State), a distance of 1,260km completed in 10hr 10min.

Faced with the military authorities' reluctance to grant her wish to join up as a pilot, Katherine Stinson decided to leave for Europe where she thought that she might be of more use. It was the wrong decision. Not only was she unable to convince anyone, but also went down with Spanish flu, from which she just about recovered, but then succumbed to tuberculosis, which required several stays in a sanatorium. After this, she had to give up flying and instead set up an architect's practice. Falling victim to a stroke in 1959, she was bedridden from 1962, dying on 8 July 1977, aged 86.

appeared at a fair where a few thousand Sioux Indians had gathered under Chief Waukessa, who made her a Sioux princess.[2] On 18 July 1915, at the controls of her 80hp biplane, Katherine Stinson became the first woman to loop the loop, following this up, on 21 November, with eight successive loops. Better still, on 15 December, she achieved the first night-time loop and traced the first three letters of the word California with magnesium flares in the night sky.

Katherine was not the only member of the Stinson family to be flying at this time. Her sister Marjorie and brother Eddie had also joined her.[3] Seeing

1. Max Lillie was a Swede, whose real name was Maximilian Liljestrand; he owned an aerodrome in Chicago.
2. She was given the name 'Keyahidewee', which in Sioux means 'the girl who flies away and returns.'
3. Marjorie Stinson (1896-1975) became the youngest licensed female pilot (18 years old). Eddie Stinson was to lose his life in an air crash on 26 January 1932.
4. Red Cross Liberty Loan.

Katherine Stinson when she was carrying the mail between Edmonton and Calgary in an LWF biplane. (Library of Congress)

Katherine Stinson in Tokyo with her Laird Looper biplane, powered by an 80hp Gnome engine. (Library of Congress)

Marjorie Stinson poses in a LePere-USAC-11 biplane during a visit to a US Army base in 1918. (Library of Congress)

The 'tomboy of the air': Blanche Scott

(1889-1970)

Blanche Scott at the controls of a Curtiss Pusher (with a pusher propeller) of the type she used in her aerial stunt work. (Library of Congress)

Blanche Scott with May Andrews and Bill Badger at one of the numerous air meetings in which she starred. (Library of Congress)

In 1910, Blanche Scott, the daughter of a wealthy veterinary surgeon, signed a publicity contract with the Willys Overland Company with the aim of achieving the first transcontinental crossing by a woman, between New York and San Francisco, driving a car named 'Lady Overland'. During the 9,500km journey, the reporter Gertrude Lyman Phillips, whose task was to give a day-by-day account of the trip, accompanied Miss Scott. As she passed through Dayton, the 'fiefdom' of the Wright brothers, Blanche came across their flying school and when she arrived in San Francisco, on 23 July 1910, she had the chance to make her maiden flight in an aeroplane piloted by Charles Willard.

The crossing, an impressive achievement for the time[1], made her the subject of much attention. She was approached by Jerome Fanciulli, the head of the Curtiss Exhibition Company, who suggested teaching her to fly so that she could join his team. She accepted on the spot. A little later, at Hammondsport, she met Glenn Curtiss who, despite his lack of enthusiasm for the idea of teaching a woman to fly, agreed nonetheless to give her a few lessons. On 2 September 1910[2], Blanche Scott made a first unintended flight, followed by a proper one, obliging Curtiss to recognise the ability of his pupil, who took little time to become a member of the show team.

Blanche Scott appeared in public for the first time at Fort Wayne, Indiana, on 24 October 1910. That autumn, she married the press attaché to whom she owed so much for the success of her transcontinental expedition, and gave up flying. However, this was not to be for long. Itching to get back into the air, she was back in her Curtiss biplane by July 1911 at Mineola (New York), accompanied by Thomas Scott Baldwin. Taking part in numerous meetings and calling herself by the nickname of 'tomboy of the air', she became increasingly bold, flying upside down at ground level, flying under bridges and doing her famous 'death dive' where she would plunge from 1,200m, pulling out of the dive only at the very last moment. 'A thrill every second' announced the publicity posters, which also described her as 'the most famous aviatrix in the world'!

After this, Blanche joined the Ward Show Team in Chicago, where she flew a Baldwin Red Devil. On 31 May 1913, at Madison, as she was executing low-altitude stunts, a stay broke and her plane crashed in a bog, a fact that fortunately mitigated her injuries. She was out of flying for a year after this and it wasn't until 1914 that she was back in the air. In addition to her usual stunts, she started to undertake test flights on behalf of the Curtiss and Glenn Martin companies. Around this time, air-show spectators began to exhibit a morbid interest in crashes. Disgusted by the public's attitude and by the lack of opportunity for women in the aeronautical industry, she decided to retire from aviation for good. She was just 27 years old. Selling her plane to the government, she turned towards radio[3] and film, working as a scriptwriter for RKO, Universal and Warner Bros., and ended her career in the 1950s as a consultant for the US Air Force Museum. In the meantime, on 6 July 1948, she had flown in a Lockheed TF-80 jet piloted by Charles E. Yeager, thus becoming, in the eyes of the media, the first American woman to fly in a jet plane.[4]

1. This was a truly remarkable achievement, as it is known that, outside the cities, there were only 400km of paved roads at this time.
2. The date varies according to the source.
3. Radio station KFI in Los Angeles, WVET and WARC in Rochester and WLEA in New York.
4. This is almost certainly not the case; the first American woman to fly in a jet was the wife of Colonel Harvey C. Dorney, in a captured Me262B.

The first qualified women pilots

Name (country)	Licence date	Aero-Club	Licence no.
Raymonde de Laroche (F)	8 March 1910	ACF	36
Lydia V. Zvereva (Rus.)	8 August 1910	AC Russia	31
Marthe Niel (F)	29 August 1910	ACF	226
Hélène Dutrieu (B)	23 August 1910	ACB	27
Marie Marvingt (F)	8 November 1910	ACF	281
Jeanne Herveu (F)	7 December 1910	ACF	318
M.-L. Martin Driancourt (F)	15 June 1911	ACF	525
Harriet Quimby (USA)	2 August 1911	ACA	37
Matilde Moisant (USA)	17 August 1911	ACA	44
Hilda Hewlett (GB)	29 August 1911	RAC	122
Melli Beese (Ger.)	13 September 1911	AeCvD	115
Eudocie V. Anatra (Rus.)	3 October 1911	AC Russia	54
Béatrice De Rijk (NL)	10 October 1911	ACF	652
Bozena Láglerová (Cz.)	10 October 1911	AC Austria	37
	19 October 1911	AeCvD	125
Cheridah de Beauvoir Stocks (GB)	7 November 1911	RAC	153
Lyoubov A. Golanchikova (Rus.)	19 November 1911	AC Russia	56
Winnie Buller (GB)	3 May 1912	ACF	848
Julia Clark (USA)	11 June 1912	ACA	133
Katherine Stinson (USA)	24 July 1912	ACA	148
Eugénie Shakhovskaya (Rus.)	16 August 1912	AeCvD	274
Jeanne Pallier (F)	6 September 1912	ACF	1012
Charlotte Möhring (Ger.)	7 September 1912	AeCvD	285
Bernetta A. Miller (USA)	25 September 1912	ACA	173
Ruth Law (USA)	20 November 1912	ACA	188
Lilly Steinschneider (H)	5 August 1912	AC Hungary	4
Rosina Ferrario (I)	3 January 1913	ACI	203
Hélène de Plagino (F)	4 June 1913	ACF	1349
Marthe Richer (F)	4 June 1913	ACF	1369
Martha Behrbohm (Ger.)	4 June 1913	AeCvD	427
Helena P. Samsonova (Rus.)	13 August 1913	AC Russia	167
Florence Seidell (USA)	20 August 1913	ACA	258
Carmen Damedoz (F)	5 September 1913	ACF	1449
Hélène Caragiani (F)	6 February 1914	ACF	1591
Sophie A. Dolgoroukaya (Rus.)	5 June 1914	AC Russia	234
Elsa Haugk (CZ)	6 June 1914	AeCvD	785
Mrs Richberg Hornsby (USA)	24 June 1914	ACA	301
Gaétane Picard (F)	10 July 1914	ACF	1953
Marjorie Stinson (USA)	12 August 1914	ACA	303

ACA: Aero Club of America
ACB: Aéro-Club de Belgique
ACF: Aéro-Club de France
ACI: Aero Club d'Italia
AeCvD: Aero Club von Deutschland
RAC: Royal Aero Club (GB)

La Coupe Femina (The Femina Cup) 1910–1913

In May 1910, with the idea of encouraging women to learn to fly, Pierre Laffite, owner of the magazine *Femina*, established a prize that he named the Coupe Femina. The prize was worth 2,000 F, and was to be awarded to the aviatrix who, during the current year, had flown the greatest total distance at the controls of a plane. After several years of the competition, it was awarded outright in 1913 to Raymonde de Laroche. The table below lists the various attempts to win the trophy.

Date	Pilot	Plane	Place	Distance	Time
27 November 1910	Marie Marvingt	Antoinette	Mourmelon	42 km	53min
1910	Marie Marvingt	Antoinette	Étampes	?	45min
5 December 1910	Hélène Dutrieu	H. Farman	Étampes	60.8 km	1hr 9min
21 December 1910	Hélène Dutrieu	H. Farman	Étampes	167.2 km	2hr 35min
29 December 1910	Hélène Dutrieu	H. Farman	Étampes	?	40min
31 December 1910	Jeanne Herveu	Blériot XI	Pau	147 km	2hr 2min
19 August 1911	Jeanne Herveu	Blériot XI	Compiègne	101.6 km	1hr 45min
11 September 1911	Hélène Dutrieu	H. Farman	Mourmelon	150 km	?
12 September 1911	Hélène Dutrieu	H. Farman	Mourmelon	230 km	2hr 45min
28 December 1911	Jeanne Herveu	Blériot XI	Compiègne	97 km	1hr 4min
30 December 1911	Jeanne Herveu	Blériot XI	Compiègne	151 km	1hr 44min
31 December 1911	Jeanne Herveu	Blériot XI	Compiègne	248 km	2hr 41min
31 December 1911	Hélène Dutrieu	H. Farman	Étampes	254 km	2hr 58min
9 March 1912	Jeanne Herveu	Blériot XI	Pau	205 km	?
10 November 1913	Jeanne Pallier	Astra-Nieuport	Mourmelon	290 km	3hr 40min
25 November 1913	Raymonde de Laroche	H. Farman	Rheims	323.5 km	4hr

Hélène Dutrieu stands in front of a hangar door in one of her flying suits. This one comprised a smock and long culottes. Her hat owed more to the style of a bonnet than a proper flying helmet. (Library of Congress)

ingenious design, it can be converted instantly into a conventional dress.'

The other contemporary, high-profile American aviatrix was the ever-smiling Matilde Moisant, who also wore a suit specially made for flying. This consisted of a one-piece, cotton smock/knickerbockers outfit in a neutral colour. Wearing a corset, which Harriet Quimby had abandoned in deference to modernity, meant that she could wear a tight belt, imparting a very wasp-waisted look. Differing from her rival's outfit, this had no hood and Matilde Moisant protected her head with a sort of cotton cap. Gaining their licences within a fortnight of one another, the two women knew each other well and had several opportunities to be photographed together in their flying clothes, of which they clearly each possessed more than one set.

Turning to the other side of the Atlantic, the Belgian stunt flyer, Hélène Dutrieu, also had purpose-made clothes. She was to be seen successively wearing a hooded suit similar to Harriet Quimby's, a khaki, waterproof, serge trouser-suit accompanied by a cap not unlike Matilde Moisant's, and an outfit incorporating long culottes in a light-coloured material.

Flying and Fashion

It was not long before the arrival of women in the small world of aviation aroused the interest of couturiers, who saw in this an opportunity to exercise their inventiveness and display their modernism. At this time, there was no women's clothing specifically designed for an activity that was so open to the elements. Wilbur Wright, after all, had been obliged to tie the hem of Edith Berg's skirt when he took her up for her first flight at Auvers in September 1908. It is said that this gave the well-known couturier Paul Poiret the idea of creating what became known in the US as the 'hobble skirt', causing the wearer to adopt a geisha-like gait.

The American Harriet Quimby had no doubts: if women wanted to fly, they would have 'to say goodbye to skirts'. Strong-minded and keen for publicity, the attractive reporter for New York's *Leslie's Illustrated Weekly* had scoured Fifth Avenue's shops for an outfit suitable for her latest fad, but all in vain. So, with the help of couturier Alexander M. Grean, she set about creating something of her own. What she came up with would instantly make her stand out from any of the other pilots, both by its plum colour, much in vogue at the time, and its shape. Writing in her magazine on 25 May 1911, she said: 'My suit is tailored in quilted satin without a lining. It's made in one piece and incorporates a hood. Thanks to an

Harriet Quimby poses in her famous plum-coloured suit, with leather boots and gloves. The suit could be transformed into a dress in the blink of an eye, but has almost always been photographed in its knickerbockers form. It would appear from photographs that Harriet Quimby wore several different versions of this suit. (Library of Congress)

In some fashion parades, it was not unusual for couturiers to display special outfits for aviatrixes that were specifically designed to prevent skirts from billowing up in the wind. Pictured is a Paul Poiret flying outfit at a fashion show. (Library of Congress)

Lucky passengers

Unable at first to take the controls, women made their initial flights as passengers. How exciting it must have been to meet one of those brave aviators, whose names were front-page news. This page provides a round-up of a few of these lucky passengers.

At Turin, on 8 July 1908, Thérèse Peltier (1873-1926) was the first ever female air passenger. (ROL, M. Bénichou collection)

Mme Farman with her husband Henry at Châlons camp on 12 August 1909. (Library of Congress)

Mme Colleix, wife of Maurice Colleix, an aeronautical engineer and pilot (1880-1954), gets ready to take a flight aboard an aircraft piloted by Jean Gobron. (Library of Congress)

Glenn Hammond Curtiss's wife, Lena Pearl Neff-Curtiss (1879-1951), at the controls of a Curtiss Pusher at Hammondsport in 1910. (Library of Congress)

Women unite

On 10 February 1909, Marie Surcouf formed Stella, an association of mainly women from the Aéronautique Club de France (ACdF), not to be confused with the Aéro-Club de France (ACF). The association's intention was to award sporting pilot's certificates to balloon flyers who had completed 10 flights, including two solo and one at night. By 1912, the association consisted of around 200 members, the majority of whom were women. By the beginning of 1914, it included among its ranks such well-known pilots as Hélène Dutrieu (see p.15), Beatrix de Rijk and Jeanne Pallier. Stella's members took part in many competitions and organised some that were specifically for women. On the eve of the Great War, several of Stella's members founded the Patriotic Union of French Women Flyers (Union Patriotique des Aviatrices Françaises) whose raison d'être was to help women pilots join the French military... a lost cause (see p. 122).

Across the Channel, Lady O'Hagan had presided over the creation of the Women's Aerial League in July 1909, whose aim was 'to encourage and stimulate the invention of aerial craft and things appertaining thereto' and to show 'the vital importance to the British Empire of aerial supremacy'. Among the founder members of the League were the Countess of Dartmouth, Lord and Lady Pirrie, Lady West, Lady Marjorie Erskine, Miss Baden-Powell, Colonel and Mrs J.E. Capper, Admiral and Lady Massie Blomfield and J.T.C. Moore-Brabazon.

The first 'Ladies' Day' organised by the Women's Aerial League at Hendon in July 1912 was far from being a success. The competitions specially arranged for the women pilots – the first of their kind – all had to be cancelled in view of 'the risky conditions, particularly for women pilots' (sic). The only flying done by women that day was as passengers.

Mme Mars in a Curtiss Pusher biplane piloted by her husband, James B. Mars, in 1910. (Library of Congress)

Anthony Jannus getting ready to take two passengers (Laura Merriam on the right and Dorothy Williams on the left) over the Potomac, on 6 April 1912. Dorothy Williams was then a member of the Washington Young Women's Aero Club. (Library of Congress)

Amanda Wright-Lane, great-great-niece of the Wright brothers, flew in a replica of the Wright B biplane, at Fort Sam Houston, on 2 May 2010. (USAF/B.J. Davis)

Members of 'Stella', including Mme Blériot (third from the left). (Library of Congress)

Leading members of the Women's Aerial League. It has not been possible to identify anyone with certainty. (Library of Congress)

In the 1930s, the German flyer
Liesel Bach dominated women's
aerobatics.
(H.P. Dabrowski collection)

The Aerobats

gained public attention at the opening of the Mineola Curtiss aerodrome (New York) when she executed 87 consecutive loops before a stunned crowd. In doing so, she beat the record that had been established the previous April by the Frenchwoman, Adrienne Bolland.

Generally speaking, barnstorming became almost the only way women had of getting into aviation, and even then they initially had to put up with wing-walking or parachute jumps rather than piloting. Among these intrepid women in the United States were Helen Lach, Nellie Zabel Willhite, Lillian Boyer (formerly a waitress in a restaurant), Phoebe Fairgrave, Gladys Roy, Ruth Roland and Ethel Dare (an appropriate pseudonym for a certain Margie Hobbs, who was also popularly known as 'the Flying Witch'). These women took insane risks, transferring from one plane to another or from a car or speedboat to a plane[1], in mid-flight, while the public became daily more greedy for new sensation and excitement. A woman pilot was still something of a novelty and women soon began to organise their own 'flying circuses', as was the case with Ruth Law, whose speciality was plane-against-car races, and Mabel Cody, who was sponsored by the petrol company Woco-Pep and whose coolness earned everyone's admiration. Nicknamed 'Queen of the Air', her speciality was transferring from a car to a plane using a rope ladder.

While barnstorming did not become as big in Europe as it did in the

With the end of hostilities and the resumption of civil flights, women were once again at liberty to devote themselves to aeronautical activities. Some of them, it is true, had remained associated with the field of aviation (Marjorie Stinson, for example, had been an industrial designer in the Aeronautical Department of the US Navy), but they were few in number. This new freedom, however, proved to be theoretical, as the large number of pilots released from the military meant that jobs were hard to come by. Many pilots returned to aviation as stunt performers, an activity that became popularised under the name of 'barnstorming', one of the specialities of which was 'wing walking', first undertaken by Ormer Locklear around the end of 1918.

One of the very first women to become involved in this sort of activity was the American Laura Bromwell who had put forward her candidacy as a reservist in the New York air police, so that she could continue to fly 'for free'. On 17 February 1920, she dropped leaflets over New York announcing the release of the film *The Great Air Robbery*, and on 20 August 1920, she

The stunt flyer Ethel Dare, whose real name was Margie Hobbs, was nicknamed the 'Flying Witch'. She specialised in transferring from one plane to another. (Dettling, R. Ostborne collection)

Women's records for the number of loops

Date	Pilot	Plane	Place	No. of loops
18 July 1915	Katherine Stinson	Partridge-Keller	Chicago	1
21 November 1915	Katherine Stinson	Partridge-Keller	Chicago	8
20 March 1920	Adrienne Bolland	Caudron G.3	Le Crotoy	3
12 April 1920	Adrienne Bolland	Caudron G.3	Rouen	25
15 August 1920	Laura Bromwell	Curtiss Standard J-1	Garden City	87
15 May 1921	Laura Bromwell*	Ansaldo	Garden City	199
May 1924	Adrienne Bolland	Caudron C.127	Orly	212
19 April 1930	Florence Klingensmith	Monocoupe	Fargo	143
4 May 1930	Laura Ingalls	DH-60G	Saint Louis	344
26 May 1930	Laura Ingalls	DH-60G	Muskogee	980
21 June 1931	Florence Klingensmith	Stearman J-5	Minneapolis	1,078

Laura Bromwell was killed on 5 June 1921, at Mineola, attempting to beat her own record.

Gladys Roy got herself noticed by dancing the Charleston on a plane's wing. She is seen here on the wing of a Curtiss JN-4. She was killed on 15 August 1927 in an accident on the ground. (K.S. Holcomb collection)

Vera von Bissing (1906–2002) obtained her pilot's qualifications on 27 January 1930 and learned aerobatics with Gerhard Fieseler. In her exhibition flights, she used successively a Raab-Katzenstein KI Ic Schwalbe, a Fieseler F3 Wespe and a Messerschmitt BFW M35b. She is pictured here at a meeting at Marburg in 1933. (F. Selinger collection)

United States, there were numerous meetings and air shows where women pilots were much in demand. In France, Adrienne Bolland, at the behest of her employer, René Caudron, was the first to make an impression at meetings such as Le Touquet, Douai and Rouen. From 1928 onwards, flyers like Maryse Bastié, Léna Bernstein and, later, Régina Wincza began to take over. In the United States, the 1929 economic crisis forced many aerial circuses to close down.

Over time, aerobatics became more disciplined, and national and international aerobatics competitions started to appear. The first German

women's aerobatics championship, at Bonn-Hangelar on 29 May 1930, witnessed the victory of Liesel Bach, with the youngest pilot in the country, Luise Hoffmann, in second place.[2] On 21 May 1933, at the Paris meeting, which took place at Saint-Germain-en-Laye, Liesel Bach, at the controls of a Klemm Falke, made a great impression. In 1932, at Zürich, in a Raab-Katzenstein 'Schwalbe', the pupil of the famous Gerhard Fieseler, Vera von Bissing, was highly placed in the aerobatics competition. In October 1933, she took part in the meeting at Villacoublay, which ended with Gerhard Fieseler and Michel Détroyat being matched against each other. Liesel Bach appeared again on 29 April 1934 at Vincennes during the

The youngest German aerobatics pilot, Luise Hoffmann (1910–1935) came second in the German Championships in Bonn, on 29 May 1930, at the controls of her Raab-Katzenstein KI Ic named 'Spatz' (sparrow). Following a crash in a Bücker Jungmann, she succumbed to her injuries on 27 November 1935. (V. Koos collection)

The second world aerobatics champion, the Russian Svetlana Savitskaya, who won her title at Hullavington, Britain, later became a cosmonaut. (DR)

International Paris Air Day. The meeting opened with the International Women's Cup, in which there were just two competitors: Liesel Bach, in a Klemm L28 XIV with a Siemens 150hp engine, and Hélène Boucher, in a 230hp Salmson-engined Morane-Saulnier M.S. 230. 'Although the French aviatrix put up an exhibition that was in every way remarkable, reported *Flight* magazine in its 10 May 1934 edition, she lacked both the training and experience of her German competitor.' Vera von Bissing, who was considered one of the finest and most advanced of the German pilots, and her 120hp Siemens-engined Raab-Katzenstein Schwalbe were also present at Vincennes, but she was unable to compete after having had to undergo an emergency surgical operation a few days previously.

Although it was not considered an Olympic discipline at the 1936 Berlin Olympic Games[3], aerobatics did feature on the margins of the Games, with a world championship held at Tempelhof airport. No women took part in this event[4], but Vera von Bissing won the special women's prize at the Olympic Games Celebration competition, flying her Messerschmitt BFW M35b monoplane.

Alexander Yakovlev at Tuchino, in August 1966, in conversation with the Soviet aerobatics team, including Galina Kortschuganova. In the background is the Yakovlev Yak-18PM no. 3. (Yakovlev)

However, the worsening political situation was to put a serious damper on international aerobatics contests for quite a few years. It was not until the mid-1950s that there was a renaissance of aerobatics at the international level, and we had to wait until 1960 for the first proper world aerobatics championships to be held in Bratislava. Women pilots had to wait until the fourth of these championships, which took place at Tushino, near Moscow, before they had their own events. The winner that year was the Russian Galina Kortschuganova flying a Yakovlev Yak-18PM. The ensuing years saw a distinct domination of the event by Soviet women and, to a lesser extent, Americans. It was only in 1988, at the 14th championships, that a Frenchwoman took first place: Catherine Maunoury at the controls of a Sirius SR-230 (see table p. 31), an achievement she repeated in 2000 at the 20th championships. From 1980 to 2000, this long-haul hostess with Air France took ten French aerobatic championships, as well as many other trophies. She gave up competitive flying in 2000 so as to devote herself to coaching pilots[5] and putting on displays at meetings.[6]

Meanwhile, another Frenchwoman, Christine Genin, had stepped up to the podium, winning the world championship in 1994 flying an Extra EA3005. The most recent champion at the time of writing is the Russian Svetlana Kapanina, who won her seventh title at the 26th championships held at Foligno, Italy in 2011.

In a quite different field, wingwalkers have reappeared since the early 1990s, especially in the United States with teams such as the American Barnstormers, but also in Europe with Crunchie, Team Guinot, the Butterly Barnstormers (commonly known as the UtButs), and more recently the Breitling team. Faithful to tradition, the 'walkers' are chiefly women and the

Women's world aerobatics champions

WAC*	Year	Place	Champion	Aircraft
4th	1966	Tuchino, USSR	Galina Kortschuganova, USSR	Yak-18PM
6th	1970	Hullavington, GB	Svetlana Savitskaya, USSR	Yak-18PM
7th	1972	Salon-de-Provence, France	Mary Gaffaney, USA	Pitts S-1 Special
8th	1976	Kiev, USSR	Lidia Leonova, USSR	Yak-50
9th	1978	Ceske Budejovice, Czch.	Valentina Yaikova, USSR	Yak-50
10th	1980	Oshkosh, USA	Betty Stewart, USA	Pitts S-1 Special
11th	1982	Spitzerberg, Austria	Betty Stewart, USA	Pitts
12th	1984	Bekescsaba, Hungary	Khalide Makagonova, USSR	Yak-55
13th	1986	South Cerney, GB	Lyubov Nemkova, USSR	Sukhoi Su-26M
14th	1988	Red Deer, Canada	Catherine Maunoury, France	Sirius SR-230
15th	1990	Yverdon, Switz.	Natalia Sergeeva, USSR	Sukhoi Su-26
16th	1992	Le Havre, France**	-	-
17th	1994	Debrecin, Hungary	Christine Genin, France	Extra EA300S
18th	1996	Oklahoma City, USA	Svetlana Kapanina, Russia	Sukhoi Su-26
19th	1998	Trencin, Slovakia	Svetlana Kapanina, Russia	Sukhoi Su-26
20th	2000	Muret, France	Catherine Maunoury, France	CAP 232
21st	2001	Burgos, Spain	Svetlana Kapanina, Russia	Sukhoi Su-31
22nd	2003	Lakeland, Florida, USA	Svetlana Kapanina, Russia	Sukhoi Su-26
23rd	2005	Burgos, Spain	Svetlana Kapanina, Russia	Sukhoi Su-26M3
24th	2007	Burgos, Spain	Svetlana Kapanina, Russia	Sukhoi Su-26M3
25th	2009	Silverstone, GB	Elena Klimovich, Russia	Sukhoi Su-26M3
26th	2011	Foligno, Italy	Svetlana Kapanina, Russia	Sukhoi Su-26M3

* The first World Aerobatics Championship (WAC) took place in 1960 at Bratislava.

** Competition cut short by poor weather conditions.

Left Catherine Maunoury filling up the CAP.10 in EMS Chronopost colours, in June 1989. (A. Bréand)

Top right Catherine Maunoury with the astronaut Patrick Baudry and the aerobatics aircraft manufacturer Auguste Mudry.
(A. Bréand)

Bottom right Catherine Maunoury prepares to take a child up for a flight at the Young Pilots' Air Tour. (A. Bréand)

Women's results in the 25th world aerobatics championships

Rank	Name (country)	Plane	Registration	No. of points
1st	Elena Klimovich (Rus)	Sukhoi Su-26M3	RA-01059	5,851.10
2nd	Svetlana Kapanina (Rus)	Sukhoi Su-26M3	RA-01059	5,841.26
3rd	Kathel Boulanger (F)	Sukhoi Su-26	HA-HUR	5,407.91
4th	Aude Lemordant (F)	CAP-232	F-GODV	5,027.58
5th	Debby Rihn-Harvey (US)	CAP-232	F-GXCP	4,837.84
6th	Heike Sauels (Ger)	Extra 300SP	D-EXHS	4,737.63
7th	Gabi Schifferle (Switz)	Extra 300S	N600YS	3,129.14

aircraft used are generally Boeing Stearman A75 biplanes powered by Pratt & Whitney 450hp engines.

Around the turn of the 21st century, the more open policy of armed forces towards women gave them the opportunity to join the various national aerobatic teams. The first to do so was the Australian, Flight Lieutenant Joanne Mein, who flew with the Roulettes during the 1999 season. She was followed by the Canadian, Captain Maryse Carmichael. In the ensuing years, some of the most prestigious teams (the Thunderbirds, Blue Angels, Red

The Russian Svetlana Kapanina has been world champion seven times, flying Sukhoi Su-25s, 26s and 31s. (S. Kapanina)

Svetlana Kapanina does a low-altitude inverted pass at the controls of a Sukhoi Su-31. (S. Kapanina)

Right *Using Stearman biplanes with 450hp R950-14B engines, the Breitling Wingwalkers are specialists in synchronised aerial choreography. (Breitling)*

Below right *Betty Skelton flew solo for the first time when she was 12. She began her aerobatics career in 1946 and bought a Pitts biplane in 1948. Her speciality is cutting through a tape held above the ground with the plane's rudder as she flies upside down. (DR)*

Below far right *Born in 1971 in Quebec, Maryse Carmichael joined the Canadian Forces in 1990 and gained her 'wings' in 1994. In 2000, she was selected to become the no. 3 in the 431st Air Demonstration Squadron, better known as 'The Snowbirds'. (Canadian Forces)*

Arrows and Patrouille de France) welcomed women among their numbers. In France, Flight Lieutenant (since promoted to Squadron Leader) Virginie Guyot, who formerly flew Mirage F1CRs in 2/33 'Savoie' reconnaissance squadron, joined the Patrouille de France in October 2008, flying in second position behind the leader during the 2009 season. She moved into the leader's spot in 2010, becoming the first woman to occupy that position in an aerobatic team.

1. *Ethel Dare made her first such transfer in November 1919.*
2. *The full results were: 1st Liesel Bach, 2nd Luise Hoffmann, 3rd Elly Beinhorn, 4th Marga von Etzdorf.*
3. *Only gliding was an approved sport in the 1936 Olympics.*
4. *It was won by the German Otto von Hagenburg in a Focke-Wulf Fw 44.*
5. *Via the Centre Passion Catherine Maunoury (CPCM) that she set up in 1993.*
6. *Catherine Maunoury was appointed director of the French Air and Space Museum in August 2010.*

The latest 'Thunderbirds' recruit, Kristin Hubbard, arrived in time for the 2010 season of air meetings. Before that, she had been an F-16 instructor with the 62nd Fighter Squadron. (USAF)

Nicole Malachowski was the first of three women who, at the time of writing, have flown in the legendary 'Thunderbirds' aerobatic team. Born in 1974 and nicknamed Fifi, she made her first public appearance in March 2006, flying a Lockheed-Martin F-16 Fighting Falcon. (USAF)

Women in national aerobatics teams

Rank, First name, Surname	Team	Aircraft	Years
Flt. Lt. Joanne Mein	Roulettes (Australia)	MB326	1999
Major Maryse Carmichael	Snowbirds (Canada)	CT-114	2001-2002
Major Nicole M. E. Malachowski	Thunderbirds (USA)	F-16	2006-2007
Major Samantha Weeks	Thunderbirds (USA)	F-16	2007-2008
Lieutenant Amy Tomlinson	Blue Angels (USA)	F/A-18	2008-2010
Commandant Virginie Guyot	Patrouille de France (France)	AlphaJet	2009-2010
Flt. Lt. Kirsty Moore	Red Arrows (GB.)	Hawk	2009-2010
Captain Kristin Hubbard	Thunderbirds (USA)	F-16	2010

The pilots of aerobatic teams are always popular with the public at air meetings. Here, Major Samantha Weeks of 'The Thunderbirds' answers children's questions at an open day at Goodfellow Base, Texas. (USAF)

Until she joined the famous Red Arrows in May 2009, Kirsty Moore (now Stewart) was a Tornado pilot with the RAF's no. 13 Squadron. (MOD/EPA)

Virginie Guyot joined the Patrouille de France in 2008. In 2010, she was appointed leader. She is pictured here with the other members of the team. Prior to this, she flew Mirage F1CRs at Rheims. (H. Lecinski/EPAA)

During a briefing before a training mission, Squadron Leader Virginie Guyot rehearses manoeuvres with her team. (H. Lecinski/EPAA)

'Showing the men a thing or two': Ruth Law

(1887-1970)

Ruth Law at the controls of the Curtiss model D that she had had modified to have controls identical to those of a Wright B. (USAF)

Looking relaxed, Ruth Law stands in front of her Curtiss whose wings had been painted with her name in large letters. (Curtiss Museum)

For her distance record, Ruth Law had some modifications made to her Curtiss Pusher, such as this sheet-metal leg cover. (Curtiss Museum)

Ruth Law displayed the same boldness in pursuing her aeronautical career as her brother Rodman Law, the parachutist, did in his. In June 1912, she enrolled at Starling Burgess's flying school in Boston. Undeterred by Harriet Quimby's fatal crash at which she had been present on 1 July, Ruth persevered with her plans, made her first solo flight the following month and received her licence on 12 November. During the winter months, she made use of her pilot's skills in Florida, on behalf of the Clarendon Hotel, doing demonstration flights and ferrying guests. As this assured her of a comfortable income, Ruth did the same thing in summer 1913 at Newport, accumulating sufficient money to buy her own plane, a model B Wright biplane, on which she had her name printed in giant letters. Flying this aircraft, she made the first night flight by a woman, on 6 November.

Between 1913 and 1916, her husband, Charles Oliver, negotiated contracts with a variety of hotel groups. By this time, feeling limited by the performance of her plane, Ruth sold it in 1915 to buy a 100hp Curtiss model D, which she had fitted with the Wright-type controls with which she was familiar. With her new steed prepared, Ruth was ready to do her first public aerobatics, on 17 January 1915 at Daytona Beach. She set off on a series of exhibitions at air meetings and, at the opening of the 1915 baseball season in Daytona Beach, she set things in motion by throwing a ball (it turned out to be a grapefruit!) from her plane. Ruth also got involved in other exploits, notably in the field of long-distance flying. On 19 and 20 November 1916, she flew non-stop between Chicago and New York, covering the 950km in 5hr 45min.[1] After this flight, she was received by President Wilson and his wife at the Waldorf Hotel. In January, she was sent to Europe to gauge the progress that had been made in aviation there.

With the return of peace, and following a six-month tour of Japan, China and the Philippines,[2] Ruth Law seriously considered making an attempt to cross the Atlantic from west to east. She made the first announcement of her plans to the *New York Times* of 28 May 1919. 'Yes', she declared, 'I intend to show these men a thing or two.' She and her mechanic, James B. 'Big Jim' LaMont, planned to use a Curtiss biplane powered by two 400hp Kirkham engines, but the project failed to come to fruition. Ruth then set up Ruth Law's Flying Circus[3], appearing with it over a number of years at meetings and air fairs all over the United States.

In March 1922, Charles Oliver officially put an end to his wife's career by publishing an announcement in the press. Ruth explained the decision, saying: 'I'm a normal woman. I want a home, a baby and everything that goes with married life.'

1. Thus beating the distance record set on 2 November 1916 by Victor Carlstrom with 727km.
2. During which she took the first airmail to the Philippines.
3. Among the pilots who made up the 'Flying Circus' was Laura Bromwell, who was killed trying to beat her own record for the number of consecutive loops (see p. 28).

Ruth and her Curtiss at Govis Island, at an unknown date. Among the stunts that her 'flying circus' offered the public were races between cars and aeroplanes. (Library of Congress)

'Queen Bess': Bessie Coleman
(1893-1926)

Bessie Coleman with Robert Thelen at Aldershof in 1922, as she was preparing to fly a German LFG biplane. (J. Underwood collection)

Hailing from Atlanta, Texas, and the tenth child of a family of 13, Bessie Coleman was to become the first qualified black woman pilot in the history of aviation. After finishing her primary-school studies at the top of her class, Bessie started work in a laundry in the hope of earning enough money to pay for her secondary education. In 1910, she joined preparatory classes at Langston Agricultural and Normal University, but her savings ran out in the first term and she had to return to the laundry. In 1915, fed up with her lot, she decided to join her brother in Chicago where, after training, she managed to find work as a manicurist. In a very short time, she established an unrivalled reputation and soon had among her clients such influential men as Robert S. Abbott, the owner of the daily *Chicago Defender*.[1]

The first female black pilot, Bessie Coleman had to struggle against discrimination. She refused to take part in meetings where blacks and whites were admitted separately. (Corbis/Bettman)

It was at this time that Bessie discovered her true vocation. Under the influence of the stories her brother told her about the aviators of the Great War, she decided that she wanted to become a pilot. After having to put up with numerous rejections from local flying schools, and on Abbott's advice, she set out for France on 20 November 1920. Once there, she joined the Caudron brothers' flying school at Le Crotoy and, seven months later, on 15 June 1921, she gained her flying licence. She spent a further three months in France practising, before setting sail for New York on 16 September 1921.

Her return was a triumph and she made the front page in many papers. However, Bessie soon realised that if she was to make a living from being a pilot, she would have to learn to do stunt flying and aerobatics, in neither of which did she have any skills. There was only one solution: she would have to go back to France. Landing at Le Havre on 28 February 1922, she spent the next two months working on learning advanced manoeuvres. Before returning to the US on 13 April 1922, she visited Germany, where she was able to fly the big LFG aircraft at Staaken and a Dornier seaplane at Friedrichshafen. She also made a trip to Amsterdam where she met Anthony G.H. Fokker.

Bessie Coleman made her first public appearance at a meeting in New York, on 3 September 1922. The *Chicago Defender*, her main sponsor, described her as 'the greatest aviatrix in the world'. Flush with this initial success, she appeared at meeting after meeting: Memphis, Chicago, Houston etc., though not without coming up against segregation as well as prejudice against women. Despite this, she was always able to win over the public, not simply because of her aerobatic displays, but by her eloquence and sense of public relations. For many, she became 'Queen Bess'.

She soon made known her intention to open a flying school for black pilots. Among her first pupils was the head of publicity for a big rubber firm[2], Robert P. Sachs, to whom she proposed a deal: she would do aerial advertising for his company if he bought her a plane. The deal was struck and she acquired a second-hand Curtiss JN-4 for the modest sum of $400.

Unfortunately, only a few days after she had taken possession of it, the JN-4 stalled and crashed. As a result of this mishap, Bessie spent three months in hospital. Discouraged by what had happened, she let a year and a half go by until, in some need, she managed to put together a series of displays for the 1926 season, at the same time doing lectures, which turned out to be much more lucrative. But it was still not enough. On the advice of a friend, she opened a beauty salon in Orlando, Florida and managed to scrape together the funds necessary to buy a new plane[3] from army surplus.

On 30 April 1926, while practising for a meeting due to take place the following day in Dallas, Bessie took off accompanied by the mechanic, William D. Wills. He took the controls while Bessie, who was new to the area, scouted out the lie of the land. Suddenly Wills lost control of the plane, which went into a spin and flipped over. Bessie Coleman fell out of the plane and hit the ground a few hundred metres below.

The death of 'Queen Bess' made the front pages of the 'black' press across the whole country, while most 'white' newspapers ignored it. Thousands of people turned out for her funeral. Three years later, in 1929, the flying school she had dreamt about became a reality when William J. Powell set up the Bessie Coleman Aero Club in Los Angeles.

1. Robert Sengstacke Abbott (1870-1940), founder of the Chicago Defender, was one of the first African-American millionaires.
2. The Tire and Rubber Company, with its head office in California.
3. Most probably another JN-4.

An accident while she was flying this Curtiss JN-4 put Bessie Coleman into hospital for nearly three months. (Aerospace Adventures collection)

Do a loop, win the plane: Adrienne Bolland

(1895-1975)

Adrienne Bolland in front of her G.3 at a tourist plane competition, on 3 September 1921. (H. Gérard, H. Hazewinkel collection)

One of two Caudron C.127s bought by Adrienne Bolland in February 1924. This one is no. 5534.8, registration F-AGAQ. The other was no. 5534.7, registration F-AGAP. (Farman)

One fine day in 1920, Adrienne Bolland barged into the office of the 'boss' – René Caudron – to demand no less than a plane of her own. Caudron, who had foreseen this request, allowed Adrienne to bend his ear for a while before laying down a challenge: if she could do a loop in a G.3, the plane would be hers. Not only did she do it, but carried away by her success, she followed it up with a second. True to his word, René Caudron let her have the plane.

Undisciplined, cantankerous, quarrelsome, in short, an enfant terrible, Adrienne Bolland, the youngest in a family of six children, had got herself into aviation on a whim, after losing money at the races. Through sheer chance, she had learned that Caudron's company was planning to recruit pilots. She had turned up a week later, clutching the 2,000F needed to pay for her training, at Le Crotoy flying school. 'I'm sure I was lucky, being a woman', she said later. 'It was good publicity for Caudron'. This was on 16 November 1919. With Caudron as her instructor, she had done just a dozen hours of flying before she was 'let loose' on a G.3. A few weeks later, having gained her certificate, Caudron took her on as a professional pilot at the fixed salary of 1,500F a month. She thus became the first French salaried woman pilot, given the job of delivering aircraft to customers and to do demonstration flights. But she had quickly decided that she wanted her own plane. And now her wish was granted.

Having completed a Channel crossing from France to England on 20 August 1920, an event that was barely noticed,[1] and taken part in a few small

Adrienne Bolland described herself as 'a woman of no account who just happened to become a pilot'. (DR)

meetings, Adrienne Bolland achieved her greatest feat with the crossing of the Andes, a flight that would become legendary. She left France with her plane on 4 December 1920, heading for South America, where she arrived in January. At this point, there seemed no chance of her crossing these fearsome mountains, her G.3 being thought quite incapable of flying at such high altitudes,[2] so she contented herself with doing a demonstration tour. However, Adrienne soon changed her mind and decided to attempt the impossible. Legend has it that a woman came to her full of useful advice about the best route to take across the mountains in her plane. The precious advice turned out to be right as, on 1 April 1921, after a flight of 4hr 17min the G.3 touched down in Espejo, on the other side of the cordillera.

On her return to France, Adrienne Bolland lost her job and, after buying a Caudron C.127 biplane, took part in numerous meetings in which, working on behalf of the Air Ministry, she worked with two other pilots (Charles Robin and Maurice Finat) doing aerobatic demonstrations and maiden flights. The star turn at these shows was a display called 'Adémaï-Aviateur', in which the pilot pretended not to know how to fly.[3] In 1924, still seeking fame, she made an attempt on the record for the number of loops, but it was American pilots who were to have the last word in this field (see p. 28).

Losing her Caudron in a crash in April 1933, she bought a Morane-Saulnier AS, followed by a Gourdou-Lesseure B7 with a 300hp engine, which she flew until 1939. While no longer flying by the time of the Second World War, Adrienne Bolland showed she had not lost her appetite for a fight, joining the resistance with her husband and becoming head of a network.

1. On 25 August 1920, to commemorate the 12th anniversary of Louis Blériot's historic flight.
2. This was G.3 no. 77 with a 80hp engine, registered as F-ABFY.
3. A reference to the film Noel-Noel.

Adrienne Bolland preparing to take up a passenger in Caudron G.3, registration F-AFDC at Le Touquet. This was the very plane she used to cross the Andes in 1921. (K. Holcomb collection)

'Tree-Tops': Florence Klingensmith (1904-1933)

Florence Klingensmith poses in front of the little, single-engined Monocoupe that she bought in April 1929, christening it Miss Fargo after the town in North Dakota where she had it based. (T.C. Weaver, John Underwood collection)

Chicago, Illinois on 3 September 1933, with Florence Klingensmith in confident pose for the photographers. (Kenneth M. Sumney, John Underwood collection)

'I don't know that I'll win, but I do know I will place. The plane is fast enough and I can fly it,' announced the charming Florence Klingensmith to the reporter from the *Chicago Daily News* who had come to interview her. The Gee Bee model Y was certainly fast enough, as its owner, one Arthur Knapp of Jackson, Michigan, had had the original 216hp Lycoming R-680 engine replaced with a Wright J6-9 Whirlwind of 450hp!

The context was the Chicago International Air Races, on Monday 4 September 1933, taking place there for the first time and Florence was about to get into this powerful machine and measure herself against the cream of the male pilots. The 29-year-old aviatrix was certainly not unknown to the watching crowds. The daughter of a school-bus driver from Oakport, North Dakota, Florence Gunderson had married Charles Klingensmith in June 1927. Known to her entourage as an inveterate daredevil, she soon got herself a plane and went around the state fairs doing death-defying stunts. Her low-level aerobatics quickly earned her the nickname of 'Tree-Tops'. Among her exploits was the extraordinary record for the number of consecutive loops. On 22 June 1931, flying a Stearman biplane in front of 50,000 spectators gathered at the Minneapolis aerodrome, Florence Klingensmith made a total of 1,078 loops over four and a half hours, smashing the previous record set the previous year by her compatriot, Laura Inglis, who had managed a mere 980! In August 1931, she had participated in the prestigious National Air Races and entered ten or so competitions at the controls of a number of different aircraft (Monocoupe, Cessna, Waco and Swallow). She won four of them, picking up some $4,200 in prize money. In 1932, she was back, on this occasion taking the Amelia Earhart Trophy, flying her little Monocoupe named *Miss Fargo*.

The following year, Florence Klingensmith decided that rather than go to Los Angeles for the National Air Races, she would instead attend the first International Air Races being held at Curtiss-Reynolds airport in Chicago. On Sunday 3 September, she took part in the all-category international women's race and came second, behind Mae Haizlip, at an average speed of 304.17kph, a feat that earned her $625.

In the late afternoon of the following day, a Monday, she once again mounted her fiery steed, this time to match herself against the men in the Phillips Trophy, with prize money of $10,000[1] at stake. With the Whirlwind engine working flat out, Florence Klingensmith soon found herself among

Florence Klingensmith receives the Amelia Earhart Trophy from E.W. Greeve, president of the National Air Races, on 3 September 1932. (NASM)

Florence Klingensmith at Chicago on 4 September 1933. The photograph was taken barely two hours before the crash that would cost her life. (AAHS)

With no time to use her parachute, she was killed on the spot. She had just celebrated her twenty-ninth birthday.

Although all the evidence pointed to a failure of the plane's structure rather than pilot error as the cause of the crash, the opportunity was seized to claim that pitting women against men in such races presented too great a danger. This view carried the day and, the following year, women were barred from entering the legendary Bendix Trophy. As a result, to show her disapproval, Amelia Earhart refused to bring the actress Mary Pickford to Cleveland to open the 1934 National Air Races. A few days after the tragic accident, many pilots joined the silent congregation in the Presbyterian Church at Fargo to render final homage to this extraordinary aviatrix.

the race leaders, holding her position over the first eight circuits, cutting close to the marker pylons on the 13km triangular course. It was then that, under the enormous stress, the Gee Bee's structure began to fail and a piece of the right wing covering tore off. She immediately left the race, so as not to risk a collision with any of the other competitors, and struggled to keep control of her plane. She headed towards the south-east, but a few kilometres further on hit a tree at the Glenview and Shermer crossroads.

1. The race was 100 miles (160km) long, over a 13km triangular course marked out by pylons.

The fallen angel: Laura Ingalls
(1901-1967)

Laura Ingalls at Lockheed in Burbank, California, on the occasion she had brought in her Air Express to exchange it for the Orion seen in the background. (Lockheed)

'Why does everything always turn into a matter of life and death for me?' A degree of resignation had begun to pervade the thoughts of Laura Ingalls on that Thursday, 12 September 1935. It was a little after 5.00am in Burbank and it was still dark. In the Union Air Terminal's hangar, mechanics were busy working on the black-painted Lockheed

Laura Ingalls in front of her English-built De Havilland D.H.60G Gipsy Moth. It had been registered on 14 November 1928 and bought by Heyer Products Company. It was in this plane that she made her record-breaking 980 consecutive loops. (J. Underwood collection)

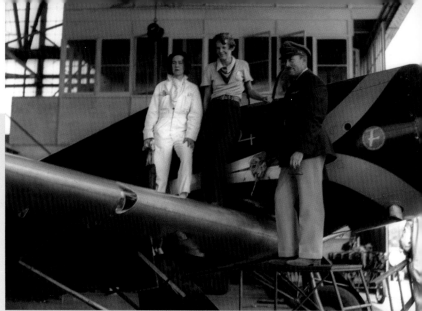

Laura Ingalls takes over the Lockheed Orion with which she was to break the record for crossing the United States. (Lockheed)

Laura Ingalls secured the support of two famous pilots who had been regular users of Lockheed aircraft, Amelia Earhart and Roscoe Turner. (Lockheed)

Orion, with which the American aviatrix was once again planning to break the record for the west-to-east crossing of the United States. It was proving impossible to repair a defective valve. 'Cancel your cables to New York, please,' she told the journalists. She'd made her decision: abandonment, yet again! But at this late hour, hope was returning. The relentless efforts of the mechanics were paying off. Laura Ingalls was going to be heading east after all. At 5.15 that morning, the big plane rose from the runway and set course for the east, guided by 'Little Elmer' as Laura liked to call the Sperry automatic pilot. The droning of the engines became steadily more distant as the plane disappeared into the darkness. As she swallowed up the miles, Laura Ingalls noted one by one the passage of the time zones: Seligman, Tucumcari, Indianapolis... After precisely 13hr 35min 5sec, she touched back down on American soil,

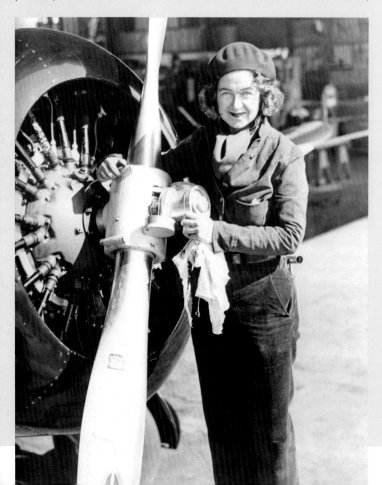

smashing Amelia Earhart's record by 5hr 30min. She was just 7min short of the male record held by Frank Hawks. Unfortunately, her achievement was to be eclipsed the very next day by the new world air speed record of 567kph set by the media-friendly Howard Hughes. It was also to be Laura's final aviation exploit.

Things had begun well for Laura Houghtaling Ingalls, the daughter of a wealthy New York family. Nothing was too good for her. After piano lessons and language studies in Paris and Vienna, she had been, successively, a pianist, a dancer, a nurse and a secretary, but had then been seized with a passion for aerobatics, a notion that was not to everybody's liking. Aerobatics was not a suitable activity for someone of her background! Ignoring the title-tattle, Laura had got her head down and gone ahead with it. One of the first women to gain an airline pilot's licence (12 April 1930), she had keenly sought media attention, making record numbers of loops and flick rolls her speciality. She started doing loops after acquiring a De Havilland Gipsy Moth: at first just a few, then 47 followed by 344, until the day in May 1930 when she had spent 3hrs 40min amassing a total of 980 successive loops, earning a dollar for each! Avid for more, she had accomplished a similar feat over St Louis, managing a modest 714 flick rolls. After this, she had turned to the record for crossing the United States. In October 1930, at the controls of her red and silver Gipsy Moth, she had established the record for the return transcontinental crossing.[1]

In May 1931, the Atlantic Exhibition Company of New York had conceived the idea of sponsoring the first transatlantic flight by a woman, acquiring for the purpose a Lockheed Air Express Special with a 2,460-litre fuel capacity. They had also set their sights on the blue-eyed aviatrix as the pilot. Unfortunately, various technical problems had delayed the project and in the event it was Amelia Earhart who accomplished the feat (see p. 138).

Laura had bought this plane on 5 April 1933, with the idea of an Atlantic crossing still in the air, but as nothing came of it, she had opted for a solo tour of South America. It was the first time that an aviatrix had ventured this far south. She had also added a few more records to her list of achievements, including the longest solo flight by a woman (27,187km) and being the first American woman to fly over the Andes. This flight had won her the much-coveted Harmon Trophy (see p. 186).

On 1 February 1935, she had exchanged her Air Express for an Orion,

Wearing her ever-present beret, Laura Ingalls pampers her Lockheed Orion, named 'Auto-da-fé'. (DR)

to which she had given the name *Auto-da-Fé* (act of faith). Not ready in time for the England–Australia race, she had decided to try and beat the record for the quickest crossing of the United States from east to west. On 11 July 1935, after two fruitless attempts, she had managed to achieve this. And, on 12 September, she had tried again, this time in the opposite direction. Laura Ingalls made use of the Orion for a further year before it was sold and headed for Spain[2]. Without any new sponsors, she was obliged to do aerobatics shows at meetings, using either a Fairchild biplane or a Ryan ST monoplane. In September 1939, while looking for a more powerful aircraft than the Orion, she managed to get a flight at the controls of a brand-new fighter aircraft designed by Jerry Vultee's team, the AB-2, but it is not known what use for it she had in mind.

Across the Atlantic, Europe was slipping steadily into war, with Britain and France trying to persuade America to join the conflict. Laura Ingalls had become a member of the Women's National Committee, an association lobbying against America joining the war, and became one of its spokespersons. She was also a member of the America First Committee. On 18 September 1939, she flew over the White House and the Capitol dropping anti-interventionist leaflets. She was accused of being an agent in the pay of Baron Ulrich von Gienanth, one of the staff at the German Embassy in Washington (but in reality a member of the Gestapo), from whom, it was claimed, she had received substantial sums of money. Denying charges that she was an agent in the pay of the Nazis, she was nevertheless arrested by the FBI on 18 December 1941 and convicted on 13 February 1942 of being in violation of the Foreign Agents Registration Act.[3] Unable to raise the $7,500 bail, she was imprisoned in the District of Columbia and later in Alderson, West Virginia, where she spent 18 months before being released on parole on 5 October 1943. A fallen angel, she was never to shine again in the firmament of aviatrixes.

With its 1200hp Pratt and Whitney engine, the Vultee AB-2 was twice as powerful as the Lockheed Orion. Laura Ingalls test-flew it at Downey, California, in March 1939. (G. Balzer collection)

1. In 30hr 25min outwards, from Roosevelt Field and Glendale, and 25hr 20min on the return.
2. In 1936, using the Orion, Laura Ingalls came second in the Bendix Trophy, some way behind Louise Thaden in a Beech C17R.
3. At her trial, Laura Ingalls was found guilty of being an agent of the Third Reich by a 12-person jury.

Laura Ingalls' Lockheed Orion 9D Special was a big monoplane with a retractable undercarriage and a Pratt and Whitney 550hp Wasp engine turning the variable-pitch Hamilton propeller. (Lockheed)

Before her test flight on the Vultee AB-2, Laura Ingalls listens to the company test pilot's suggestions. (G. Balzer collection)

At 5.10am on 16 April 1935, Laura Ingalls prepares for take-off on her record-breaking flight. (WWP, H. Hazewinkel collection)

Liesel Bach (left) with her compatriots Thea Rasche and Elly Beinhorn (right). (DR)

In the service of propaganda: Liesel Bach

(1905-1992)

Liesel Bach was useful propaganda for the Nazis. With the swastika visible in the background, she is seen here in a posed shot preparing for a flight with a 'passenger'. (H. Hazewinkel collection)

Liesel Bach was known for maintaining her own aircraft. In this posed shot, she is checking the engine of a Klemm L25d VII. (H. Hazewinkel collection)

On Sunday 29 April 1934, in beautiful weather, 150,000 spectators had gathered at the Polygone de Vincennes to watch the stars of aerobatic flying: Michel Détroyat and Marcel Doret.[1] The competition started at 11.00am with the Women's International Cup, in which the two top celebrities were to go head-to-head: Hélène Boucher in a Morane-Saulnier MS.230, and Liesel Bach in a Klemm L28 XIV. Although the French pilot put on a great display, her level of training was well behind that of the German pilot, who won the competition by some margin.

Liesel Bach was then at the peak of her fame. A native of Bonn, the 29-year-old had sport in her blood. Keen on sport from a very young age, she had a passion for hockey, tennis, horse riding, athletics, and especially swimming, a discipline in which she had won several competitions. She was not far from being selected for the 1928 Olympic Games.

Her first encounter with flying came at Hangelar, near Bonn, where an acquaintance gave her her maiden flight. Immediately falling in love with this new experience, she signed on with the local DLV association and the gliding group, of which she was to be the sole female member. By these means, she was able to take part in the tenth Rhön championships in the Wasserkuppe.

Shortly afterwards, with Jacob Möltgen as her instructor, she started her pilot's training, which ended in November 1929 when she gained her A2 certificate. She quickly showed herself to be a gifted pilot and specialised in aerobatics. In April 1930, she obtained her aerobatics qualification and not long afterwards took part in the first German women's aerobatics championships flying a Klemm L26a[2] lent by her club. This took place on 29 May 1930 and, novice though she was, Liesel Bach won against competitors who were, for the most part, highly experienced.

In her early competitions she was still flying the plane she had been lent, but was soon in a position to pilot her own Klemm L26a[3] with an Argus AS 8 engine. With this, she attended a variety of meetings, not just in Germany, but also in France (St-Germain-en-Laye, Vincennes, Deauville, Clermont-Ferrand, Bordeaux etc) and other countries (Italy, Netherlands, Luxembourg, Poland, Switzerland, Czechoslovakia etc), amassing wins and trophies as she went. Very confident and precise, she flew with great fluidity. 'Who would believe that this shy, quiet girl could become, at the controls of her aircraft, a formidable competitor to the stronger sex?' was one contemporary comment.[4]

Liesel Bach advertised herself by having her name or initials marked on her plane and her clothes. She even designed an outfit that she described as 'the international uniform of the aviatrix'. Deeply patriotic, she considered herself as the flag-bearer of her country whenever she appeared abroad, and she was soon taking up the ideas advocated by the National Socialists. We have to 'make it clear that what is said about Germany in the foreign press is nothing

The RAAB Katzenstein RK 26a Tigerschwalbe used by Liesel Bach was a small, very powerful biplane specially designed for aerobatics. The aircraft hasn't yet had the swastika applied to the fin. (H.P. Dabrowski collection)

but lies and calumnies... We want only peace and justice,' she declared at an aerobatics tournament in Milan in 1931.[5]

Liesel Bach continued her lightning rise. In late 1931, she made a long-distance flight to Sardinia, where she was unable to land because of bad weather. This was a probing flight for a round-the-world project for which she had requested the assistance of the Ministry of Foreign Affairs. The plan came to nothing, but the following year she once again took the European women's aerobatics title.

She became increasingly committed at the political level, becoming an ardent supporter of Adolf Hitler. Her achievements were exploited for propaganda purposes and photos appeared in the press of her giving the Nazi salute.[6] She was quick to appear in public with leading members of the NSDAP, such as Joseph Goebbels or Colonel Bruno Loerzer, the Reich's aerial sports director (Reichsluftsportführer).

Little is known about Liesel Bach's activities during the Second World War, other than that she worked in no. 1 ferrying squadron flying planes from the factories to assembly airfields. It is said that she flew planes up to the size of a Junkers Ju 87, for which she held the appropriate licence.

With the return of peace, she was invited to go to India, spending three years there. In this way, she was able to continue flying, which would have been strictly forbidden in Germany at that time. In February 1951, she took part in the Asian Aerobatic Championships at Kanpur (Uttar Pradesh). Flying

a Gipsy Moth in front of 100,000 spectators, she won the trophy, which was presented to her by the President of the Indian Republic, Rajendra Prasad. To help her realise her dream of flying across the Himalayas, the Prime Minister of the United Provinces, Govind Ballabh Pant, put his personal Beech 18 at her disposal. In late March 1951, she became the first woman to fly across the Himalayas. By this time, the Indian Army had sufficient confidence in her to permit her to make a number of flights in a Spitfire. She was able to defend her aerobatics title the following year in Ceylon, although she was obliged to compete in the men's category, as no competition specifically for women had been organised. She nevertheless took second place in the general classification.

In 1953, back in her own country, she was invited by the Divina-Film company to do some flying scenes for its film *Sterne Über Colombo*[7], and even played a small part in it. Once Germany had regained control of its airspace, in 1955, Liesel Bach bought a new plane, a Klemm Kl 35B with a 160hp Hirth HM 506 engine. With this, she took part in a variety of competitions, such as the Deutschlandflüge, the tenth German Aerobatics Championships and, in 1963, the European Women's Aerobatics Championships, which she duly won. She was 58 years old.

Liesel Bach continued to fly until she was 70, accumulating a total of 21,000 hours, before returning to her first sporting interest, tennis. She settled in the south of France at Bandol in the Var, where she died in 1992.

1. This meeting, known as the 'International Paris Air Day', was organised by Air Propaganda under the auspices of the daily newspaper Le Petit Parisien.
2. Klemm L26a II, no. 184, registration D-1798, built in March 1930.
3. Klemm L26a II, no. 230, registration D-1916, built in July 1930.
4. Taken from the programme of the Saint-Germain-en-Laye meeting, 21 May 1933.
5. Quoted by E. Zegenhagen, in Schneidige Deutsche Mädel, p. 330.
6. Photo taken at the 1935 Leipzig meeting, where she appeared in company with the Nazi parachutist, Inge Brumann.
7. Directed by Veit Harlan, the film was released in Britain in 1953 under the title of Stars Over Colombo.

Three of the best aerobatics pilots of the pre-war period: from left to right, Marcel Doret, Liesel Bach and Gerhard Fieseler. (V. Koos collection)

Liesel Bach poses in front of her Tigerschwalbe at one of the many meetings where she performed. The plane is registered as D-EVUK. (H.P. Dabrowski collection)

For the 1929 'Powder Puff Derby', Marvel Crosson's Travel Air Speedwing carried the number 1.
The plane had been lent to her by Walter Beech. (J. Underwood collection)

The Competitors

In the aftermath of the First World War, hundreds of pilots returned to civilian life. In this essentially masculine world, there was barely any room for female flyers. Marginalised by events, they took a while to find their place in the competitive flying events that marked the inter-war years. In Britain, aviation contests were the exclusive preserve of male pilots, mostly from the armed forces. It was eight long years before a woman would take part in a meeting on this side of the Channel. Sophie Eliott-Lynn was the first British woman to take part in an aviation meeting. On the weekend of 21 and 22 August 1926, she competed in four of the six events making up the Bournemouth Summer Aviation Race Meeting organised by the Royal Aero Club. At the time, Eliott-Lynn had two planes available to her: a standard, light-blue D.H.60 Moth biplane with a 60hp Cirrus engine, and a silver RAF S.E.5a fighter with a 200hp Hispano-Suiza engine. On 30 July 1927, she was again the only female pilot to be on the start line for the soon-to-be-famous King's Cup Race, at the controls of an Avro Avian II. Unfortunately, she was forced to pull out, but took the Grosvenor Challenge Cup, pipping Lady Bailey at the post by just a couple of metres. By November 1927, six British aviatrixes owned at least one plane. Lady Heath stood out from the crowd with three, to which would soon have to be added the Avro Avian (G-EBUG) that she had just ordered for a trip to South Africa. Mrs Maia Carberry, as well as having a Moth, had recently acquired a Fokker Universal for her husband.

In 1928, Winifred E. Spooner was the only woman among the 37 competitors lining up at the start of the King's Cup Race at Hendon on 20 July, yet despite being so outnumbered, she came in third. There were three challenging for the King's Cup at Heston in 1929, against 38 men, but the highest-placed (W. E. Spooner) was only fifth. The women were to take their revenge the following year at Hanworth. There had never before been so many competitors: 101 had registered, with 88 actually taking part. There were six women and even though F.M. Woods had to withdraw and Diana C. Guest abandoned the race, Winifred S. Brown came in first at the controls of her Avro Avian III, ahead of Alan Butler, whose wife, Lois, had also taken part. This was the only occasion an aviatrix was to win the coveted trophy. In the 1931 competition, it was a wipeout. Of the four women to take part, three had to drop out of the race and the fourth, Miss F.J. Crossley, came in 20th.

In the United States, following Charles Lindbergh's achievement, ocean fever had taken hold of many women, whose sole ambition was to get noticed, even at the risk of endangering their lives. Most of them could not fly, so were content to be co-pilots, or even passengers, so they had to find both a pilot and a plane. In this crazy quest, which lasted from the spring of 1927 to June 1928, several crews went missing. The slaughter was brought to an end by Amelia Earhart's successful crossing. On 17 June 1928, aboard a Fokker

British aviatrixes owning their own plane (1927)

Name	Plane	Registration	Date registered
Duchess of Bedford	D.H.60 Moth X	G-EBRI	18 May 1927
Lady Bailey	D.H.60 Moth	G-EBPU	1 January 1926
Miss S. O'Brien	D.H.60 Moth	G-EBOS	2 August 1927
Mrs Maia Carberry	D.H.60 Moth X	G-EBSQ	11 August 1927
Mrs Maia Carberry	Fokker Universal	G-EBUT	19 October 1927
Lady S. Heath	Avro Avian	G-EBQL	20 September 1927
Lady S. Heath	SE.5a	G-EBPA	30 July 1926
Lady S. Heath	D.H.60 Moth	G-EBMV	11 July 1927
Miss W.E. Spooner	D.H.60 Moth	G-EBOT	2 August 1927

Amelia Earhart was the first woman to cross the Atlantic by air. Though dressed like a pilot, she was just a passenger in the Fokker, which was piloted by Wilmer Stultz, with Louis Gordon as co-pilot. (Wide World, H. Hazewinkel collection)

Transoceanic attempts by women

Co-pilot/Passenger	Pilot	Plane	Comments
Pauline Rich	Garland Lincoln	Unknown	Planned, 1927
Constance Erwin	William P. Erwin	Unknown	Planned, 1927
Mabel Boll	Charles Levine	Wright-Bellanca WB-2	Planned, 1927
Mildred Doran*	John A. Pedlar	Buhl CA-5	Went missing, 16 August 1927
Alice Lowenstein	Leslie Hamilton	Fokker F. VII	Went missing, 31 August 1927
George Haldeman	Ruth Elder	Detroiter	Ditched, 13th October 1927
Frances Grayson	Wilmer Stultz	Sikorsky S-36A	Flight cut short, 17 October 1927
Frances Grayson	Oskar Omdahl	Sikorsky S-37	Went missing, 23 December 1927
Amy Phipps-Guest	Wilmer Stultz	Fokker Trimotor	Planned, 1927
Mabel Boll	Oliver Boutiller	Wright-Bellanca WB-2	Flight cut short, 12 June 1928
Amelia Earhart	Wilmer Stultz	Fokker Friendship	Successful crossing, 17 June 1928
Edna Newcomer	William Ulbrich	Bellanca CH-400	Went missing, 14 September 1932

*This was an attempt to cross the Pacific (Dole Race).

Mildred Doran was the first woman to pay for an attempted Atlantic crossing with her life. A passenger on the single-engined Buhl, christened Miss Doran and piloted by J. Pedlar (left) and V. Knope (right), she was lost without trace on 16 August 1927. (W.K. Ogata, DR)

in a competition that would not lose its urgency until 1933 with Frances Marsalis's performance of 237hr 42min. The superstitious Gentry had set herself the target of 13hr 13min 13sec. Her first attempt, on 28 December 1928, was a little over eight hours, but was almost immediately bettered by Evelyn 'Bobbie' Trout. The race was on.

There was a similar battle for the altitude record, begun by Louise Thaden on 7 December 1928.

In continental Europe, it was not until August 1929 that a competition of any significance arose: the first European Tourist Plane Contest organised by the daily, *Le Journal*, and the ACF. The 25 stages (a total of 5,942km) started at Orly and covered 11 countries. Among the 82 registered competitors, the

Having taken part in the first attempted Atlantic crossing on 17 October 1927 with Wilmer Stultz as the pilot, Frances Grayson tried again on 23 December 1927 with Oskar Omdahl in a Sikorsky S-37. The last sight of the aircraft was at 7.10pm off Cape Cod then it disappeared. Frances Grayson is seen here at Le Bourget with the pilot Laulhé, on 21 November 1927. (ROL, H. Hazewinkel collection)

Friendship piloted by Wilmer Stultz and Louis Gordon, she was the first woman to cross the Atlantic by air. She was greeted as a heroine and her exploit, in which she hadn't been the principal actor, brought her to the front stage and marked the beginning of a dazzling career.

With one challenge coming after another, aviatrixes now turned their attention to the endurance record, with Viola Gentry firing the starting pistol

Mabell Boll, a wealthy heiress from Rochester, was nicknamed 'The Queen of Diamonds'. An opportunist, she offered the tidy sum of $25,000 to any pilot who would fly her across the Atlantic. She is seen here on 27 October 1927, posing for the photographer while travelling on the liner France. (DR)

Women's endurance records 1929–33

Date	Aviatrix	Performance
28 December 1928	Viola Gentry	8 hr 6 min 37 sec
2 January 1929	Bobbi Trout	12 hr 11 min
31 January 1929	Elinor Smith	13 hr 16 min 45 sec
10–11 February 1929	Bobbi Trout	17 hr 5 min 37 sec
16–17 March 1929	Louise Thaden	22 hr 3 min 12 sec
23–24 April 1929	Elinor Smith	26 hr 21 min 32 sec
28 July 1929	Maryse Bastié	26 hr 47 min 30 sec
27 November 1929	B. Trout & E. Smith	42 hr 5 min
2 May 1930	Léna Bernstein	35 hr 46 min
4–9 January 1931	B. Trout & E. Cooper	123 hr
14–22 August 1932	L. Thaden & F. Marsalis	196 hr 5 min
20–30 December 1933	F. Marsalis & H. Richey	237 hr 42 min

Bobbi Trout was noted for repeatedly breaking endurance records. An enthusiast for motorised sports, she also took to motorcycling. She is seen here in Los Angeles on 22 June 1933, as she was preparing to take part in the National Air Races. (Bettmann/Corbis)

It was probably Viola Gentry's endurance record that unleashed the wave of records that characterised the late 1920s. On 20 December, at 5.44am, she took off from Curtiss Field at the controls of a Travel Air lent to her by Grace Lyon. Bad weather caused her to cut short the flight. She had, nevertheless, been in the air for 8hr 6min 37sec. (AAHS)

only women were the British pair, Winifred Spooner and Lady Bailey, both piloting Gipsy Moth D.H.60G biplanes. When the results came in, Winifred Spooner was in tenth place. The second European Contest, organised by the German Aero Club and starting from Berlin on 20 July 1930 was bigger still with 98 pilots, 47 of them German, and covered a total distance of 7,560km

Women's altitude records

Date	Aviatrix	Altitude
7 December 1928	Louise Thaden	6,175 m
28 May 1929	Marvel Crosson	7,315 m
18 November 1929	Ruth Alexander	4,791 m
20 October 1930	Mary E. Conrad	4,103 m
10 March 1930	Elinor Smith	8,357 m
6 March 1931	Ruth Nichols	8,761 m
March 1931	Elinor Smith	9,929 m
2 August 1933	Hélène Boucher	5,900 m

On 28 May 1929, Marvel Crosson reached 7,315m in a Ryan Broughman B-3 monoplane, beating Louise Thaden's record. Here, she is seen trying out the oxygen system held by its designer, John V. O'Connell. (Curtiss Museum)

over 28 stages. Once again appearing along with Lady Bailey, W. Spooner was the top woman, being placed fourth. She achieved the same position that year in the very first Tour of Italy (Giro Aereo d'Italia).

The first Air Tour of France, organised in 1931 by the French Civil Pilots' Union, saw the names of Maryse Hilsz and Maryse Bastié appear for the first time in a competition of national significance. Piloting a Moth-Morane,[1] Maryse Hilsz came in eighth having completed the 3,700km circuit at an average speed of 139.68kph.

The first exclusively female competition took place in the United States. A year after Phoebe F. Omlie's low-key participation in the fourth National Air Tour,[2] the ninth National Air Races were organised in Cleveland, Ohio, from 24 August to 2 September 1929. A great novelty that year was an exclusively female race, the Women's Air Derby, which was soon dubbed 'The Powder Puff Derby' by reporters. To qualify to take part, the aviatrixes had to have accumulated at least 100 hours of solo flying on a suitably certified aircraft.[3] From the 70 qualified aviatrixes at the time, only around 40 fulfilled the conditions and 20 or so took part in two categories: aircraft designated as 'light' and those designated as 'heavy'.[4] Among those taking part were some already well-known flyers, such as Ruth Elder (see p. 70), Amelia Earhart, Marvel Crosson, and the German Thea Rasche (see p. 60). Departing from Santa Monica on 17 August, by the time they got to Cleveland on Monday 26 August, there were just 14 left, with Louise Thaden arriving in first place over an hour ahead of the second-placed Gladys O'Donnell.

The National Air races allowed aviatrixes, who until then had been widely dispersed, to get to know each other and share their experiences. Several of them perceived the need to create an organisation that would make it possible to maintain contact and bring other women into aviation. It was Clara Trenchman who was the driving force behind the movement that was to lead to the creation of the famous 'Ninety-Nine'.[5] The competition was repeated

the following year, with the Transcontinental Handicap Air Derby, from which Phoebe Omlie was to emerge victorious at the controls of a Monocoupe 110, with Louise Thaden managing only fifth place.

At this time, pilots involved in the renaissance of aviation in Germany faced each other in an annual competition known as the 'Deutschlandflug', in which only German light planes powered by German engines competed against each

Some of the contestants in the 1929 Women's Air Derby posing with their trophies. From left to right are: Louise Thaden, Bobbi Trout, Patti Willis, Marvel Crosson, Blanche Noyes, Vera Walker, Amelia Earhart, Marjorie Crawford, Ruth Elder and Pancho Barnes. (NASM)

The '99' club, formed after the first 'Powder Puff Derby' to allow American aviatrixes to get to know each other and exchange experiences. Taken in Los Angeles before the 1933 National Air Races, the photograph shows, from left to right: Genevieve Haugen, Edna Crumrine, Hilda Jarmuth, Ruth Elder, Adoree Neville, Esther Jones, Kathleen Truett, Clema Granger, Esther Johnson, Margaret Perry Cooper, Elliott Roberts, Georgialee McGaffey, Jean Allen and Edith B. Clark. (Bettmann/Corbis)

Flying a Travel Air at the 1929 Women's Air Derby, Blanche Noyes came fourth in the DW category. She came into aviation after marrying the mails pilot Dewey Noyes. (Cleveland Airshow)

British pilot Winifred Spooner took part in many competitions. She came third in the 1928 and 1929 King's Cup Races and fourth in the 1930 European Circuit. (H. Hazewinkel collection)

other. On 15 and 16 April 1931, after submitting to rigorous tests, 30 pilots, two of whom were women (Liesel Bach and Elly Beinhorn), took part in a race over 2,150km, divided into eight stages and taking two days. On this, her first attempt, Liesel Bach came fourth, 1hr 49min behind the winner, Oskar Dinort.

In France, 1933 witnessed the birth of a competition that, over the four times it was run, gained steadily in fame: the Angers Twelve Hours (Les Douze Heures d'Angers). Organised by the Aéro-Club de l'Ouest, the race consisted essentially in covering the greatest distance possible in a 12-hour flight period, inclusive of stops. There was a total of 100,000F in prize money, 40,000F going to the winner. The first race, on 2 July 1933, saw the aviatrix Alex Plunian, teamed with Maurice Finat in a Farman 359, come in second place behind the Burtin/Langlois team. A young novice flyer by the name of Hélène Boucher was in 14th place.

The 1934 'Douze Heures' was marked by the appearance of the Caudron Rafales and by an increase in the number of women contestants, with teams consisting of H. Boucher/M.L. Becker in a Caudron 530, V. Elder/P. Gautier in a Farman 400 and M. Charnaux/Y. Jourjon in a Miles Hawk. The four Rafales that had been entered swept the first four places, and Hélène Boucher, piloting one of them, came second. In 1935, there were four women's teams on the start line, three of whom were placed sixth, seventh and ninth, a long way behind the winner, Maurice Arnoult. In 1936, with the object of raising interest by increasing the number of participants, the race was opened up to planes with 4- and 2-litre engines. On 5 July 1936, over a course that had been reduced to six hours because of the weather conditions, 19 planes were ready for the start. Of the three women's teams, the Andrée Dupeyron/Gracieuse Lallus pair was forced to abandon the race in the fifth hour, but Elisabeth Lion and her fellow crewmember, Mme Roumenteau, came second in the eight-litre category.

In Britain at this time, female participation in the King's Cup Race remained limited. The competition most popular in the media was undoubtedly the

One of the lesser-known participants in the 1930 National Air Races was Jane LaRene, flying a Reawin 2000-C. She finished third in the Women's Pacific Derby. (AAHS)

Women's world records in 1934

At 1 July 1934, women pilots held the following records:

Class C aeroplanes

- Distance in a straight line: 3,939.245km by Amelia Earhart (USA), in a Lockheed Vega, between Los Angeles and New York, on 24-25 August 1932.
- Altitude: 9,791m by Maryse Hilsz (Fr), in a Morane-Saulnier M.S. 222, at Villacoublay, on 19 August 1932.
- Speed: 405.92kph by May Haizlip (USA), in a Wedell-Williams, at Cleveland, on 5 September 1932.
- Speed over a closed 100km circuit: 281.47kph by Amelia Earhart (USA), in a Lockheed Vega, at Detroit, on 25 June 1930.

Light planes, class 2 (single-seaters of less than 450kg)

- Distance in a straight line: 2,976.91km by Maryse Bastié (Fr), in a Klemm L.25al, between Le Bourget and Urino (Russia), on 28-29 June 1931.
- Altitude: 5,900m by Hélène Boucher (Fr), in a Mauboussin-Peyret-Zodiac, at Orly, on 2 August 1933.

Light seaplanes, class 2 (single-seaters of less than 570kg)

- Altitude: 5,554m by Carina Negrone (It), in a Breda 15, at Genoa, on 5 May 1934.

Flying a Miles M.2H Hawk Major, Elyse Battye was, along with Ruth Fontes, one of two women to take part in the 1935 King's Cup race. Both had to abandon the race. (Mundopress, H. Hazewinkel collection)

Aircraft competing in the 1935 Hélène Boucher Cup, with, in the foreground, Miles Hawk Major G-ADAB and Caudron Aiglon G-ANZR. (GPPA)

England–Australia race, known as the MacRobertson Race. No fewer than six well-known aviatrixes decided to take part in this 18,000km-plus race, which was organised by the RAC, but this number was soon sharply reduced, with four of them having to scratch (Ruth Nichols, Jessie Keith Miller, Laura Ingalls and Louise Thaden). After her Northrop Gamma was damaged, Jacqueline Cochran opted for a Gee Bee QED, but was forced out of the race at Bucharest following mechanical trouble. Amy and Jim Mollinson, in a D.H.88 Comet named *Black Magic*, were obliged to pull out of the race at Allahabad, India.

Organised jointly by the ACF and the Cannes Aero-Club in 1935 and 1936, and offering 51,000F in prize money, the Hélène Boucher Cup rewarded the aviatrix who could achieve the best speed over the Paris–Cannes route. In the first of the two that took place, three out of the 10 registered crews withdrew, three pulled out during the race and, of the four who touched down in Cannes, it was Maryse Hilsz who had raced her way into first position at an average speed of 277.263kph flying a Breguet 27-4 sesquiplane. She again won the competition the following year, but this time in a Caudron C.680.5 Super Rafale with a 220hp engine.

Across the Atlantic, besides the inevitable National Air Races and numerous local competitions, a much-coveted trophy had made its appearance. In 1931, Clifford W. Henderson had managed to persuade the

industrial magnate Vincent Bendix to sponsor a transcontinental race that would encourage engineers to design faster and more-reliable planes. Thus was the Bendix Trophy race born. While no, or very few, aviatrixes entered this testing race between 1931 and 1935, the situation began to change at the end of this period when Amelia Earhart came fifth, flying a Lockheed Vega, having covered the 3,287km separating Burbank and Cleveland in under 14 hours.[6] It was just the first step. In 1936, women dominated the Bendix Trophy, taking three of the first five places. Flying a Beech C17R

Contestants in the 1935 Hélène Boucher Cup, from left to right, seated: Mlle de Franqueville; standing: Lucienne Saby, Maryse Hilsz, Raymond Delmotte and Andrée Dupeyron. (ROL, H. Hazewinkel collection)

The team of Béatrice McDonald/Elyse Battye in a Miles Hawk came third in the 1935 Hélène Boucher Cup. (Mundopress, H. Hazewinkel collection)

With an average of 209.359kph in her Maillet 20, Yvonne Jourjon was fourth in the 1935 Hélène Boucher Cup. She was third in 1936. (ROL)

Marthe de la Combe getting into her Caudron Simoun, at Buc on 30 August 1935, to take part in the Hélène Boucher Cup. She later had to abandon the race. (ROL)

Staggerwing biplane, Louise Thaden and her co-pilot, Blanche Noyes, were the first to be surprised by their victory. After coming third the following year in the same type of aircraft, Jacqueline Cochran set the bar very high in the 1937 event. Flying a Seversky AP-9 racer, derived from a fighter plane, she linked the two coasts in a little over 8hr 10min, 23min ahead of the next plane, of the same type.

In that same year, a more exotic competition took place in the Middle East: the International Oasis Circuit, which pitted 44 crews against each other, flying planes of highly contrasting performance, ranging from the little Miles Hawk to the big, twin-engined Junkers Ju 86. Among the teams who registered were six aviatrixes from five different countries, including the solitary Egyptian pilot, Loftia Al-Nadi (see p. 77). The winner in the women's category was the Irish pilot, Lilly Dillon, flying a Klemm 25c-1a.

As war drew closer air races began to lose their allure and high-

For the 1946 Bendix Trophy race, Jacqueline Cochran used a North American P-51B Mustang fighter, finishing second. (J. Underwood collection)

King's Cup Race was relaunched in 1949 and the first entirely female races were organised in France by the ACF starting in 1953, with the International Women's Rally, which in that year was won by Jeanette Poujade at the controls of a SNCAN Nord 1203 Norécrin, and the year after by Marie Nicolas in the same type of plane. Unsurprisingly, Germany revived the Deutschlandflug somewhat later, because of the restrictions imposed by the Allies. The first post-war event was not until 1956, when Elly Beinhorn and her Piper Club finished in second place.

Slowly, the competitions became fewer and further between, eventually disappearing altogether, thanks to a lack of sponsors and spectators. Nowadays, the only races to have survived are in America. Taking place annually in Reno, Nevada, the National Championship Air Races see a few aviatrixes each year, such as Lynn Farnsworth, Mary Dilda and Leah Sommer, competing in the Super Sport category. In 1990, Erin Rheinschild competed and won in the 'Unlimited' category for the first time, flying a P-51D Mustang.

performance planes became much less in evidence as they were kept from public view for security reasons. In Europe, the last significant competitions took place in 1937, and in the US in 1939 with the 19th National Air Races, which took place in Cleveland from 30 August to 2 September. On this occasion, Arlène Davis, flying a Spartan Executive, came fifth in the Bendix Trophy race.[7]

At the end of hostilities, it was these very National Air Races that were the first to reappear, with Jacqueline Cochran at the peak of her form. Flying a P-51B Mustang, she took second place in the Bendix Trophy. This was to be the last time that a woman would achieve such a performance in this competition. However, the race for the Halle Trophy was to see aviatrixes facing each other for many more years flying only North American AT-6/SNJ aircraft.

In Europe, aeronautical competitions made a slower start. In Britain, the

1. The Moth-Morane was a version of the De Havilland D.H.60 built under licence by Morane-Saulnier.
2. The National Air Tour was first and foremost a test of endurance and reliability.
3. Namely, in receipt of an Approved Type Certificate (ATC) issued by the Department of Commerce.
4. The light planes (category CW) had engines of less than 8,360cm3 and the heavy planes (DW) had engines between 8,360cm3 and 13,100cm3.
5. The '99s'. This designation was chosen only after some thought. Amelia Earhart suggested basing it on the number of founder members. The association was thus successively named the '86s', the '97s' and finally the '99s'.
6. Earhart was, however, more than five hours behind the winner, Ben Howard.
7. The last Bendix Trophy race was to take place in 1951.

Jacqueline Cochran poses in front of the Beech D-17W in which she has just taken third place in the 1937 Bendix Trophy race, having completed the crossing of the United States in 10hr 29min 8sec. (Odlum Photo)

Leah Sommer with her Pitts S-15 no. 10 at the 2008 Reno races. (Jim Dunn)

Erin Rheinschild at the controls of her jointly-owned P-51D Mustang, taxies towards the parking area after her win on 23 September 1990. (Jim Dunn)

The height of elegance: Lady Heath

(1897-1939)

Sophie C. Eliott-Lynn (left) with Thea Rasche (right) at their first meeting, in London, 1927. (DR)

Erin Rheinschild was the first woman to compete in the 1990 Reno 'Queen of the Races' category and win the 'Bronze Unlimited Final'. (Jim Dunn)

Lady Heath at the Rotterdam Meeting, flanked by M. Plesner, the managing director of KLM (left) and Fris Koolhoven (right). (Geen, H. Hazewinkel collection)

'She made the wings fast in flying position, climbing around the plane like a great cat,... She was clad in a colorful cretonne smock and wore high, soft leather boots... She spun the propeller and started the engine herself while a score of men and boys stood open-mouthed in a semi-circle.'[1] The aviatrix in question was Sophie Mary Heath, commonly known as Lady Heath, probably one of the best-known Britons of the period. She had been born in Ireland, at Knockaderry, and her real name was Sophie Catherine Theresa Mary Pierce-Evans.

By the time she began her career in aviation, Sophie had already forged a name for herself in athletics, making a few records (in the javelin and high jump), taking part in the seventh Olympic Games and writing a book on the subject.[2] It was at this time that she married her first husband – becoming Sophie C. Eliott-Lynn – and started her first flying lessons, gaining her private pilot's licence by 1924 and, in 1926, becoming the first British woman to gain a commercial pilot's licence.

In August 1926, she took part in the Bournemouth Meeting flying an old S.E.5a and, on 26 May 1927, she broke the British altitude record with 4,880m. In the summer of the same year, she acquired an Avro Avian[3] and signed a contract with its builder to go on a 2,000km demonstration tour around England. The same year marked the death of her husband. Keen to go to South Africa, she bought a second Avro Avian[4] and had it sent over, with the intention of doing a tour during the winter of 1927-1928. In fact, she used the plane to return to England. Taking with her just a Bible, a gun, a pair of tennis rackets, six evening dresses and a fur coat, she left Cape Town on 12 February 1928, hoping to reach London in three weeks. In the event, the journey was to take her three months. It was during this trip that she came across Lady Bailey in Khartoum (see p. 58). She arrived in Croydon on 17 May,

suitably dressed in one of her gowns! The same year, she married the 75-year-old Sir James Heath, who was rolling in money, a union that permitted her to take the title of Lady Heath.

In July, Lady Heath took part in the Rotterdam Meeting, where she met the managing director of KLM. A week later, on 27 July, she was hired as a co-pilot, allowing her the opportunity to fly on virtually any of the Dutch company's routes. This new occupation was short-lived: in January 1929 she began a demonstration tour of the Avian in the United States, in which she ended up visiting some 40 manufacturers and doing 125 demonstration flights. To cap this tour, she planned to take part in the National Air Races at Cleveland. Unfortunately, on 29 August, as she was practising landing, the engine cut out and her plane crashed, leaving her seriously injured. After this brush with death, she was stuck on the ground while she slowly recovered and did not fly again until the beginning of 1931. She returned to her native Ireland with her third husband, G.A.R. Williams, a rider and pilot from the Caribbean, and ran a small aviation firm at Kildonan, near Dublin. She was to die in London, in 1939, after falling from the platform of a tramcar.

1. In the Jacksonville Journal 5 January 1929.
2. Athletics for Women and Girls: How to Be an Athlete and Why (1925).
3. The Avro Avian had folding wings, so that it could be kept in a garage.
4. This Avro Avian was sold on to Amelia Earhart at the end of 1928.

One of the English cigarette cards depicting aviators, dating from the 1930s. This is one of a series of 50 cards entitled 'Famous Airmen and Airwomen' distributed by Carreras Ltd. in 1936. (Author's collection)

Lady Heath, on the left, wearing a leopard-skin coat, and her personal secretary, with her D.H.60 Moth at the Rotterdam Meeting from 20 to 22 July 1928. (Geen, H. Hazewinkel collection)

No-nonsense flying: Lady Bailey

(1890-1960)

Calm, relaxed and modest, sometimes excessively so, Lady Mary Bailey had her status in the world of aviation recognised by the award of the Hammond Aviatrix Trophy in 1927 and 1928. (Wide World Photos)

The only daughter of Derrick Westenra, the fifth Baron of Rossmore, Mary Westenra married the South African millionaire, Sir Abe Bailey, in 1911. In 1926, after having given birth to five children, Lady Bailey decided to learn to fly. In February of the following year, she received her pilot's licence, thus becoming the second British woman to do so. On 5 July 1927, accompanied by Mrs Geoffrey De Havilland, Mrs Bailey got herself noticed when she broke the light-plane altitude record, with 5,268m. A little later, she also became the first woman to cross the Irish Sea. These two exploits brought her the title of Champion Woman of the Air, bestowed upon her by an American association.

At the end of that July, along with Sophie C. Eliott-Lynn, she became the first woman to start in the King's Cup Race, organised by the Royal Aero Club, but was unfortunately forced to abandon the race when a valve broke on her De Havilland biplane. Continuing along the path she had set for herself, she became the first woman to gain a licence for low-visibility flying.

On 9 March 1928, flying a D.H.60 Moth,[1] she took off from Croydon heading for Cape Town in South Africa. Arriving in Khartoum, she met Lady Heath and the two aviatrixes were invited to a reception put on in their honour. The difference in style between the two women could hardly have been more marked. Lady Heath arrived in an evening dress, while Lady Bailey, straightforward and not remotely sophisticated, turned up in her flying suit. Continuing her journey, she crashed near Tabora. It hardly mattered: her husband immediately sent her a replacement aircraft, in which she managed to get to Cape Town a little after midday on 30 April and to leave again for London on 12 May, arriving there on 16 January 1929, though not without another accident at Hummansdorp and having covered a total of 28,960km. Despite the length of time the journey took, the press was full of praise for her achievement.

In July of the same year, Lady Bailey was once again on the start line of the King's Cup Race, alongside two other British aviatrixes: Mrs Winifred E. Spooner and A.S. Butler. All three were flying D.H.60G Gipsy Moths. Mary Bailey came in 21st place. Following closely came the first Light Plane Tour of Europe, starting at Orly on 4 August 1929 and pitting the contestants against each other over a 5,940km course, but she and her co-pilot turned up too late for the start! A few months later, Mary Bailey managed to finish in the 1930 King's Cup Race, though she achieved only 53rd place, and also finished 31st in the second Tour of Europe. Ever pugnacious, even a little stubborn, she made her final attempt on the King's Cup race in 1931, at the controls of a D.H.80A Puss Moth, but was forced to abandon the race.

In 1933, Lady Bailey attempted to repeat her flight to the Cape, but in a shorter time, using her D.H.80A Puss Moth. Leaving Croydon on 15 January, she went missing in the Tanezrouft desert and, for a while, it was thought she had met her end. On 20 January, she decided to return to London, via Poitiers and Le Bourget, where a journalist from *Les Ailes* (Wings)[2] reported: 'Great aviatrix though she is, Lady Bailey's adventures show what a demanding test the flight from London to the Cape really is.'

1. A standard production aircraft with a 75hp ADC Cirrus Mk II engine and a reserve fuel tank in the forward cockpit.
2. In Les Ailes, 2 February 1933.

Mary Bailey accomplished most of her feats flying various De Havilland D.H.60 biplanes, registered as G-EBQH, G-EBSF and G-EBTG. (DR)

Louise Thaden wears a broad smile after breaking the women's altitude record. (NASM)

Recordbreaker of the Golden Age: Louise Thaden

(1905-1979)

Louise Thaden at the time of the first Women's Air Derby. (Curtiss Museum)

'The indisputable fact that I was first into Cleveland, winner of the derby, could not penetrate. Before the ship rolled to a stop a crowd swarmed around us. Alarmed, I cut the switch. Sunburned field mechanics grinned, showing white teeth. Picking the Travel Air and me up bodily, they carried us over in front of the grandstand.'[1] It was 26 August 1929 and Louise Thaden had just won the first competition exclusively for women, the famous 'Powder Puff Derby', by covering the 4,439km from Santa Monica to Cleveland in 20hr 19min 2sec.

Louise McPhetridge Thaden was not completely unknown at the time. On 7 December 1928, she had beaten the women's altitude record, reaching 6,175m, and on 16 and 17 March 1929, she had taken the women's endurance record, staying aloft for 22hr 3min 12sec.[2]

The daughter of Roy and Edna McPhetridge, Iris Louise was born at Bentonville, Arkansas, one fine day in November 1905. After pursuing journalistic studies, she had turned towards physical education and then found a job at the J.H. Turner Coal and Building Materials Company. Turner had introduced her to Walter Beech who had taken her on at the San Francisco subsidiary of the Travel Air Corporation, then a renowned aircraft brand. It was there that she met the man who would become her husband: Herbert von Thaden.[3] Finding herself increasingly enthused by flying, she had taken lessons and gained pilot's licence no. 850 on 16 May 1928, following this up the following year with commercial pilot's licence no. 1943. She was the fourth American woman to receive such a licence.

Louise Thaden in March 1929 at Oakland airport at the time of her first endurance record. (NASM)

Louise Thaden in front of the Beech C17R Staggerwing in which she won the Bendix Trophy. (Beech)

After her victory in the 'Powder Puff Derby', which earned her $3,600, Louise Thaden, with her friend Amelia Earhart, was one of the founders of the '99s' group, serving first as treasurer (from 1930 to 1934) then as vice-president (from 1934 to 1936).

Having competed in the 1931 Women's Air Derby, she teamed up with Frances Marsalis from 14 to 22 August 1932 to break once again the endurance record. Flying a Curtiss Thrush monoplane[4] she stayed airborne for 196hr 5min, during which she was refuelled no fewer than 78 times. But it was her victory in the 1936 Bendix Trophy race that most stunned the aviation world. Flying a Beech C17R Staggerwing biplane with a 420hp Wright engine, with Blanche Noyes as co-pilot, she brought down the time for the crossing of the US to 14hr 54min. For this achievement, the women pocketed $9,500. The performance also saw them awarded the 1936 Hammond Trophy. The following spring, Louise Thaden took her final record, with the American speed record over 100km, flying at an average of 318.514kph.

From 1938 onwards, Louise Thaden withdrew from competition to devote more time to her family. Nonetheless, during the Second World War, she took an active part in the Civil Air Patrol and in 1950, with her daughter Patricia, she entered one final competition; the International Women's Air Race between Montreal and West Palm Beach in which she came fifth.

1. In High, Wide and Frightened, Louise Thaden's autobiography (1938).
2. The plane used in this performance was Air Travel 3000, no. 07, registered as NC5426.
3. Herbert von Thaden was an ex-US Army pilot who was then working as an engineer at Warren's, designing an entirely metal transport plane.
4. The Curtiss Thrush J was a 225hp, Wright J6-5-engined monoplane. The one used by L. Thaden was registered as NR9142.

Here displaying her ever-present smile, Thea Rasche was nicknamed 'Rasche Thea' (Fast Thea), 'Königin der Asse' (Queen of the Aces) and 'Aristokratin der Lüfte' (The Aristocrat of the Air) in her own country. She is seen here in the cockpit of the Flamingo owned by her instructor, Paul Baumer. (DR)

'The Flying Fraulein': Thea Rasche

(1899-1971)

Thea Rasche was solicitous of her image and readily gave interviews to journalists. She is here seen posing with her Udet U12a biplane, at a Berlin-Tempelhof meeting. (H. Hazewinkel collection)

Louise Thaden with a Travel Air biplane. It was in a similar plane that she reached an altitude of 6,175m on 7 December 1928. (DR)

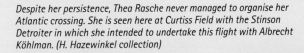

Thea Rasche went to the United States with her Flamingo, seen here at Roosevelt Field, Long Island, accompanied by her mascot, a toy monkey. (H. Hazewinkel collection)

As the handful of Calexico locals approached the pilot of the biplane that had just come down, its engine cut, in a nearby field, they were astonished to hear her address them in a strong German accent. Once over their surprise, they helped the aviatrix – Thea Rasche, or the 'Flying Fräulein' as she was nicknamed – to repair her plane and set off again for Fly Field, not far from Yuma, Arizona.

Thea was one of the 19 aviatrixes taking part in the 'Powder Puff Derby' between Santa Monica, California, and Cleveland, Ohio (see p. 177). Despite this unfortunate setback, she finished fourth in her category, in a race that was just one of thirty competitions that made up the National Air Races taking place from 24 August to 2 September 1929. Still better was to come when, on 31 August, she came first in the Australian Pursuit Race for Women, winning the tidy sum of $1,250.[1]

Born in Westphalia, the daughter of a wealthy brewer, her rounded features were always illuminated with a smile. She had secretly started to learn to fly under Paul Baumer, a veteran of the Great War, and had received her private pilot's licence in 1925, followed by her aerobatics certificate. As the first

German stuntwoman, she had taken part in numerous meetings. In 1926, she had been given her first plane by her father, an Udet Flamingo with a bright-red fuselage.

In May 1927, swept up in the enthusiasm over the Atlantic, she had met Clarence D. Chamberlin[2] when he came to Berlin. He had invited her to go to Paris, where she came across the polar explorer, Richard E. Byrd (1888-1957) and his team,[3] who had persuaded her to come with them to the east coast of the United States. Taking her Flamingo with her, she set sail on the SS *Leviathan*.

As the only woman present, Thea Rasche had got herself in the public eye at several meetings (Providence, Rhode Island, Worcester etc). She had been received at the White House by President Coolidge in person, but had unfortunately lost her precious Flamingo while attempting to fly under the Albany Bridge on her birthday.[4] Six months later, she had returned to Germany, with the idea of attempting an Atlantic crossing. After three months spent in Berlin, she had set off again for America where she began the search for a sponsor and a plane, having set her heart on a Bellanca monoplane. After several arrangements that had not worked out, Mrs Fifi Stillman had bought the said plane, named it *North Star* and taken on Thea as a pilot. After much red tape, Thea had tried to make the 'great leap' from Canada, but never managed to get off the ground. Obliged to return to Germany in August 1928, she had come back the following March to make a further attempt, this time from Orchard Beach, Maine, but in the meantime, the Bellanca had been sold on for an attempt to fly to Rome.[5]

This was at the time the First Women's Air Derby was announced, due to take place from 18 to 26 August, between Santa Monica and Cleveland. Thea

Thea Rasche and her BFW M23b monoplane, registered as D-1858, which she acquired in June 1930. (V. Koos collection)

Despite her persistence, Thea Rasche never managed to organise her Atlantic crossing. She is seen here at Curtiss Field with the Stinson Detroiter in which she intended to undertake this flight with Albrecht Köhlman. (H. Hazewinkel collection)

Thea Rasche on the liner SS Leviathan, on her way to the United States in July 1927. (ROL)

In 1934, Thea Rasche took part in the famous London–Melbourne race as a reporter aboard a KLM Douglas DC-2, which finished second. She is seen here in Hawaii, camera in hand, with Reeder Nichols, the navigator of the Boeing 247D that came in third. (Hawaii Aviation)

Rasche, who had sold her Flamingo,[6] had agreed to compete on behalf of the Moth Aircraft Corporation[7] flying a Gipsy Moth.

Thea Rasche returned to Germany in November 1929 and, in the following June, bought her third plane, a BFW M-32b. In 1932, she took her hydroplane certificate, becoming the first German woman to obtain one.

When the Nazis came to power, in 1933, she sold her plane, became the editor of the aviation magazine *Die Deutsche Flugillustrierten* and, in May of that year, joined the National Socialist Party. In 1934, she took part in the well-known London–Melbourne race, though not as a pilot, but as a reporter, on board a KLM Douglas DC-2 piloted by K.D. Parmentier and J. Moll. The only entrant to carry passengers, the DC-2 created a sensation when it came in second. Once in Australia, she continued her world tour aboard the SS *Mariposa* and arrived in Los Angeles in December 1934. While there, she gave a series of lectures and was received at the White House by Mrs Roosevelt before returning to Germany.

The Nazis then banned her from continuing her job as an editor, and the three books she had published were suppressed on the grounds that they were too indulgent towards the Anglo-Americans. Thea Rasche then became a professional photographer, remaining in Berlin until the end of the war. In December 1951, she emigrated to the United States, returning to Germany in September 1953. She died in Essen on 25 February 1971.

1. Worth about $15,000 today.
2. Between 4 and 6 June 1927, Clarence D. Chamberlin made a non-stop flight from Roosevelt to Eisleben, a distance of 6,293km, in 42hr 31min.
3. Balchen, Acosto and Noville.
4. During the attempt, the Flamingo's engine stalled and Thea Rasche was forced to come down in the Hudson River. Being insured, she was able to take delivery of a new Flamingo.
5. This flight was undertaken by Roger Q. Williams and Lewis Yancey, who took off on 8 July 1929.
6. Thea Rasche was dissatisfied with the new Flamingo and sold it on to DVS-Berlin for 16,000 Marks.
7. The Moth Aircraft Corporation had been established in 1929 at Lowell, Massachusetts to sell the De Havilland Gipsy Moth in the United States. It was bought by Curtiss-Wright in 1930.

'Records are made to be beaten': Ruth Rowland Nichols

(1901–1960)

Ruth Nichols posing in front of a Curtiss Robin on 19 March 1929, just after she had arrived in Washington at the end of a tour of the United States that she had undertaken with Robb C. Cortel to promote national aeronautical clubs. (Library of Congress)

Ruth Nichols at the time she was breaking records. She is wearing her usual lavender-coloured flying jacket. (AAHS)

During a stopover at Cincinnati in late 1930, Ruth Nichols used everything she could to get the powerful Powell Crosley to lend her his Lockheed Vega so she could beat a series of records, which in return would provide some excellent publicity for his firm: Crosley was persuaded. Ruth started from the principle that 'records were made to be beaten, and the more women could get hold of good planes, the more records they would beat... and the more the public would have confidence in flying. Given that we are considered the weaker sex,' she added, 'flying would look easy.'

Ruth Rowland Nichols was born on 23 February 1901 in New York. When she had finished her studies, her father, Erickson Norman Nichols, had treated her to a flight aboard a plane flown by Eddie Stinson, the brother of the well-known Stinson sisters (see p. 19), thereby awakening her interest in aviation. In February 1922, while she was still a student, Ruth secretly began flying lessons and obtained her qualifications in 1924. Her first exploit took place on 2 January 1928 when, as co-pilot to Harry Rogers (her instructor), she made a flight from New York to Miami in a single-engined Fairchild.[1] This led to her being hired by the Fairchild Airplane and Engine Company as director of sales promotion.[2] This, however, was short-lived, for as soon as she heard about the First Women's Air Derby, she wasted no time in signing up. Her participation did not leave her covered in glory, however, ending in two forced landings and the destruction of her plane.

Far from being disheartened, Ruth Nichols approached Clarence Chamberlin, a specialist in long-distance flights. She had conceived of nothing less than a round-the-world solo flight, but Chamberlin dissuaded her, suggesting she start with an Atlantic crossing. As she did not have the means to buy a plane, she got Powell Crosley[3] to lend her his Lockheed Vega. The day after her return to New York, she took off for Los Angeles, where she landed 16hr 59min later, establishing a new women's record. It was a record she beat again on her return flight with just 13hr 20 min.

Ruth then went after records: the women's altitude record, which she broke on 31 March 1931 with 8,761m, and the speed record on 13 April 1931, which she took from Amelia Earhart with 338.992kph. She now felt ready to make the great leap across to Europe. On 22 June 1931 at 15.30, she took off from Floyd Bennett Field at the controls of her Vega, but while landing at St Johns, New Brunswick, she overshot the runway and crashed, breaking five vertebrae. Ignoring doctors' advice, after just four months' convalescence she made her comeback and established a new women's distance record by flying the 3,182km from Oakland to Louisville on 24 and 25 October 1931. With the height of ill luck, her Vega caught fire the following day as she was preparing to take off for New York. Once more, Clarence Chamberlin lent all his support to get the Vega back in order. In the meantime, she borrowed the diesel-engined Vega from

On 6 March 1931, Ruth Nichols broke the altitude record at the controls of a Lockheed Vega 5 Special no. 619, registered as NR496M, which had been lent to her by Powell Crosley, the chairman of the powerful Crosley Radio Corporation. (Wide World Photos, H. Hazewinkel collection)

Chamberlin Flying Services[4] using it to set the altitude record for this type of aircraft, with 6,074m. This string of achievements gained her the award of 'Aviatrix of the Year 1931' bestowed by the prestigious FAI (Fédération Aéronautique Internationale). Her greater public profile allowed her to start raising money for the transatlantic attempt. However, on 21 May 1932, Amelia Earhart beat her to it. Ruth Nichols, after her initial disappointment, resolved to go one better, by completing the first New York–Paris flight by a woman, effectively repeating Lindbergh's exploit.

By August 1932, she was ready to go, but the weather was uncooperative. While waiting, she planned various long-distance flights, including one from New York to Los Angeles undertaken on 4 November 1932. Unfortunately, while taking off from Floyd Bennett Field, her Vega

Like many aviators of her time, Ruth Nichols was used in advertising campaigns such as this one for Goodrich tyres. (DR)

Lockheed Vega NR496M after its reconstruction following a fire on 26 October 1931. Ruth Nichols christened it Atika, a word used by South Dakota Indians to mean 'explorer'. (Lockheed)

Los Angeles: the National Air Races on 6 July 1933, Ruth Nichols and Amelia Earhart sit relaxing on the running board of a magnificent Cord cabriolet. (Bettmann/Corbis)

On 25 September 1960, suffering from depression, she died from a barbiturate overdose at her home in New York.

1. The plane used for this flight was a Fairchild FC-2 with a 200hp Wright J-4 engine.
2. In doing so, Ruth Nichols became the first woman in the US to occupy a senior executive position in the aeronautical industry.
3. Powell Crosley Jr was the managing director of the mighty Crosley Radio Corporation.
4. This was Lockheed Vega 1 no. 14, registered as NR7426, with a 225hp Packard DR-980 diesel engine.
5. The crash occurred when she was co-piloting a Curtiss Condor, on which one of the engines had failed.

overturned and was irreparably damaged. Without a plane or money, Ruth Nichols found herself grounded. Chamberlin gave her a position in his aviation firm. On 21 October 1935, at Troy, New York, she was again seriously injured in a crash, preventing her from flying for nearly a year.[5] This difficult period marked a turning point in her career. Once she had recovered, Ruth joined the Emergency Peace Campaign organised by a Quaker group then, in 1939, she joined the Civil Air Patrol, taking the rank of lieutenant colonel. With the return of peace, she became involved in various humanitarian enterprises, notably within UNICEF.

Over her career, Ruth Nichols flew in 71 different types of aircraft: aeroplanes, gliders, autogyros and even a jet fighter. Indeed, in 1958 when she was 57, she co-piloted a supersonic Convair TF-102A Delta Dagger fighter. Later, she was involved in the Mercury space programme.

May 1927: Ruth Nichols speaking on the place of women in aviation at the National Aviation Forum. (Library of Congress)

Best aviatrix of 1930: Elinor Smith (1911–2010)

Enthused by flying from a very early age, Elinor Smith was, in her time, the youngest qualified aviatrix. (DR)

Elinor Smith broke her first endurance records flying a Bellanca CH monoplane. (Bettmann/Corbis)

Nowadays, she is almost forgotten, but in 1930 her peers voted her the best aviatrix of the year. Overshadowed by the media barrage put up around Amelia Earhart by George P. Putnam, Elinor Smith had more than one achievement to her name, the first of which was to have gained her pilot's licence at the age of 16, making her the youngest aviatrix in the world. In truth, the young Elinor[1] had been crazy about planes ever since she and her brother Joe had flown aboard a Farman biplane piloted by Louis Gaubert. She was then barely six years old.

Elinor had made her first solo flight when she was 15[2] and, three months later, she had set an altitude record, climbing to 3,624m at the controls of a Waco 9 biplane that her father had bought. In October 1928, she had made the front pages by flying, one after the other, under the four bridges spanning the East River in New York. She then set a string of records: the endurance record on 31 January 1929, with over 13 hours, a figure she had increased to over 26 hours by the following April, flying a Bellanca CH. In May, piloting a Curtiss, she had beaten the women's speed record with 307kph. In June, the Irving Chute Company took her on to do a 9,700km promotional tour around the country, which had culminated in the simultaneous dropping of seven parachutists at the National Air Races in Cleveland. Teaming up with Bobbi Trout, she had then set the long-distance record using in-flight refuelling. Now in full flow, she had smashed the altitude record, climbing to 8,357m in March and, the following May, when only 18 years old, she had gained her commercial pilot's licence. It is not difficult to see why, that October, she was voted 'Best American Aviatrix' for the year 1930.[3]

In March 1931, she again broke the altitude record, coming within an ace of 10,000m but, much to her annoyance, the achievement was invalidated because of a technical problem. To cap it all, the economic crisis removed all hope of her being able to make a solo Atlantic crossing flying a Lockheed Vega.

Her marriage to Patrick H. Sullivan in 1933 cut short her aeronautical career as she turned to devoting herself fully to her family. Only after her husband's death, in 1956, did she return to aviation, when she joined the Air Force Association, a move that gave her the opportunity to fly jet planes. Active until the end, Elinor Smith was the last surviving aviatrix from the 'Golden Age'.

1. Her original full name was Elinor Regina Patricia Ward. Her father changed his name to Smith.
2. She had begun flying lessons at the age of 10.
3. The title of 'Best American Aviator' was awarded that year to Jimmy Doolittle.

Elinor Smith planned to cross the Atlantic solo in this Lockheed Vega Special 5C, christened Mrs ?. (DR)

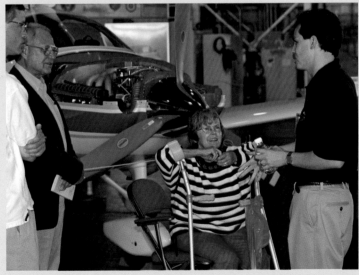

Born on 17 May 1911, Elinor Smith died on 19 March 2010. Over the years, she maintained her contacts with the aviation world. She is seen here at an Open Day at NASA's Langley Center, on 28 April 2001. (NASA/LaRC)

Raymonde de Laroche, Amelie Beese, Hélène Dutrieu, Harriet Quimby, Katherine Stinson, Blanche Scott, Ruth Law, Bessie Coleman, Adrienne Bolland, Florence Klingensmith, Laura Ingalls, Liesel Bach, Lady Heath, Lady Mary Bailey, Louise Thaden, Thea Rasche, Ruth Rowland Nichols, Elinor Smith, Ruth Elder, Carina Negrone, Paulina Denisovna Ossipenko, Hanna Reitsch, Marcelle Choisnet, Maryse Bastié, Léna Bernstein, Amy Johnson-Mollison, Anne Morrow-Lindbergh, Marga Von Etzdorf, Maryse Hilsz, Beryl Markham, Elly Beinhorn, Jean Batten, Elisabeth Lion, Helen Richey, Eugénie M. Shakhovskaya, Cecil W. "Teddy" Kenyon, Pauline Gower, Nancy Harkness Love, Maria Ivanovna Dolina, Amélia Earhart, Hélène Boucher, Jacqueline Cochran, Jacqueline Auriol, Eileen Marie Collins, Anna Walker, Ellen Church, Clara Adams, Harriet Quimby, Marjorie Stinson, Mrs Eyman, Fay Gillis, Virginia Waibel, Eleanor Blevins, Aniwegi Boudinot, Helen Clifford, Janett Moffett, Bernetta Miller, Ruth Fontes, Jeanne Pallier, Blossom Miles, Emily Schaeffer, Raymonde de Laroche, Amelie Beese, Hélène Dutrieu, Harriet Quimby, Katherine Stinson, Blanche Scott, Ruth Law, Bessie Coleman, Adrienne Bolland, Florence Klingensmith, Laura Ingalls, Liesel Bach, Lady Heath, Lady Mary Bailey, Louise Thaden, Thea Rasche, Ruth Rowland Nichols, Elinor Smith, Ruth Elder, Carina Negrone, Paulina Denisovna Ossipenko, Hanna Reitsch, Marcelle Choisnet, Maryse Bastié, Léna Bernstein, Amy Johnson-Mollison, Anne Morrow-Lindbergh, Marga Von Etzdorf, Maryse Hilsz, Beryl Markham, Elly Beinhorn, Jean Batten, Elisabeth Lion, Helen Richey, Eugénie M. "Teddy" Kenyon, Pauline Gower, Nancy Harkness Love, Maria Ivanovna Dolina, Amelia Earhart, Hélène Boucher, Jacqueline Cochran,

The shooting stars

Myrna Loy looks angelic with her white flying helmet and perfect makeup, as she plays opposite Cary Grant in Wings in the Dark. *(DR))*

Between 1918 and 1929, Edna Mae Cooper acted in 20-odd silent films, several of which were directed by Cecil B. De Mille. She disappeared from the scene with the advent of the talkies. (DR)

The year of 1927 was a fruitful one for both aviation and the cinema. Charles Lindbergh crossed the Atlantic and, on the silver screen, *Wings*, the first big production devoted entirely to flying, was being shown, with Clara Bow and Buddy Rogers in the lead roles. The link between women's aviation and the cinema dated back barely ten years at that point. On 12 July 1919, Edna Purviance, Charlie Chaplin's favourite actress, took an active part in the Syd-Chaplin-Air-Line's inaugural flight aboard a Curtiss Seagull.[1] Right from the early 1920s, Hollywood made use of stunt flyers in the making of its films. Among the best-known of these was certainly Ruth Roland, who was responsible for some of the aerial stunts in *The Timber Queen* (Pathé, 1922), *Around the World in 18 Days* (Universal, 1923) and *The Eagle's Talons* (Universal, 1923). In September 1919, the *New York Herald* announced that the theatre actress Hope Eden had acquired a Curtiss JN-4D biplane, as well as a pilot, to get her to her various engagements on time.

The Lindbergh effect created a stampede of self-appointed aviators and aviatrixes, some of whom came from the world of cinema. This was the case with Ruth Elder, who took on the task of crossing the Atlantic, but without success. For a long time, she vacillated between the two careers, in the end succeeding in neither. Blanche Noyes, whose career as a theatre and film actress had made a promising start, married a pilot in the air-mails service and gave it all up to take her pilot's licence and buy a plane. At the same time, the youthful Loretta Young, who was to have a shining career in the cinema, was in Arizona taking flying lessons from Ace Bregunier. Another actress, Edna Mae Cooper,[2] already with 22 films to her credit, joined Evelyn 'Bobbi' Trout to take the endurance record. On 2 January 1931, flying a Curtiss Robin named *Lady Rolph*, the two women made an attempt on the record, but were forced to call it off after three hours following a problem with the refuelling process.

The actress Linda Darnel poses at the controls of a Lockheed P-38 fighter at Muroc in 1945. (AFFTC)

Edna Mae Cooper at the time she and Bobbi Trout broke the endurance record. (H. Hazewinkel collection)

The actress June Travis learned to fly for one of her films. She was taught by Amelia Earhart who is seen here helping her to put on her parachute. (IFP, H. Hazewinkel collection)

Two days later, they made a further attempt. This time, Trout and Cooper remained aloft for 122hr 50min, being obliged to stop when a piston fractured in the Curtiss Challenger engine. During their almost-five-day flight, they made 11 in-flight refuellings and nearly tripled the previous women's record.[3] They had covered 11,858km and used 4,300 litres of fuel and 128 litres of oil.

1933 saw the first feature-length film depicting a woman pilot. This was

Katherine Hepburn, in a leather jacket and helmet, gets ready to climb into her plane, in Christopher Strong. *(RKO)*

Miss Beatrix Thomson in the cockpit of a De Havilland Puss Moth in March 1935. This British actress, who was a qualified pilot, was then having a runaway success in London, at the Duke of York Theatre, in the play For the Defence *by John Hastings Turner. (F.A. Srapf)*

Loretta Young (right) and Geraldine Fitzgerald (left) in Ladies Courageous, *a feature-length film made in 1943 by John Rawlins, based on an original story by Virginia Cowles. (Universal)*

Christopher Strong directed by Dorothy Azner (one of the few Hollywood female directors) and with none other than Katherine Hepburn topping the bill. *Wings in the Dark* appeared in 1935, with Myrna Loy playing the part of an aerial stuntwoman called Sheila Mason. The following year, in *Sky Parade* (Paramount), Katherine DeMille is seen next to Jimmie Allen at the controls of a Stearman while, in France, the actress Gaby Morlay took the test for her airship pilot's licence.

With the advent of war, Hollywood paid tribute to the female pilots of the US Army Air Force. Loretta Young and (her sister) Geraldine Fitzgerald played two such WAFS in *Ladies Courageous* (Universal, 1944), while many women stars of the big screen toured air bases, boosting the morale of the aircrews.

In France, aviatrixes appeared in a few films such as *Le Ciel est à Vous* (1943), a comedy of manners inspired by the true story of Andrée Dupeyron, and particularly *Horizons sans Fin* (1952), a Jean Dréville film based on the life of Hélène Boucher, with Gisèle Pascal in the role of the famous French aviatrix.

The coming of television witnessed the disappearance of aviatrixes from the big screen, while TV films cashed in on the lives of a number of them, including: Pancho Barnes (*Pancho Barnes*), Beryl Markham (*A Shadow on the Sun*), and Amelia Earhart (*The Final Flight*). It was not until 2009 that a new major production about a female flyer would be made. The film, simply entitled *Amelia*, was shot in 2009 by Mira Nair, with Hilary Swank playing the part of Amelia Earhart.

1. *Founded by Charlie Chaplin's brother Sydney Chaplin, the Syd-Chaplin-Air-Line started up on 4 July 1919 using Curtiss MF hydroplanes.*
2. *Edna Mae Cooper (1900–1966) got her first part in 1918 and played her last in 1956.*
3. *The previous record was 42hr 16min and was set by Bobbi Trout and Elinor Smith on 27 November 1929, with 42hr 3min 30sec.*

Ruth Elder at the controls of the Stinson American Girl. (Curtiss Museum)

The starlet in the sky: Ruth Elder

(1902-1977)

On 11 October 1927, just before the transatlantic crossing attempt, Ruth Elder poses with the pilot George W. Haldeman (right) and her manager, T.H. McArdle (left). She is wearing the headband that would soon become fashionable under the name of 'Ruth Ribbon'. (WWP, H. Hazewinkel collection)

'A quarter of a million dollars slipped through my fingers and soon there was none left,' claimed Ruth Elder with a sense of disillusionment after having been for so long the darling of the showbiz and aeronautical media. In the mid-1920s after playing a dozen or so middling roles in silent films,[1] Ruth Elder, a dental-practice secretary who had started taking flying lessons, found herself missing the fame.

On 21 May 1927, Charles Lindbergh made his historic Atlantic crossing, an exploit that unleashed a swell of competition among aviatrixes. There was much talk about who would become the first to cross the ocean, if not as the pilot, then at least as a passenger. Who would gain the coveted title of 'Lady Lindy'? Ruth Elder asked her instructor and friend, George Haldeman, to attempt the feat with her.

Two months earlier, the disastrous Dole Race over the Pacific had cost the lives of 10 flyers, including the young Mildred Doran.[2] Far from being discouraged by this, the two partners had sought several sponsors, raising $35,000 and procuring a bright-yellow Stinson Detroiter monoplane that they christened American Girl.

Although it was not the right season for the exploit, Ruth Elder was keen to do it before the year was through. On the chosen Tuesday 11 October, the forecast was hardly propitious and there was no hope of its clearing. However, Ruth and George decided to try their luck and took off. A worrying 48 hours later there was still no news from them. Fortunately, on Friday, radio messages were received confirming that they were still alive. A sudden fall in oil pressure had forced them to seek the help of a ship in the area. They had managed to locate the Dutch tanker Barendrecht and, flying over it at low altitude, they dropped a message: 'How far are we from land and in which direction?' By way of response, the captain painted on the deck: 'Due south, 40 west, 360 nautical miles, Terceira, Azores.' Rather than press on and risk the engine failing completely, the two of them took the wise decision to ditch in the sea near the ship. It was just as well that they did, for hardly had they been hauled on board than the Stinson exploded and sank. According to various sources they had been in the air for between 28 and 36 hours

After their arrival in Paris on 27 October 1927, Ruth Elder and George W. Haldeman were invited to a banquet held by the 'Vieilles Tiges' (an association of pioneer aviators), in the presence of M. Delsol, chairman of the municipal council. (ROL)

and covered some 4,220km. Ruth had been at the controls for nine hours in all. It was the longest distance ever covered by a woman pilot.

Knowing that it could easily have turned to tragedy, some male journalists went on the attack. The Belfast Irish News commented: 'A woman had no business to attempt such a flight. It was perfectly ridiculous to read of this young person's chatter, of her preparations for the event: her vanity bag, Chinese ring, knickerbockers, red and black four-in-hand tie and pastel-shaded band over dark brown hair, and to remember that she was going to risk her life just to gratify her stupid vanity. She is a married woman. Her

On one of her public relations outings, Ruth Elder visited NACA's large wind tunnel at Langley, California. She is seen here with, on her left, the director of the Langley Research Center, Dr H.J.E. Reid. (NASA-LaRC)

Roosevelt Field, New York in December 1927; Ruth Elder wishes Frances Grayson luck just before her ill-fated Atlantic crossing to Denmark. She and her crew disappeared without trace on 23 December 1927. (WWP, H. Hazewinkel collection)

Ruth Elder at Roosevelt Field, New York, on 12 October 1927. (H. Hazewinkel collection)

At Long Beach, Ruth Elder poses on her Swallow F28W biplane, with its 200hp Wright J-5A Whirlwind engine, which she flew to fifth place in the first Powder Puff Derby. (J. Underwood collection)

Ruth Elder on arrival in Lisbon from the Azores after she had been fished out of the Atlantic by a cargo ship. (C. Gulbenkian Lib.)

husband wisely remained at home. If Ruth has any sense left she will join him now and keep house for him.'

After going ashore in the Azores, the two Americans arrived in Paris on 27 October, where they were received by the chairman of the city council, M. Delsol and were feted at various ceremonies and banquets in their honour. Back in the United States, Ruth Elder was presented with the medal of the Spanish Legion of Honour, which had been awarded to her by the King of Spain.

High on this sudden fame, Ruth used the publicity to try to obtain a first film role. Her attempts bore fruit as, on 7 April 1928, with flashguns popping all around, she announced the signing of a contract with Florenz Ziegfeld of Paramount Pictures for her first part in a film with the grand-sounding title of *Glorifying the American Girl*. At the same time, she signed a contract for a tour of 100 performances of the musical comedy *The American Girl*, for a fee of $100,000. The tour ended on 5 June 1928, and she set out on an aerial journey across the United States, starting in New York and finishing in Los Angeles on 1 July.

In October 1928, the Paramount film *Moran of the Marines* was released, in which Ruth Elder played opposite Richard Dix, but *Glorifying the American Girl* was made without her, Ziegfeld preferring Mary Eaton. In the meantime, between 18 and 26 August, Ruth Elder had taken fifth place in the famous Powder Puff Derby, flying a Wright-engined Swallow F28W biplane that she bought on 3 February 1930.

Her varied aeronautical and cinematic activities earned her a small fortune, estimated at $250,000, but it was to melt away like snow in the sun. Without obvious prospects in either field, Ruth Elder decided to leave the bright lights for good, even going so far as to change her first name to Susan. In March 1933, she sold her plane to the Pacific School of Aviation (whose vice-president she then was) and, in place of collecting trophies, went in for collecting husbands instead.[3] Ruth Elder died at home, in San Francisco, on 9 October 1977 and her ashes were scattered over the Golden Gate Bridge.

1. Among the silent films in which Ruth Elder performed are: The Bridal Bouquet, Helen Intervenes, A Man of Iron, A Scientific Mother, Love and Money, The Marvelous Marathoner, Susie of the Follies, Triumph and Thirty a Week.
2. Mildred Doran, a 22-year-old primary-school teacher from Flint, Michigan, had obtained permission to be a passenger aboard the Buhl biplane that was lost at sea on 16 August 1929.
3. Ruth Elder had six husbands: C.E. Moody (schoolteacher) in 1922, Lyle Womack (a member of the Byrd expedition to the South Pole) in 1925, Walter Camp Jr. (director of Madison Square Garden) in 1929, G.K. Thackery, Arnold A. Gillespie in 1933, and Ralph King (cameraman).

Pictures Inc., with screenplay by Oliver H.P. Garrett and S.K. Lauren, depicting the life of Amelia Earhart (called Tonie Carter in the film), starring Rosalind Russell (Tonie Carter) and Fred MacMurray (Randy Britton).

Le Ciel est à Vous (1943)
A 102min, black and white film directed by Jean Grémillon, with screenplay by Albert Valentin, starring Madeleine Renaud (Thérèse Gauthier), Charles Vanel (Pierre Gauthier) and Jean Debucourt (M. Larchet).

Ladies Courageous (March 1944)
An 88min, black and white film directed by John Rawlins for Universal Pictures Co., based on a screenplay by Norman Reilly Raine and Doris Gilbert, starring Loretta Young (Roberta Harper), Geraldine Fitzgerald (Virgie Alford) and Diana Barrymore (Nadine).

Horizons sans Fin (1952)
A 144min, black and white film directed by Jean Dréville and based on a screenplay by Raymond Caillava, depicting the life of Hélène Boucher, starring Gisèle Pascal (Hélène Boucher), Maurice Ronet (Marc Caussade) and Paul Frankeur (Soupape).

Amelia Earhart (1976)
A TV film directed by George Schaefer for Universal Television Entertainment, with screenplay by Carol Sobieski, depicting the life of Amelia Earhart, starring Susan Clark (Amelia Earhart), John Forsyth (George Putnam), Stephen Macht (Paul Mantz), Bill Vint (Fred Noonan) and Susan Oliver (Neta Snook).

A Shadow on the Sun (May 1988)
A 192min TV film directed by Robert K. Lambert for CBS, with a screenplay by James Fox and Allan Scott, depicting the life of Beryl Markham, starring Stefanie Powers (Beryl Markham) and Claire Bloom (Lady Florence Delamere).

Pancho Barnes (1988)
A 150min TV film directed by Richard T. Heffron for CBS, with a screenplay by John Michael Hayes depicting the life of Pancho Barnes, starring Valerie Bertinelli (Pancho Barnes) and Sam Robards (Gene McKendry).

Amelia Earhart: The Final Flight (June 1994)
A 95min TV film directed by Craig Hosking for Turner Home Entertainment Co., with a screenplay by Anna Sandor and based on the biography of Amelia Earhart by Doris L. Rich, starring Diane Keaton (Amelia Earhart), Bruce Dearn (George Putnam), Rutger Hauer (Fred Noonan) and Paul Gilfoyle II (Paul Mantz).

Amelia (October 2009)
A 111min colour film directed by Mira Nair for Fox Searchlight, with a screenplay by Susan Butler and Mary Lovell, starring Hilary Swank (Amelia Earhart), Richard Gere (George Putnam), Ewan McGregor (Gene Vidal), Christopher Eccleston (Fred Noonan) and Mia Wasikowska (Elinor Smith).

Aviatrixes on the screen

While the theme of women in aviation has not been ignored by the film industry, feature-length and TV films on the subject are not plentiful. Here is a list of them.

Christopher Strong (1933)
A 78min black and white film directed by Dorothy Azner for RKO, based on a screenplay by Zoë Akins (from a novel by Gilbert Frankau), with Katherine Hepburn (Cynthia Darrington) and Colin Clive (Christopher Strong).

Wings in the Dark (May 1935)
A 75min black and white film directed by James Flood for Paramount, with scenario by Philip D. Hurn and Nell Shipman, starring Myrna Loy (Sheila Mason), Cary Grant (Ken Gordon), Roscoe Karns (Nick Williams), Hobart Canaugh (Mac) and Dean Jagger (Top Harmon).

They Flew Alone (September 1942)
US title: Wings and the Woman
A 96min black and white film directed by RKO Radio British Productions Ltd, from a scenario by Miles Malleson and inspired by the life of Amy Johnson, starring Anna Neagle (Amy Johnson) and Robert Newton (Jim Mollison).

Flight for Freedom (April 1943)
A 99min black and white film directed by Lothar Mendes for RKO

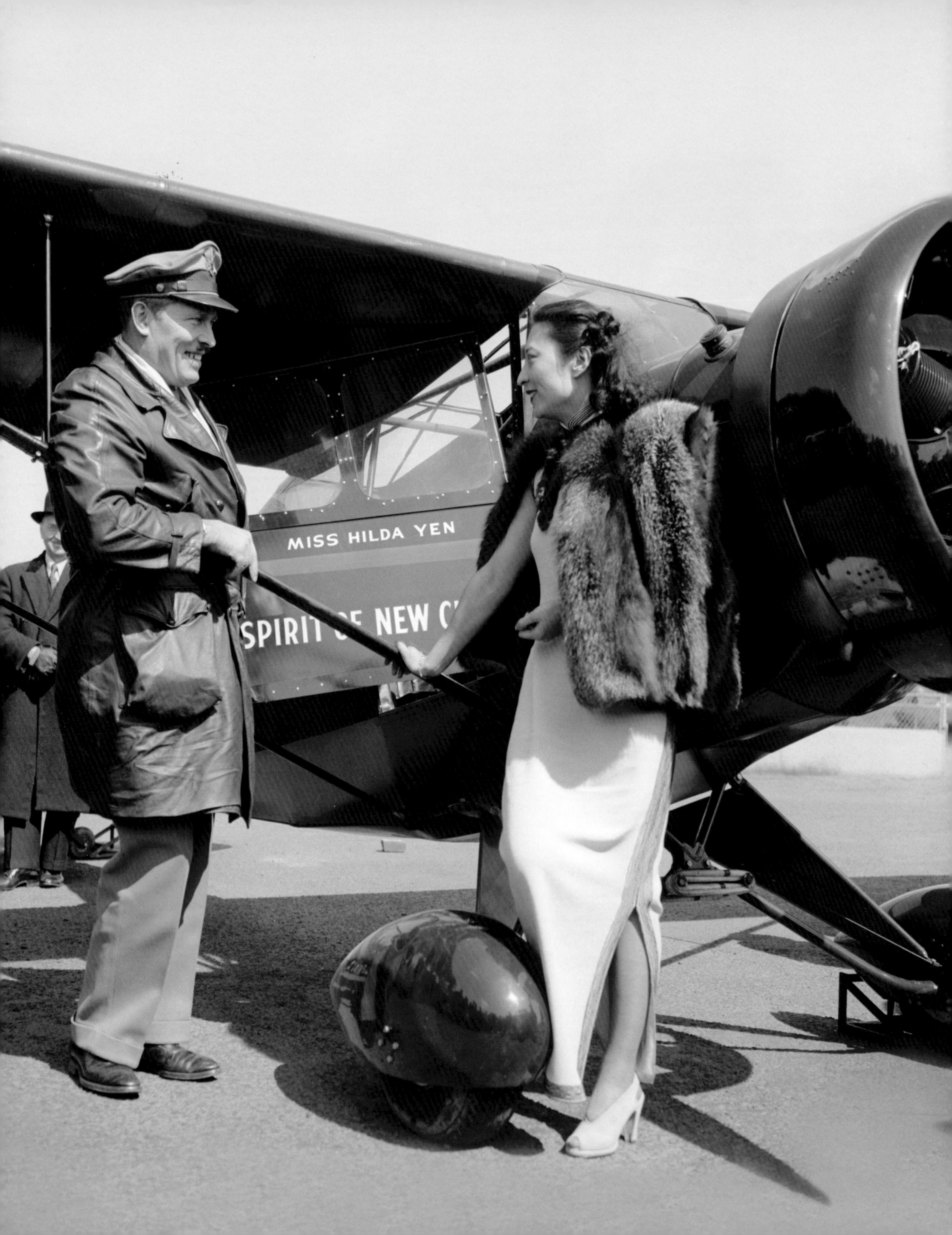
MISS HILDA YEN
SPIRIT OF NEW C

Dutrieu, Harriet Quimby, Katherine Stinson, Blanche Scott, Ruth Law, Bessie Coleman, Adrienne Bolland, Florence Klingensmith, Laura Ingalls, Liesel Bach, Lady Heath, Lady Mary Bailey, Louise Thaden, Thea Rasche, Ruth Rowland Nichols, Elinor Smith, Ruth Elder, Carina Negrone, Paulina Denisovna Ossipenko, Hanna Reitsch, Marcelle Choisnet, Maryse Bastié, Léna Bernstein, Amy Johnson-Mollison, Anne Morrow-Lindbergh, Marga Von Etzdorf, Maryse Hilsz, Beryl Markham, Elly Beinhorn, Jean Batten, Elisabeth Lion, Helen Richey, Eugénie M. Shakhovskaya, Cecil W. "Teddy" Kenyon, Pauline Gower, Nancy Harkness Love, Maria Ivanovna Dolina, Amélia Earhart, Hélène Boucher, Jacqueline Cochran, Jacqueline Auriol, Eileen Marie Collins, Anna Walker, Ellen Church, Clara Adams, Harriet Quimby, Marjorie Stinson, Mrs Eyman, Fay Gillis, Virginia Waibel, Eleanor Blevins, Aniwegi Boudinot, Helen Clifford, Janett Moffett, Bernetta Miller, Ruth Fontes, Jeanne Pallier, Blossom Miles, Emily Schaeffer, Raymonde de Laroche, Amelie Beese, Hélène Dutrieu, Harriet Quimby, Katherine Stinson, Blanche Scott, Ruth Law, Bessie Coleman, Adrienne Bolland, Florence Klingensmith, Laura Ingalls, Liesel Bach, Lady Heath, Lady Mary Bailey, Louise Thaden, Thea Rasche, Ruth Rowland Nichols, Elinor Smith, Ruth Elder, Carina Negrone, Paulina Denisovna Ossipenko, Hanna Reitsch, Marcelle Choisnet, Maryse Bastié, Léna Bernstein, Amy Johnson-Mollison, Marga Von Etzdorf, Maryse Hilsz, Beryl Markham, Elly Beinhorn, Jean Batten, Elisabeth Lion, Helen Richey, Eugénie M. Shakhovskaya, Cecil W. "Teddy" Kenyon, Pauline Gower, Nancy Harkness Love, Maria Ivanovna Dolina, Amélia Earhart, Hélène Boucher, Jacqueline Cochran, Jacqueline Auriol, Eileen Marie Collins, Anna

Aviatrixes around the world

Bozena Láglovavá, known as 'Miss Lagler' (1888-1941), was the first Czech aviatrix to qualify as a pilot, as well as being the first woman to receive a licence from the Aero-Club of Austria. She is seen here with someone named Richter. (Library of Congress)

The world of aviation pioneers is far from being confined to the handful of countries with which we are familiar. Besides the American, British, French and German aviatrixes, there are others, such as the first licensed Belgian woman pilot, Hélène Dutrieu[1] and the first Czech, Bozena Láglerová, who obtained licences, just a few days apart, from both the Austrian Aero Club[2] and the German Aero Club (on 19 October 1911). Known in Germany as Lagler, she was a native of Prague and learned to fly under Hans Grade. At the same time, the first Dutch aviatrix, Beatrix de Rijk, a pupil of the Hanriot School at Rheims-Bétheny, successfully took her licence and, thanks to a small personal fortune, bought her own Duperdussin monoplane in which she appeared at many meetings.

In 1912, the Hungarian Lilly Steinschneider, a pupil of Karl Illner, became the fourth aviator (and the first woman) to receive a pilot's licence from the Hungarian Aero Club. In Italy, at Vizzola Ticino, the 24-year-old Rosina Ferrario was training at the Giovanni Batista Caproni School and, on 3 January 1913, took pride in being the first Italian woman to obtain a pilot's licence. The final few weeks of peace in Europe witnessed the Swiss Elsa Haugk join the small circle of women pilots, with a licence from the German Aero Club.

In Romania, Elena Caragiani-Stoenescu stirred a wave of indignation when Prince George Valentin Bibescu's flying school flatly turned down her entry request for a pilot's licence. In the end, it was only by going to France that she was able to get hold of a precious licence, at Mourmelon on 22 January 1914. With her own country refusing to go back on its decision and barring her from participation in any meetings, she gave up on flying and became a correspondent for a major French daily.

Flying fever was not long in reaching South America, particularly in Argentina, where Amalia Celia Figueredo de Pietra, more commonly known as Amalia Figueredo, was preparing her debut. She first flew at Villa Lugano, Buenos Aires, on board a 25hp, Anzani-engined monoplane piloted by Paul Castaibert. She needed no further incentive to fling herself into the adventure. She took lessons in a Farman biplane at the San Fernando school and by 6 September 1914 was ready to take her pilot's test, but an accident obliged her to retake it on 1 October 1914, when she obtained licence no. 58 from the Aero Club Argentino. Until her marriage to Alexandre Carlos Pietra, Amalia Figueredo flew her plane at many shows, but her husband persuaded her to curtail her aeronautical career.

The First World War put an end to the ambitions of women hoping to become pilots. In Brazil, it was 1922 before women made their appearance on the aeronautical scene, starting with Teresa de Marzo who gained her licence on 18 April and soon afterwards opened a flying school in Ypiranga. It lasted a year before being shut down and having its planes confiscated in the revolution of 1924. On 9 April 1922, the Aeroclube do Brasil awarded licence no. 77 to Anesia Pinheiro Machado who, the following September, piloting Caudron G-3 named Bandeirante, made the first flight between Sao Paulo and Rio de Janeiro, to mark the centenary of independence.

In July 1930, the Club de Aviación de Cuba granted a licence to the country's first aviatrix, Berta Moraleda. Six months later came the first Spanish aviatrix, Maria Peper Colomer Luque (19 January 1931), who for a few years appeared at various meetings before joining the military flying school (Escuela de Pilotos Militares, founded on 1 October 1936) as an instructor and then taking part in propaganda activities within the republican air force. At the end of the war, she left for exile in England, where she lived until her death on 24 May 2004.

In the United States, Katherine Sui Fun Cheung became the first woman of Chinese origin (she was born in Canton on 12 December 1904 and had emigrated in 1921) to be granted a pilot's licence (1932) and become a member of the '99s'. She began her career in itinerant meetings during which she did aerobatic demonstrations. In 1934, with a 125hp Fleet biplane that the Chinese community had bought for her at the modest sum of $2,000, she entered the Ruth Chatterton Air Sportsman Pilot Trophy Race from Los Angeles to Cleveland, coming in next to last. It didn't matter; what counted was that she was flying. Despite all her best efforts, she failed to realise her dream of establishing a flying school in China. She gave up flying for good in 1942 and died in 2003 aged 99.

Amalia Celia Figueredo (1895-1985) obtained licence no. 58 from the Aero Club Argentino on a Farman biplane, but she learnt to fly on a 25hp monoplane built by Paul Castaibert. (Smithsonian)

Rosina Ferrario (1888-1959) was the only Italian woman to gain her licence before the outbreak of the Great War. She took her first steps at Come, on the 'Circuit of the Lakes', flying a monoplane. (G. Apostolo collection)

Katherine Sui Fun Cheung (1904-2003) learned to fly with encouragement from her father, becoming the first Asian-American to gain a pilot's licence. (NASM)

In Europe in 1932, a 20-year-old Italian, Gabriella Angelini, having just earned her licence, undertook a tour of the continent, taking her via Vienna, Prague, Stockholm, Copenhagen, Amsterdam, Heston, Paris, Lyon and Cannes to Geneva, an exploit that established her international fame. Shortly after this, she set out on an attempt to link Milan and Delhi, but was killed when her plane crashed at Wadi-al-Qaltah, in Libya. The best-known Italian aviatrix at this time, however, was Carina Negrone who, flying a Caproni monoplane beat the women's world altitude record with 12,043m, on 20 June 1935 (see p. 79).

During the 1930s, on the other side of the world, a number of Australians were making news, starting with Maude Rose Bonney, known as 'Lores' Bonney, who completed a circuit of Australia between August and September 1932. From 15 April to 21 June 1933, flying a Gipsy Moth D.H.60G (VH-UPV), she made the first solo flight from Australia (Darwin) to England (Croydon), the reverse of Amy Johnson's historic flight, and finally, she flew a Klemm Kl.31 from Australia to South Africa in June 1939.

The best-known Australian aviatrix is undoubtedly Nancy Bird-Walton. She learned to fly in 1933 at the age of 17 under the instruction of the celebrated Charles Kingsford Smith. Two years later she was flying a Gipsy Moth as an air ambulance, carrying nurses deep into the outback. She soon added a further string to her bow by appearing at travelling air shows, a more entertaining, and lucrative, activity. In 1936, Nancy Bird entered the first Brisbane to Adelaide race, but in 1938, under pressure from conservative political figures, she was forced to put her aeronautical activities on the back burner. Years later, in 1950, she would establish the Australian Women Pilots' Association, of which she was the president until 1990. Another Australian worthy of mention is Peggy Kelman. Born in Glasgow in 1909, Margaret Mary 'Peggy' McKillop received her private pilot's licence in 1932 and her commercial licence in 1935. Taken on by Nancy Bird, she began her career at meetings and it was while at one of these that she met Colin Kelman, marrying him in 1936. The couple acquired a twin-engined plane and took off for Australia, taking from 19 December 1936 until 15 January 1937. From that moment onwards, Peggy Kelman spent her time flying around the country until well into her eighties.

In the Near East, the 26-year-old Loftia Al-Nadi became the first Egyptian qualified woman pilot in September 1933, after learning to fly at the Misr Aero Club without her father's knowledge. The following year, she took part in the Oases Rally then went to England with the intention of beating the England to Australia record set by Jean Batten, but nothing came of the plan. In 1937, she again took part in the Oases Rally flying a DH-87B Hornet Moth and finished in eighth position. A legendary figure in her own country, Loftia died in Switzerland in 2002.

Not far away, in Iran, the opening of the Iran Aero Club on 7 November 1939 saw no fewer than 630 trainees enrolled, among whom were several women, such as Fakhrotaj Monfaredi, Ozra Rahimi, Drakhshandeh Malakooti, Safieh Partovi and Effat Tejertachi; the latter, after serving her apprenticeship on a De Havilland Tiger Moth, becoming the first Iranian aviatrix.

India had its first aviatrix in the person of Sarla Thakral. Born into a family of aviators, it was with the encouragement of her husband, P. D. Sharma, that she obtained her pilot's licence in 1936 at the age of 21. She then planned to take her commercial pilot's test, but her husband's death in a plane crash cut the project short, and she turned, with some success, to painting and fine arts.

Czechoslovakia, with its renowned aeronautical industry, held a number of records in women's aviation. On 29 November 1937, M. Dubkova and Svobodova with a fourth-category Praga Baby single-seater broke the

The Italian Gabriella Angelini in front of the Breda 15 that she bought from Sesto S. Giovanni. The plane had the appropriate registration of I-TALY. (G. Apostolo collection)

In a conservative country like pre-war Australia, Nancy Bird-Walton (1915-2009) faced many obstacles in getting recognition for her flying skills. (DR)

Sarla Thakral was the first qualified female pilot from the Indian subcontinent, although she did not make a career in aviation. (DR)

women's 100km speed record with 143.13kph and on 29 November, in the same plane, they raised the record to 143.85kph.

The Soviet Union, not wanting to be outdone, saw Russian aviatrixes taking part in what were principally propaganda efforts, notably in the fields of altitude, long distance and gliding records. Thus from 22 to 25 May 1937, Paulina D. Ossipenko, flying a Beriev MP1bis hydroplane, broke several women's altitude records (see p. 81). On 15 October of the same year, Valentina Grisodoubova took the women's altitude record with 3,267m, complementing it on 24 October with the straight-line distance record of 1,444.722km, achieved in collaboration with Marina Raskova in an AIR-12. On 2 July 1938, a three-woman team of Paulina D. Ossipenko, Vera Lomako and Marina Raskova, flying a MP-1bis seaplane, established the speed record over the Sebastopol–Kiev–Novgorod–Archangel route with 2,416km covered in 10hr 33min at an average speed of 228kph. On 24 September, a slightly different team (Valentina Grisodoubova, Paulina D. Ossipenko and Marina Raskova) flying a Tupolev ANT-37 named *Rodina* (Fatherland) took the women's straight-line distance record between Tchelcovo and Amgun with 5,908.61km. The day before, C. Mednikova, at the controls of a Yakovlev UT-1 light hydroplane, had beaten the 100km speed record with 197.271kph. Two days later, in the same plane, she beat the altitude record with 4,086m.

On 3 April 1939, Hilda Yen, the daughter of Dr W.W. Yen, the Chinese ambassador to Russia, was provided with a single-engined plane by Colonel Roscoe Turner in which, accompanied by Miss Lee Ya-Ching, she set out on a tour of the United States to raise funds to help the Chinese peasant victims of the war against Japan. Known as 'the Chinese Amelia Earhart', she was seriously injured when her plane crashed at Prattville, Alabama, on 1 May 1939. After recovering from her injuries, she went to China with her aid funds and did not return to the United States until 1944.

1. Patent no. 27 on 23 August 1910.
2. Patent no. 37 on 10 October 1911.

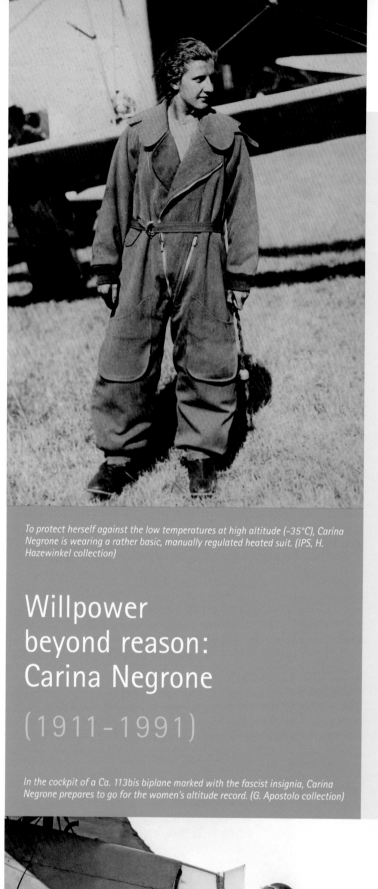

To protect herself against the low temperatures at high altitude (-35°C), Carina Negrone is wearing a rather basic, manually regulated heated suit. (IPS, H. Hazewinkel collection)

Willpower beyond reason: Carina Negrone (1911–1991)

In the cockpit of a Ca. 113bis biplane marked with the fascist insignia, Carina Negrone prepares to go for the women's altitude record. (G. Apostolo collection)

Having got out of her plane, still numb from her record-breaking flight, Carina Negrone is congratulated by General Giuseppe Valle, Air Marshall and Chief of Staff of the Reggia Aeronautica, and General Oppizzi, president of the Aero Club of Italy. (G. Apostolo collection)

On Thursday 20 June 1935 at 7.17am, a Caproni biplane[1] lifted off from the Montecelio runway, powered skywards by the 1,100hp of its Alfa Romeo engine. At the controls, wrapped in a rudimentary flying suit and equipped with an oxygen cylinder, was the blue-eyed, blond, 24-year-old Carina Negrone. Her aim was to beat the altitude record that had been set a week previously by Maryse Hilsz. At exactly 8.56, the Caproni touched down again, having climbed to 12,043m. Carina Negrone had just beaten the Frenchwoman's performance by 754m.

Born in Genoa on 20 June 1911, Carina Negrone was married to Ambrogio Negrone. Adoring all sport, and especially flying, she had taken her second-level licence in 1933 and in March 1934 set the altitude record for class C hydroplanes by climbing to 5,544m. But women pilots were not welcome in fascist Italy, where their role was to propagate large families. Be that as it may, Carina Negrone was determined to set other records, particularly the altitude record. She had managed to gain the friendship of the media-wise Italo Balbo, a well-known pilot and influential member of the fascist hierarchy. It was on his orders that she had been able to undergo intensive training at the Guidonia Montecelio military base, near Rome. However, the doctors who had followed her progress remained convinced that she would not be able to go any higher than 11,000m, but they had reckoned without Carina Negrone's willpower which, though she was on the verge of blacking out, had driven her to exceed their predictions by 1,000m. Her performance that day would see her being awarded the Harmon Trophy (see Appendix 5, page 186).

On the outbreak of war, Carina Negrone had offered her services as a pilot to the Air Ministry, but as had happened almost everywhere else, she was turned down point blank. Like it or not, she had to sit it out until the end of hostilities before she could fly again and take part in the re-establishment of

Italian light aviation. Elected president of the Genoa Aero Club, she landed the first plane (a Stinson L5) on the potholed runway. She became involved once more in a variety of competitions, winning the first one, organised by the Milan Aero Club, flying a Lombardi FL5.

In 1951, she teamed up with Ada Marchelli in a Macchi MB.308 to be one of the three Italian[2] entries in the Tour of Algeria, on a 6,000km-plus route over the desert. In 1954 she added another record to her list of achievements when, on 19 June, she broke the speed record for amphibious aircraft between Ghedi (Brescia) and Luxor (Egypt), a distance of 2,987km covered in 13hr 34min at an average speed of 299kph.

1. The Caproni Ca.113bis was a biplane with a turbocharged Alfa Romeo Pegasus engine fitted with a governor. In a modified Ca.113, Renato Donati had beaten the world altitude record with 14,433m on 11 April 1934.
2. Out of a total of 80 teams entered.

From farm to the Kremlin: Paulina D. Ossipenko (1907–1939)

Among the ashes deposited in the funerary urns of the Kremlin wall are those of the 32-year-old aviatrix, Paulina Denisovna Ossipenko. Virtually unknown in Western aeronautical circles, she had a notable career. What is known about her begins in 1907 in the little village of Novospassovsk, somewhere in the Ukraine. The ninth child of a peasant family, Paulina Doudnikest was born on 8 October. After a period at the local parish church school, she worked on the farm and met Stepan Goviaz, a military flyer whom she married in 1926. In 1929, after training in aviculture, Paulina Goviaz became responsible for chicken rearing at the Katovsk kolkhoz, but in 1931 decided to go and join her husband who was based at Katcha. She failed the Miasnikov flying school's entry exam and had to content herself with working in the canteen. Choosing to make the best of it, she began to practise flying the Polikarpov U-2 biplane that delivered the meals. Gaining slowly in confidence, Paulina renewed her application to the flying school during a visit by a defence commissar. This time, she was accepted. She rose steadily through the ranks to become an inspector in the spring of 1935. In 1936, at a Kremlin meeting for Red Army women, she publicly committed herself to taking the world altitude record. In the same year, she was divorced and, the following year married Lieutenant Alexander Ossipenko, then commander of the 40th Air Regiment.

Having committed herself, Paulina Ossipenko set three altitude records in the MP-1bis seaplane's category: the first, 8,864m, on 22 May in an empty plane; the two others, of 7,605m and 7,009m, were in aircraft with 500kg and 1,000kg payloads, respectively (25 May).

In July the following year, Paulina and two other women (Marina Raskova and Vera Lomako) decided to make an attempt on the distance record over the Sebastopol–Novgorod–Archangel route, using the MP-1bis. By the end of

Accompanied by a pilot from the Reggia Aeronautica (Italian Air Force), Carina Negrone walks towards her plane. (G. Apostolo collection)

Paulina Ossipenko was the victim of a fatal accident while undertaking a nil-visibility flight in 1939. (A. Zablostky collection)

Warmly dressed, the Russian crew pose in front of the unique MP-1bis seaplane. (A. Zablotsky collection)

To achieve her record, Paulina Ossipenko's team used the prototype of the civil version of the Beriev MP-1bis short-range reconnaissance seaplane with an M17 pusher engine. (A. Zablotsky collection)

June, the authorities still seemed unwilling to make up their minds about permitting the flight. Tired of waiting, Paulina took her courage in both hands and called Marshal Klementi Voroshilov to ask for his agreement, which was duly given and confirmed by telegram: 'I authorise this flight...Check all equipment thoroughly...I wish you success...Voroshilov.' It was a response that filled the three women with joy. On 2 July, they set off on the long journey that would lead them to Archangel. The weather conditions were not ideal, with thick, dark clouds covering the high ground. As a safety precaution, they had decided to fly at 5,000m and avoid using their oxygen except in case of extreme necessity. Nearing Novgorod, they had great difficulty in making out the city, so decided to descend to ensure that they were on the right course. Down to 700m, they recognised Lake Ilmen south of the city and were able to fly over Novgorod's Kremlin as planned. The final part of the flight to Archangel was undertaken in difficult conditions. The cloud cover over Lake Ladoga was thicker than ever and the three women suffered from violent headaches as a result of the lack of oxygen. When the seaplane finally came down, they had covered a record distance of 2,416km at an average speed of 228kph. Once on land, and assisted by her two colleagues, Ossipenko dictated a telegram: 'To Moscow...the Kremlin... Joseph Vissarionovich Stalin...Non-stop flight Sebastopol–Archangel completed...Are ready to undertake any further mission...Ossipenko, Lomako, Raskova.'[1]

Indeed, it was not long before Paulina was off again. On 24 and 25 September the following year, teamed up with Marina Raskova and Valentina Grisodoubova, she made up the crew of the Tupolev ANT-37 that beat the world non-stop distance record with 5,908km. On 2 November 1938, in recognition of her achievements, Paulina Ossipenko was awarded the title of Hero of the Soviet Union. In the ensuing months, she was made an inspector of military aviation instructors and acted as a delegate at the 18th Communist Party Congress. Sadly, she was to meet her death on 11 May 1939 when her plane crashed on a low-visibility training flight accompanied by the inspector general of aviation, Serov. Their bodies were brought back to Moscow and for two days and two nights, the public and members of the government filed past the urns before they were buried in the Kremlin walls. An extraordinary journey for the aviatrix who begun her career as a poultry farmer.

1. For this exploit, the three women were awarded the Order of Lenin.

'She who belongs to the heavens': Sabiha Gökçen

(1913-2001)

In 1938, Sabiha Gökçen made a five-day flight over the Balkans, creating quite a sensation in her own country. (Corbis)

Turkey has its flying legend in the form of Sabiha Gökçen, a young woman who was 'found' by Mustafa Kemal Atatürk himself, but whose origins remain obscure. Some claim that she was a Turkish orphan of the Great War, others that she was an Armenian orphan. Atatürk is said to have adopted her on one of his visits to Bursa in 1922 or 1925 and brought her back to Ankara, where she studied at the American School. In 1934, Atatürk bestowed on her the surname Gökçen (she who belongs to the heavens) and, the following year, she enrolled at the civil aviation school recently set up by the Türk Hava Kurumu (THK, or Turkish Aeronautical Association).[1] After training on gliders, Sabiha was sent to the USSR to complete her training and become a gliding instructor. The following year, she joined the military aviation school at Eskisehir, becoming the first Turkish woman to obtain a pilot's licence and the first female military pilot in the world. She remained at Eskisehir, where she flew Breguet 19s, Curtiss Hawks and Vultee V-11s and in 1937 took part in the major manoeuvres that were held in Thrace and the Aegean. Flying her Vultee as part of the first Air Regiment, she was active in the Dersim operations against the Kurds, in one episode assisting in the taking of some forty prisoners. Subsequently appointed as head of the Türkkusu Flying School, Sabiha Gökçen remained in this post until 1954. She ceased flying in 1964,[2] but continued to teach. Throughout her career she amassed no fewer than 10,000 hours of flying at the controls of around 15 different types of aircraft.[3]

1. The school, 'Türk Kusu' (Turkish bird) was founded on 5 May 1935.
2. In 1975, according to some sources.
3. On 7 November 2002, at the suggestion of the THK, the general assembly of the FAI agreed to the creation of the Sabiha Gökçen Medal to be awarded to women who had achieved remarkable exploits in aerial sports.

The MP-1bis crew, with, from left to right: Marina Raskova, Vera Lomako and Paulina Ossipenko. Marina Raskova was to distinguish herself in the Second World War. (A. Zablotsky collection)

Not long after her marriage to Charles Lindbergh, Anne Morrow took up gliding on the advice of her husband (seen here from behind) and William Hawley Bowlus (left). She is seen here at the controls of a Bowlus glider as she is about to be towed up. (J. Underwood collection)

The glider pilots

Although the details of her flights are not known, Maxine Dunlap, a native of Burlingame, California, was the first qualified American female glider pilot, in late 1929 or early 1930. (World Wide Photo)

The German aviatrix Hanna Reitsch dominated gliding in the inter-war years. She is seen here in her famous red and white outfit, in discussion with Flugkapitän Knoetsch in front of her DFS Habicht glider at Kassel on 17 July 1938. (Fieseler Archives)

A s gliding had not been explicitly banned in any of the Treaty of Versailles' clauses, it saw a greater growth in Germany than it did elsewhere. The competitions that took place at the Wasserkuppe in the Rhön massif had an international, as well as national impact. It was here that the first female pilots distinguished themselves, and among their leading lights was Hanna Reitsch. At the Wasserkuppe International Championships in July 1937, the three women glider pilots taking part came sixth (Hanna Reitsch in a Reiher glider, with 1,104 points), 11th (the Austrian Emmy von Roretz in a Röhnsperber glider, with 442.9 points) and 21st (the English Joan Price, with 127.3 points).

In the United States, just as in Europe, gliding offered a cheaper way into flying in these times of crisis. The first American woman to gain her third-class glider-pilot's licence[1] was the Californian, Maxine Dunlap, at around the end of 1929 or early 1930, probably using a Ferguson glider. On 26 January 1930, she was joined by another woman in the shape of Peaches Wallace, from San Diego, using a Bowlus glider. It was Hawley Bowlus who taught Anne Morrow-Lindbergh the art of flying gliders. On 29 January of the same year, Morrow-Lindbergh became the first woman to obtain a first-class licence after a six-minute flight. Inspired by this, Peaches Wallace founded the 'Anne Lindbergh Gliders Club', whose other founder members were Ruth Alexander and Guinevere Kotter. Ruth Alexander, who was already an aeroplane pilot and was known for having broken several altitude records, was unfortunately killed in a crash at the end of that year, and Peaches Wallace died from a burst appendix.

At the end of the 1940s, glider pilots came together to compete in national championships. Among those who contested the American championships were Virginia Bennis, Alberta Brown, Naomi Allen, Betsy Woodward, Betty Boles, Margaret McDougall and Ruth Petry. In Spain in 1952, Hanna Reitsch came third and in France in 1954 she was sixth. Competitions solely for women started in Poland in 1949 with the People's Socialist Republics Championships. These championships, which took place every two years until 1989, were an opportunity to show off top pilots such as the Russian Valentina Toporova, the two Poles, Pelagia Majewska and Adela Dankowska, the Hungarian Maria Bolla and the East

Germans Monika Warstat and Irmgard Morgner.

From 1973, these championships went international with the first International Women's Championships held at Leszno in Poland, in which 21 women from 12 countries took part. The Pole Pelagia Majewska, the Australian Susan Martin and the Czech Jindra Paluskova emerged as winners of the competition which, in 1979, changed its name to become the European Women's Gliding Championships.

While these competitions were going on, other women were looking to break endurance, altitude and distance records. Among these were Marcelle Choisnet (see p. 86), Jacqueline Mathé, Yvonne Gaudry, Denise Trouillard and Suzanne Melk. On 9 September, the last named of these beat the endurance record held by Marcelle Choisnet since 29 April 1945, flying an Avia 40P, and then went on to beat her own record on 6 October 1946 with 16hr 44min 12sec. On 25 and 26 March 1947, in a Castel C.242 with Thérèse Bucquet, she became the women's world endurance champion for a twin-seater glider with 16hr 3min, breaking the record

After taking lessons at the Bowlus Glider School, Ruth Alexander, who was already the holder of a private pilot's licence, became the first American woman to qualify as a glider pilot. (World Wide Photo)

held since 13 June 1946 by the pairing of Madeleine Renaud and Thérèse Bucquet. In the autumn of 1947, she emigrated to the United States looking for atmospheric conditions more conducive to record breaking. She took part in the Sanford Contest with an Air 100 glider from 15 to 18 January 1948 and won the Challenge Trophy. Sadly, she died of leukaemia at Durnham on 4 February 1951.

However the dominant figure in women's gliding down to the 1980s was unquestionably the Pole, Pelagia Majewska (1933–1988). After discovering gliding in 1949 and training on a German SG38 glider, she started on a string of international records on 23 May 1956 when, flying a PZL-Bielsko SZD Bocian, she took the record for an out-and-back flight to 341.9km.

The very next day, she added the speed record over a 200km triangular course, with 66.55kph. In 1957, she took part in the Polish Championships, adding several world records to her list of achievements. During the 1960s, Pelagia Majewska set no fewer than 17 records. In 1973, at the Women's International Gliding Championships, and facing the best glider pilots of the time, she won outright, repeating this feat in 1977. She captured a final record on 14 May 1980 when, accompanied by Violetta Malcher, she beat the out-and-back, two-seater distance record, with 617.43km. Unfortunately, health problems obliged her to withdraw from competition, but she continued to fly, notably delivering firefighting aircraft. It was on one such flight that she lost her life in a crash at Lisbon in 1988.

1. At this time, to gain a first class licence, a pilot had to remain airborne for at least five minutes at a higher altitude than the point of take off. The third class licence required only 30 seconds of flight.

On 25 March 1947, French aviatrix Suzanne Melk (1908-1951) broke the international endurance record for a two-seater glider, remaining aloft for 16hr 3min. (DR)

The Third Reich encouraged women to take up gliding. Hermann Göring is seen here congratulating some German glider pilots during a meeting at Berlin-Tempelhof, in 1934. (Deutsche Flugillustrierte)

The descent into fanaticism: Hanna Reitsch

(1912-1979)

An official portrait of Hanna Reitsch wearing the Iron Cross first class and the Luftwaffe gold brooch with diamond. (DR)

Hanna Reitsch was soon recognised for her remarkable flying skills. (Segelflug Museum)

There is often a tendency to characterise Hanna Reitsch's career by her exploits on behalf of the Third Reich during the Second World War. Yet this is to ignore her exceptional career as a glider pilot in the 1930s, which put her at the forefront of the international aeronautical scene.

Born on 29 March 1912 at Hirschberg in Silesia, Hanna Reitsch took her glider pilot's licence in 1932 at Grünau, while still continuing with her medical studies with the aim of becoming a missionary. Her instructor, Wolf Hirth (1900–1959), quickly spotted her aptitude for flying. She became the first German woman (and the 25th of any German) to gain a class C licence (15 May 1934). Hirth, who had set up his flying school in Swabia, took her on as an instructor. It was at this point that she decided to give up her studies, so as to devote all her time to gliding. She soon got herself noticed, in particular on a gliding expedition in South America (Brazil and Argentina) led by Prof. Dr Walter Georgii, for which she was awarded the silver medal for gliding.[1] She was then asked to join the Gliding Research Institute, the famous DFS.[2] For her achievements as a test pilot, Ernst Udet (1896–1941) gave her the rank of Flugkapitän, a promotion of which she was especially proud, particularly as no other woman had achieved this rank. Hanna Reitsch now began to take part in numerous gliding contests around the world, amassing a variety of records. By 1937, she had acquired an international reputation. She became the first woman to cross the Alps in a glider and beat the world distance record on 4 July, flying from the Wasserkuppe to Hamburg, a distance of 351km. In 1938, she won several championships and broke records in endurance, distance, and speed over a triangular course. On 17 November 1938 at Rangsdorf, she flew in the unusual Ho IIL flying wing designed by the Horten brothers. Meanwhile, under Ernst Udet's patronage, she had joined the noted Rechlin test-flight centre as a test pilot. The best one could say is that she was welcomed rather coolly by her exclusively male colleagues, but nonetheless managed to get herself accepted. While there, she flew Junkers

Before the war, Hanna Reitsch was not satisfied with flying gliders alone; she also gained her aircraft pilot's licence and was the first female helicopter pilot. (V. Koos collection)

Hanna Reitsch was of a fairly small stature (1.5m tall and weighing 40kg) so fitted easily into the rather tight cockpit of a glider. Here she is pictured with Heini Dittmar (1911-1960) and Thea Rasche. (V. Koos collection)

Ju 87s and Dornier Do 17s. In 1937, she paid a visit to the Focke-Wulf factory in Bremen and was the first woman to fly a helicopter.[3] The following year, she added further records to her list of achievements.

When war broke out, Hanna Reitsch was put in charge of testing the DFS 230 assault glider designed by Hans Jacobs.[4] Using a Dornier Do 17, she also carried out testing of a device intended to cut the mooring cables of British barrage balloons, and flight-tested the Messerschmitt Me 321 Gigant heavy glider. Her achievements drew the attentions of Adolf Hitler, who personally decorated her with the Iron Cross, second class. She then undertook some tricky test flights on the tail-less Messerschmitt Me 163 Komet jet interceptor designed by Alexander Lippisch, during which she suffered the most serious accident of her career. Some would have given up test flying at this point, but, unbending, Hanna Reitsch was back flying within five months.

The armies of the Third Reich were now suffering defeat after defeat and with Germany's military situation leaving no doubt about the outcome of the war, Hanna Reitsch established the S.O. Unit (Selbstopfer, or 'Self-sacrifice') composed of around 60 suicide pilots who, piloting modified V-1 flying bombs, would attack vital Allied targets. 'We contemplate this sacrifice coldly, not in a burst of fanaticism or in despair...We loved our country and knew that this was the only way left to us to save it', she wrote later in her memoirs.[5]

On 28 February 1944 at Berchtesgaden, Hitler decorated her with the Iron Cross, first class. Taking advantage of this opportunity, she revealed her insane plan to the Führer, who was initially opposed, but listening to Reitsch's arguments, he agreed that it should be tried. The tests were inconclusive and this crazy project was abandoned in October 1944.

By 25 April 1945, the end of the Third Reich was imminent. Hitler summoned General Ritter von Greim, commander of the 6th Air Wing, to Berlin to make him Commander-in-Chief of the Luftwaffe in place of Göring.

It was Hanna Reitsch, flying a Fieseler Storch, who brought the General to Hitler in a Berlin in flames and surrounded by the Russians. She also flew him back out again.

Taken prisoner by American troops, Hanna Reitsch was held as a prisoner of war for 18 months and freed in 1946. She took up gliding again almost immediately and, in 1952, came third in the World Championships in Spain. In 1956, she was the champion of Germany and, the following year, broke the women's world altitude record, climbing to 6,848m. In 1959, she was invited to India to do gliding demonstrations and host lectures, after which she went, successively, to Finland, the United States[6] and Ghana. In Ghana, at President Kwame Nkrumah's request, she founded a gliding school where she taught for a few years.

In 1971, even though gliding had been her first love, she won the first World Helicopter Championships. During the 1970s she also managed to beat various out-and-back distance records: in 1975, over the Austrian Alps (644km); in 1976, in Germany (715km); in 1979, in the Appalachians (805km). Hanna Reitsch spent her last years in Austria, where she had gained citizenship. She carried on flying gliders until May 1979 and died on 23 August when her heart stopped while she was asleep.

1. The medal (Silbernes Leistungsabzeichen) was awarded to her on 16 May 1934. She was the 25th glider pilot to receive it.
2. The DFS or Deutsches Forschungsinstitut für Segelflug was founded in 1935.
3. This was the Focke Achgelis Fa 61 that Hanna Reitsch demonstrated at the Berlin Deutschlandhalle in 1938 before the international press.
4. The DFS 230 was used for the first time during the invasion of Belgium in May 1940.
5. In The Sky, My Kingdom.
6. In 1961. During the trip, she was introduced to President J.F. Kennedy.

In November 1938, Hanna Reitsch flew in the Horten IIL flying-wing glider, designed by the Horten brothers. She is shown here in her trademark white and red outfit. On the right is NSFK-Gruppenführer von Eschwege. (DR)

Records in profusion: Marcelle Choisnet

(1914–1974)

During her career, Marcelle Choisnet broke some 30 French records and 11 world records. (GPPA, Michaud collection)

The leading figure in post-war French gliding, Marcelle Choisnet was born at Versailles on 9 May 1914. From a modest background, she was very seriously injured in an accident when she was nine years old. Displaying courage and tenacity quite out of the ordinary, she made a full recovery. There is no doubt that these aspects of her character would define her aeronautical career. It was after her first flight that she was seized with a passion for flying. After obtaining her private pilot's licence, she changed course and turned to gliding just as the Second World War broke out. On the completion of her specialised training at Beynes, she became an instructor at the Light and Sporting Aviation Service (SALS) in 1945.

The guns had not yet fallen silent when Marcelle Choisnet set out on her career as a champion glider pilot, which would ultimately lead to her amassing some 30 French records and 11 world records in different categories (distance, endurance, altitude). On Sunday 22 April 1945, she beat the women's endurance record by remaining aloft for 8hr 52min 54sec, a record that she improved upon by more than three hours just a week later.[1] Tackling the distance record next, she smashed Edmée Jarlaud's record (89km) with 139km on 9 June 1945, followed by 347km a few days later. She soon added her first international record to these national ones, with the distance record over a course with a fixed destination. All these records, to which she added the world record for the greatest distance flown with a passenger over a straight course (237km),[2] brought her the award of the first Aeronautical Medal.

Having taken the women's world out-and-back distance record on 25 July 1946 (105km), Marcelle Choisnet began the year 1947 with the women's national record for the greatest gain in altitude (2,083m on 25 March) accompanied by Jeannine Rousseau in a Kranich II glider. She ended the year by taking the French endurance record in a single-seater Meise glider, with 19hr 50min.

The most significant event of 1948 proved to be the French endurance record in a single-seater glider (Air 100 no. 5), which she took in November. Taking off from Romanin-Les Alpilles at 8.30pm on 17 November, she touched down two days later at 12.36am in the middle of the night, having been airborne for 35hr 3min. Noteworthy among her exploits in 1949 was the women's national and international distance record over a closed circuit (Fez–Boubeker–Fez, in Morocco) of 151km at the controls of a Nord 2000 glider on 27 June. The following year, on 20 July, flying her Air 100 glider no. 14, Marcelle Choisnet established a women's out-and-back distance record, covering 203km at an average speed of 36kph. The year 1951 saw the women's altitude-gain record beaten, with 6,072m, set on 18 January in a Castel-Mauboussin glider with J. Queyrel as a passenger. That autumn, on 22 and 23 November, the team of Yvette Mazellier and Marcelle Choisnet, flying Fouga CM-7 no. 1, beat the women's world endurance record with 28hr 51min, after being towed up to 450m over Castellas.

Always looking to do better, Marcelle Choisnet added to her list of achievements on 12 May 1953, with the women's world out-and-back to a fixed-point distance record of 290km, flying her Air 100. On 17 April 1954, she took the fixed-destination distance record to 507km, followed on 12 May by a new women's fixed-destination distance record of 510km. Finally, on 17 April 1955, accompanied by Nadette de Abelenda, she beat the women's free-flight distance record at Beynes with 445km, missing the world record by just 3km. In 1960, she established the Yvette Mazellier Cup in memory of her fellow crewmember that had been lost in the Agadir earthquake. The cup rewarded the best performance in a training glider. Marcelle Choisnet continued to fly over the ensuing years, but was tragically killed when her glider crashed at Chartres on 14 July 1974.

1. 12hr 20min 45sec, on 29 April 1945.
2. The record had been held since 23 July 1939 by the Russian pair of E. Velikosseltzeva and A. Voroskova.

Marcelle Choisnet in front of the VMA 200 Milan glider no. 1 at the Brive meeting in 1946. The VMA 200 was the version of the Weihe made in France by Victor Minié Aéronautique. (GPPA, Michaud collection)

Gliding performances (1929–1988)

Women's endurance records for single-seater gliders

Date	Glider pilot	Glider type	Time
February 1929	Marga von Etzdorf (Ger)	Grunau Baby	1hr 20min
Autumn 1931	Lotte Orthband (Ger)	Grunau Baby	5hr 15min
Autumn 1932	Hanna Reitsch (Ger)	Grunau Baby	5hr 30min
August 1933	Hanna Reitsch (Ger)	Grunau Baby	10hr 0min
April 1935	Martha Mendel (Ger)	Rhönadler	1hr 28min
18 April 1935	Lisel Zangemeister (Ger)	?	12hr 57min
20 May 1937	Wanda Modlokowska (Pol.)	SG-3/35	24hr 15min
17/19 November 1948	Marcelle Choisnet (F)	Arsenal Air 100	35hr 3min

Women's endurance records for two-seater gliders

Date	Glider pilot	Glider type	Time
16 May 1939	E. Zelenkova/K. Samarina (USSR)	Cheremetyev III-5	12 hr 30 min
25 March 1947	Suzanne Melk/Thérèse Bucquet (F)	Castel 242	16 hr 3 min
22 November 1951	Marcelle Choisnet/Yvette Mazellier (F)	Castel-Mauboussin CM-7	28 hr 41 min
11 January 1954	Jacqueline Mathé/Marinette Garbarino	Castel-Mauboussin CM-7	38 hr 41 min

Women's record height gain for single-seater gliders

Date	Glider pilot	Glider type	Height gained
18 April 1938	Edmée Jarlaud (F)	Avia 40-P	1,184 m
4 June 1948	Jacqueline Mathé (F)	Meise	6,730 m
20 January 1951	Yvonne Gaudry (F)	Nord 2000-12	7,746 m
14 April 1955	Betsy Woodward (USA)	Pratt-Read	8,533 m
13 January 1961	Anne Burns (GB)	Skylark 3	9,119 m
12 January 1988	Yvonne Loader (NZ)	Nimbus	10,212 m

Women's record height gain for two-seater gliders

Date	Glider pilot	Glider type	Height gained
21 January 1948	Jacqueline Mathé/Yvonne Gaudry (F)	Kranich	2,883 m
7 April 1950	Betsy Woodward/Vera Gere (USA)	Schweizer TG-3	3,291 m
18 January 1951	Marcelle Choisnet/J. Queyrel (F)	Castel-Mauboussin CM-7	6,072 m
11 December 1961	Denise Trouillard/Suzanne Suchet (F)	Wassmer Bijave	7,256 m
17 October 1967	Adela Dankowska/Maria Matelska (Pol.)	PZL Bocian	8,430 m

Women's distance records for single-seater gliders

Date	Glider pilot	Glider type	Distance
May 1934	Hanna Reitsch (Ger)	?	150 km
June 1936	Hanna Reitsch (Ger)	?	210 km
June 1937	Eva Schmidt (Ger)	?	255 km
4 July 1937	Hanna Reitsch (Ger)	Relher	351 km
6 July 1939	Olga Klepikova (USSR)	Rot Front 7	749.2 km
19 April 1977	Adela Dankowska (Pol.)	PZL Jantar 1	837 km
20 January 1980	K. E. Karel (GB)	LS-3	949.7 km

Women's distance records for two-seater gliders

Date	Glider pilot	Glider type	Distance
10 June 1938	Olga Klepikova/E. L. Rastorgoueva (USSR)	CH-10	152.6 km
19 June 1940	Olga Klepikova/V. Bordina (USSR)	Stakanovetz	443.7 km
10 August 1958	Pelagia Majewska/Jadwiga Kurka (Pol.)	PZL Bocian	518.5 km
8 August 1962	Pelagia Majewska/Irena Raze (Pol.)	PZL Bocian	540.4 km
15 July 1963	Pelagia Majewska/Maria Kempowna (Pol.)	PZL Bocian	562.4 km
27 June 1964	Zinaida Solovey/S. Ivanova (USSR)	Blanik	619.9 km
3 June 1967	T. Pavlova/L. Filomechkins (USSR)	Blanik	864.8 km

Source : Segelflug Museum.

Maryse Bastié poses in front of her plane in Tokyo at the end of her March 1937 air trip. Also in the photo, standing next to her, are the Japanese painter Fujita and his wife Yuki. (Author's collection)

The long-distance fliers

Tokyo, Saigon, the Cape, Nairobi and Antananarivo are just some of the evocative destinations chosen by early aviatrixes. Some of them made this a speciality upon which their fame was based. It was not until 1927 that a woman made an aerial journey of any substantial length, in the person of Mary du Caurroy, Duchess of Bedford. Flying a De Havilland D.H.60 Moth biplane, with Captain C.D. Barnard, she completed a circular tour of more than 5,100km between 21 April and 12 May 1927. Relatively long though it was, this flight was eclipsed by the performance of the Australian Jessie Maude 'Chubbie' Miller who, accompanied by Captain W.N. Lancaster, flew from England to Australia in 159 days between 14 October 1927 and 19 March 1928, aboard an Avro 594 Avian Mk III. The flight totalled around 18,600km, with 39 stopovers, taking them to Port Darwin, although not without suffering some severe damage at Muntok in Sumatra, where they were held up for two long months. Meanwhile, another Briton, Lady Heath, made a flight from the Cape to London (see p. 56), just as her compatriot, Lady Bailey was making the same journey in the reverse direction. The latter crashed at Tabora, Tanganyika, but her husband quickly sent her a replacement plane (see p. 58).

Though arguably less impressive, several straight-course distance records were broken in the same period, starting on 22 October 1927 with the record for a plane weighing less than 400kg, set by Maurice Finat and his wife. Flying a Caudron C. 109 biplane, they linked Paris and Berlin, a distance of 868km. This record lasted a mere 10 months, as on 13 July 1928, Maryse Bastié and Georges Drouhin, also flying a C. 109, raised it to 1,058km with a flight from Le Bourget to Treptow, Berlin. Then two Swiss flyers, H. Wirth and Mme E. Naumann, flying a Daimler-engined Klemm monoplane, took it to 1,305km. On 20 August, the record again changed hands, with Léna Bernstein (see p. 99), again in a Caudron C. 109, covering the 2,268km separating Istres and Sidi Barrani (Egypt).

All these achievements were just asking to be bettered. On 20 March 1930, Alan S. Butler and his wife Lois took off from Croydon heading for the Cape, flying a Gloster Survey,[1] where they arrived 27 days later having covered 11,900km in 16 stages. But there is no question that the Holy Grail of British aviators remained Australia. From 5 to 24 May 1930, the young Amy Johnson flew from Croydon to Darwin, a feat for which the *Daily Mail* awarded her a £10,000 cash prize. In the autumn, another English aviatrix got herself into the news: in 1930, the Honourable Mrs Mildred Bruce, an enthusiastic racing driver, had bought herself a second-hand Blackburn Bluebird.[2] Flying alone, with barely 40 hours experience under her belt, she set out on an eastbound tour of the world on 25 September 1930. She finished on 20 February 1931, after a journey of 36,000km, including two sea crossings (Korea–Vancouver and New York–Le Havre) and two accidents in the United States.

In France, things weren't going so well. Maryse Hilsz, who had flown from Paris to Saigon between 12 November and 11 December 1930, had considerable

Mrs Victor Bruce (1895-1990) gained recognition in car racing before turning to flying and record breaking. In the mid-1930s, the Honourable Mrs Victor Bruce was one of a few British aviatrixes to be depicted on cigarette cards distributed by Lambert and Butler. (Author's collection)

On 5 November 1931, the 19-year-old British aviatrix Peggy Salaman flew from London to the Cape in one day, 1 day 1hr 23min. Accompanied by Gordon Store, she used a De Havilland DH-80A Puss Moth christened Good Hope. (H. Hazewinkel collection)

difficulty getting back to France. Léna Bernstein twice failed in her attempt to beat the distance record (May and June 1931). It took Maryse Bastié until 28 and 29 June 1931 to beat the distance record (see p. 95), while Amy Johnson was flying from London to Tokyo in nine days, or more precisely 79 hours of flight. The same summer, the German, Marga Etzdorf, flew from Berlin to Tokyo in 11 days, and in autumn, Ruth Nichols took the distance record from Maryse Bastié with a flight from Oakland, California to Louisville, Kentucky, a distance of 3,182.65km.

Both 20 and 21 May 1932 were red-letter days in the history of women's flying. Amelia Earhart, in her red Lockheed Vega, became the first woman to cross the North Atlantic solo, between Harbor Grace (Newfoundland) and Londonderry. A few weeks later, she failed in an attempt to cross the United States non-stop. She tried again on 24 August, this time successfully, flying from Los Angeles to Newark in 19hr 4min. At the same time, she beat the straight-line distance record with 3,939km. London to Cape Town continued to attract British aviatrixes. Amy Johnson and Lady Bailey battled it out to achieve the shorter time, while in early 1933, the French were heading for the Far East (Hélène Boucher to Saigon and Maryse Hilsz to Tokyo). In April, the New Zealander Jean Batten attempted to reach Australia, but got no further than Karachi, while the Australian Maude Rose 'Lores' Bonney achieved the first solo from Australia (Darwin) to England (Croydon) at the controls of the legendary De Havilland D.H.60 Gipsy Moth. In early July, Amelia Earhart and

Long-distance flights provided excellent advertising material for many aviation suppliers, as shown here in a Castrol advertisement fronted by Jean Batten. (DR)

her Lockheed Vega were joining Los Angeles and Newark in 17hr 7min 30sec while, the next day, the Lindberghs were setting out on the first of their joint trips (see p. 102).

After an initially abortive attempt to cross the Atlantic on 8 June, the Mollisons, flying a De Havilland Dragon[3] tried again on the 22nd July, but crashed at Bridgeport, Connecticut, emerging with just a few scratches. Indeed, couples were making the aeronautical news at this time. On 24 January 1934, three French aviators, André Garric, his wife and a passenger, flying a Dragon,[4] completed a North African journey across the Sahara and

Maurice Finat's widow and Flight Officer Raynaud just before leaving for Madagascar on 15 January 1936. The aircraft is a Caudron Aiglon registered as F-AOGT. (ROL, H. Hazewinkel collection)

the Sudan. Three months later, a Belgian couple, Guy and Marie-Louise Hansez-Fester, in a De Havilland Fox Moth,[5] flew from Antwerp to Leopoldville in five days, arriving back on 11 April. Ten days later, Jean Batten made a second attempt to fly from England to Australia, but got no further than Rome. For her, it was to be third time lucky! Leaving on 8 May, she touched down in Darwin 14 days later, beating Amy Johnson's record by more than four days (see p. 100). In 1935, Amelia Earhart began the aeronautical year with a record flight from Hawaii to California, covering the 3,870km in 18hr 15min in her Lockheed Vega. On 19 April, she added to her achievements with a flight from Burbank to Mexico City in 13hr 32min, followed on 8 May by a flight from Mexico City to New York. Meanwhile the Garrics, with Mme de France as a passenger, had undertaken a flight from Agen (France) to Saigon and back.[6] In Germany, Elly Beinhorn was beginning to get herself noticed after a Berlin to Constantinople round trip in the same day (13 August 1935), at the controls of a brand-new Messerschmitt Bf 108 Taifun monoplane.

Ignoring the traditional destinations in the British Empire, Jean Batten headed for South America on 11 November 1935. Leaving Lympne in a Percival Gull Six, she arrived in Natal, Brazil, having almost halved the time record set by Jim Mollison two and a half years previously. In France, after Maurice Finat's death in a crash,[7] his wife, accompanied by Raynaud and flying a Caudron Aiglon, decided to undertake a flight tracing her husband's route. Leaving Paris on 15 January 1936, she arrived in Antananarivo on 1 February and was back at Le Bourget by 9 March. As for Amy Johnson, she was struggling to beat her own records. On 3 April, she set out for the Cape, but got no further than Colomb-Béchar (Algeria). Trying again on 4 May, she reached the Cape on the 7th, smashing the previous record and again beat a record on the return flight. In the autumn, Jean Batten did likewise on the England–Australia route, with her various achievements leading to her being awarded the Britannia Trophy and the Seagrave Memorial Trophy.

Maryse Bastié made a number of long-distance flights. She is seen here at Le Bourget, on 8 March 1938, with her mechanic Lendroit, after completing a journey around South America. (SAFARA, H. Hazewinkel collection)

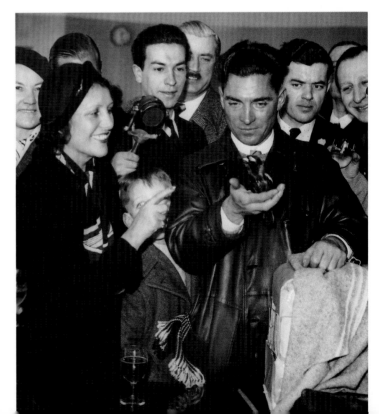

Claire Roman (right) and Alix Lucas-Naudin (left) at Le Bourget on 4 June 1937 after a Paris–Pondicherry flight undertaken between 22 April and 1 May, in a Salmson Phrygane. (ROL. H. Hazewinkel collection)

Geraldine Mock posing in front of her Cessna 180, named Spirit of Columbus, with which she broke a number of records between 1964 and 1969. (DR)

Sheila Scott (1927-1988) with her Piper Aztec Mythre, in which she completed a round-the-world journey in 1971, becoming the first person to fly over the North Pole in a single-engined plane. (NASA/GRIN)

1936 ended with a Paris–Natal flight by Maryse Bastié in a Caudron Simoun christened *Jean Mermoz*.

Increasingly numerous, these long-distance flights began to lose their appeal and gradually disappeared from the front pages. Among the flights undertaken in 1937, worthy of note are: Paris–Pondicherry by Claire Roman and Alix Lucas-Naudin (22 April–1 May), Paris–Novosibirsk by Maryse Bastié and Suzanne Tillier (15 July), Darwin–Lympne by Jean Batten (19 October), Croydon–the Cape by A.E. Clouston and Betty Kirby-Green (14–20 November) and Paris–Saigon by Maryse Hilsz (19–23 December). But the attempt that made the biggest headlines that year was undoubtedly the round-the-world flight on which Amelia Earhart set out on 1 June, with the controversial Fred Noonan as navigator and which was to have the tragic end that is so well known (see p. 140). This last flight of the American aviation icon seemed to mark a turning point in the way such long-distance flights and the women who made them were viewed. Furthermore, the steadily deteriorating international situation was pushing such exploits into the background. In France, Maryse Hilsz's distance records and those of the newcomers Elizabeth Lion and Andrée Dupeyron were now of interest only to those in the small world of aviation. Nonetheless, on 13 May 1938,

Elizabeth Lion, flying a Caudron Aiglon, took the women's distance record up to 4,100km, following this up with a flight from Istres to Dakar in 21 hours non-stop on 3 June 1939. Meanwhile, Andrée Dupeyron had taken the distance record on 15 May 1938, flying from Oran (Algeria) to Tel-el-Aham (Iraq), a distance of 4,372km. By the end of the Second World War, long-distance flights had become routine and so more or less disappeared for good from aeronautical annals. Still, a few aviatrixes managed to attract a degree of publicity. Between 19 March and 18 April 1964, the American flyer Geraldine L. Mock, in a single-engined Cessna 180 touring plane christened *Spirit of Columbus* for the occasion, completed a round-the-world flight in 29 days 11hr 59min, an average speed of 52.75kph. The following year, Sheila Scott, from Britain, in a Piper Comanche 400, beat a series of 15 records on flights linking European capitals (19 and 20 May 1965). Beginning on 18 May 1936, she set out on a 33-day 46,670km flight around the world, followed in 1969 by a second round-the-world trip, at the end of a London–Sydney race, and the legendary London to the Cape flight (July 1967). Finally, she undertook an unprecedented journey, flying around the world via the North Pole. Piloting a Piper Aztec, she flew the 54,700km using special IRLS Nimbus tracking equipment that she had agreed to test for NASA. With around 100 records to her credit, Sheila Scott ceased flying after her plane was wrecked in a cyclone. In November 1980, the British flyer Judith Chisholm flew around the world in 360hr 22min 23sec in a Cessna 210, breaking some 28 city-city records in the process.

She was the last of the great long-distance specialists. In 1994, the crossing of the Atlantic by the 12-year-old Vicki Van Meter drew a kind of line under the race for long-distance records.

1. Gloster A.S.31 Survey no. 1, registered as G-AADO.
2. Blackburn Bluebird IV, no. SB245, registered as G-ABDS.
3. De Havilland DH-84 Dragon I 'Seafarer' no. 6014, registered as G-ACCV.
4. De Havilland DH84 no. 6040, registered as F-AMTM.
5. De Havilland Fox Moth no. 4033, registered as OO-ENC.
6. Left Agen on 21 January 1935, returning on 11 March.
7. Maurice Finat was killed on 20 April 1935 returning after a flight he had led to Madagascar.

Worldwide fame: Maryse Bastié

(1898-1952)

Maryse Bastié in her early days, at the controls of a Caudron G.3 (P. Gaillard collection)

'An aviatrix who, with ten records to her name, and flying alone, has demonstrated rare skill enhanced by a complete indifference to danger' thus begins the citation of the Ordre de la Nation awarded to the French flyer, Maryse Bastié.

Born in Limoges on 27 February 1898, into a family of modest means, Marie-Louise Bombec was only 10 years old when she lost her father. As soon as she was of working age, she got employment in a shoe factory that closed down in 1914. She then became a dressmaker and married an apprentice painter. The union bore a son[1] but the father turned out to be an alcoholic. The young mother managed to get a divorce after the war and married Lieutenant Louis Bastié, her wartime adoptive son, who gave her her first flight. The new family settled in Cognac and bought a shoe shop there. On Louis Bastié's appointment as instructor at Mérignac in 1925, Marie-Louise's enthusiasm for flying took off.

Taught the basics of flying by Guy Bart, she took her pilot's licence on 29 September 1925. A week later, she attracted attention when, at the controls of a Caudron G.3, she flew under the Bordeaux transporter bridge. The following month, she decided to 'go up' to Paris, a journey she undertook in six stages, despite poor weather conditions. On 15 October 1926, she learned of her husband's death in a plane crash. This tragic event barely put her off her stride. After making a few flights in a Caudron C.59, she succeeded in getting herself taken on as a pilot at a flying school in Paris, on 1 December 1927. There she gave people their first flights and did some aerial advertising, but the school had to close in May 1928. The next month, at the Rheims meeting, she teamed up with Maurice Drouhin and the pair took second place with prize money of 25,000F. Marie-Louise then decided to buy her own plane, a Caudron C.109. As she did not have sufficient money to do this and fly it, Drouhin agreed to help her out.

From that moment, Marie-Louise Bombec, now known as Maryse Bastié, achieved a string of feats that would guarantee her fame. On 13 July 1928, with Drouhin, she beat the distance record over a straight course, flying from

Maryse Bastié was described in the aeronautical press as a brave flyer with a winning smile. (H. Manuel)

Maryse Bastié and Maurice Drouhin in the little Farman Sport F-65 no. 13 (registration F-AICP). (André, M. Bénichou collection)

Orly to Treptow in Pomerania, a distance of 1,058km. This was followed by six endurance records; on each occasion flying solo. Thus it was on 20 April 1929 that she remained aloft for 10hr 30min, establishing a French endurance record for a light plane and permitting her to acquire the Caudron, a much better plane for such performances. On 28 and 29 July, after two fruitless attempts, she took the women's world endurance record (26hr 46min) recently established by the American, Elinor Smith (26hr 33min). But Léna Bernstein quickly took it from her, remaining airborne for 35hr 44min. 'I can assure you it's a pretty monotonous business,' she declared to the reporter of *Ailes*.[2]

But her most exceptional performance was achieved soon afterwards in a

Maryse Bastié has just landed following her record endurance flight at the controls of her Klemm in 1930. A mechanic is removing the barograph from inside the fuselage. (World Wide Photo)

German Klemm L-25 monoplane with a 40hp Salmson engine that she had collected from Stuttgart in April 1930 and had had fitted with a 300-litre reserve fuel tank.[3] Taking off on the evening of 2 September 1930, she touched down again nearly two days later having been airborne for 37hr 55 min. For this, she won 50000F in prize money, enough to mount a new project. Glory was unquestionably achieved on 28 June 1931 when she took the international distance record for a light, single-seater monoplane, flying from Le Bourget (at 5.02am) to Yurino (near Nizhny-Novgorod in the USSR), a distance of 2,976km covered in 30hr 30min. At the same time, she had snatched the distance record over a straight course from the American, Zimmerly. Not only this, but while she was being feted in the newspapers and everyone was seeking her out, she was awarded not just the Harmon International Aviatrix Trophy for 1935, but also the Légion d'Honneur.

She now made a change of plane, selling her Klemm and buying a Caudron Phalène. In October 1932, she signed a contract with Potez to deliver the firm's aircraft. In June 1935, she was made redundant, but far from being downcast, she bounced back by setting up her own flying school at Orly, the Maryse Bastié Aviation School, which remained in existence until the war. Outside her purely professional activities, Maryse Bastié doggedly pursued her record-breaking exploits. Her dream was to beat the record for the South Atlantic crossing, held since 1935 by Jean Batten (see p. 112). Having obtained, not without difficulty and at the cost of numerous approaches to the Air Minister, Marcel Déat, a single-engined Caudron Simoun, a plane that she believed was the only one capable of such a performance, she set out for Dakar on Saturday 3 October 1936, accompanied by Suzanne Tillier, and arrived there after an eventful journey. On 30 December 1936, she flew solo from Dakar to Natal in 12hr 5min, thereby establishing a new record for the South Atlantic crossing, a flight which, according to her, was trouble free, apart from crossing the Doldrums. As she was to say to a journalist from *Paris Soir*: '...I was roughly battered. Below, the dark sea; overhead a threatening sky! But the engine behaved perfectly, purring away like a cat.' After being feted in Paris, she soon left again for South America. On 12 January, she was in Rio de Janeiro, shortly afterwards in Montevideo then Buenos Aires where she was given a triumphal reception and named her plane after Jen Mermoz who had recently been lost.[4]

Le Bourget on 12 August 1930: Maryse Bastié powders her nose before the next attempt on the endurance record. (DR)

After her South Atlantic crossing, Maryse Bastié gives her mechanic, Lendroit, a hug. (Meurisse)

In 1937, Maryse Bastié was at the peak of her fame. 'The pilot of charm and glory', as the aeronautical weekly *Ailes* used to refer to her, was promoted to Knight of the Légion d'Honneur on 26 February and treated to lunch with the President of the Republic, Albert Lebrun. That same year, she made a tour of Central and South America. After a short period of rest, she started out again on her travels, notably with a flight to Vladivostok[5] at the far eastern extremity of the Soviet Union, accompanied by Suzanne Tillier and the mechanic, Lendroit. The two women left Orly at 9.45am on 15 July, heading for Königsberg.[6] But by the time they got as far as Krasnoyarsk, they were forced to turn back because of the appalling weather conditions. On their return flight, they stopped off in Moscow, Königsberg, Warsaw, Budapest, Belgrade, Vienna and Prague, during a journey totalling some 25,000km. The same distance was covered in a propaganda trip that took her to the main South American capitals between November 1937 and March 1938.

On 22 December 1938, Maryse Bastié set out for Africa with her mechanic Lendroit and Maurice Reine. She was also accompanied by Lucienne Saby in another Simoun. The journey took her to Tunis, Dakar, Villa-Cisneros, and Bechar. She ended the tour on 16 January 1939 with a Mediterranean crossing from Tunis to Istres. Still not satisfied, she left on 21 March for North Africa on a month-long journey of 15,000km. When war broke out, the Quai d'Orsay entrusted her with a mission to the Scandinavian countries, after which she

On 4 September 1930, her arms laden with flowers, Maryse Bastié is overjoyed after having broken Léna Bernstein's record. (ROL)

Maryse dedicated this photo to André Allibert with the words: 'To André, the photo ace, best wishes.' (André Allibert, J. Moulin collection)

Maryse Bastié poses in front of the 40hp Salmson-engined Caudron she used to break the women's endurance record on 29 July 1929. (André Allibert, J. Moulin collection)

Maryse Bastié with Suzanne Tillier, in Tunis, on 4 October 1936, during the Paris–Dakar expedition. (André Allibert, J. Moulin collection)

offered her services to the Red Cross where, as a nurse and ambulance worker, she aided prisoners.

At the same time, she started to work for the Allies and collaborated with the 'Darius' network. She continued this clandestine activity until March 1944 when, coming under suspicion from the Germans, she was arrested. After three days of interrogation, she was released, but forbidden to leave the capital.

Joining the women's Air Force Auxiliaries as a lieutenant in November 1944, Maryse Bastié gained her military 'wings' following her training at Châteauroux and was assigned to the GMMTA.[7] She was demobilised in April 1946, but

Maryse Bastié and Lendroit are enthusiastically greeted at Orly. (Meurisse)

continued to work for the Air Ministry as an official representative.

On 14 April 1947, Flight Lieutenant Bastié was the first woman to be elevated to the rank of Commander of the Légion d'Honneur for 'exceptional conduct and acts of resistance in war', a decoration that added to her Croix de Guerre with bar, Resistance Medal and the numerous foreign honours she had received. The Air Minister, André Maroselli, obtained a post for her at OFEMA (French Aviation Export Office), a job she left in 1951 to go into public relations with the Flight Test Centre at Brétigny. In 1952, she agreed to take part in an aviation meeting at Lyon-Bron. Setting out afterwards for Paris on 6 July, aboard the prototype Nord Noratlas 2501 that she had demonstrated, she met a tragic end. Having climbed to 200m, the plane suddenly nosedived and crashed. Maryse Bastié perished along with the rest of the crew, seven people in all. The aviatrix was given a state funeral at Les Invalides and received the highest mention in dispatches.

1. Her son died in June 1935 of typhoid fever.
2. In Les Ailes of 2 May 1929.
3. This brought the fuel capacity up to 525 litres, plus 30 litres of oil.
4. Jean Mermoz disappeared in the South Atlantic on board the Latécoère hydroplane Croix du Sud (Southern Cross), on 7 December 1936.
5. At the request of the USSR, Maryse Bastié was obliged to revise her final destination to Irkutsk.
6. Now named Kalinigrad, in East Prussia.
7. GMMTA = Groupement des Moyens Militaires de Transport Aérien (Military Air Transport Organisation).

Léna Bernstein at the start of her career poses in front of a Potez VIII that she would shortly exchange for a Caudron C.109. (André Allibert, J. Moulin collection)

She has 'pluck':
Léna Bernstein

(1906-1932)

Léna Bernstein warms the 40hp Salmson engine of the Caudron C.109 lent to her by Maurice Finat. The aircraft had the number 2 and was registered as F-AIIH. (André Allibert, M. Bénichou collection)

The news resounded like a gunshot: Léna Bernstein 'has been found dead on the dunes at Biskra. The cause of her death is unknown'. This sad news filled the papers in early June 1932. Was it an accident or suicide? Nothing in her life up to then had suggested such an outcome. This 26-year-old had built for herself a solid reputation as an adventurous aviatrix. She had 'pluck', people said of her.

Léna Bernstein was born in Leipzig of Russian parents who had emigrated successively to Germany then France. She had gained her pilot's licence at Aulnat in 1928 and gone to the capital with a clear determination to take some records. To support her in this endeavour, Maurice Finat had lent her his Caudron C.109, with which she intended to go for the distance record over a straight course for a third category aircraft.[1] On 19 August 1929, after two fruitless attempts, she crossed the Mediterranean from Istres to Sidi Barrani, in Egypt, a distance of 2,268km in a single hop. The record was beaten. Unfortunately, on 5 September, while on the return flight, she flipped over as she landed at La Manoubia, but escaped unhurt.

The following year, this time at the controls of a Farman F.192, she beat Maryse Bastié's endurance record (see p. 95). On 1 and 2 May, at Le Bourget, she remained airborne for 35hr 46min 55sec, improving on her compatriot's record by nine hours. Not content with this, she attempted a flight from Paris to Saigon in 1931 with the mechanic Guitton, but this was cut short and ended prematurely by a forced landing at Baghdad. Persistent and stubborn, Léna Bernstein managed to obtain a Farman F.230 against a security of 32,000F. On 31 May at 3.00am, she attempted a take-off with her plane filled with 415 litres of fuel, but a sudden gust of wind blew her off the runway and into a heap of stones. Although she was seriously hurt, she got off lightly

Léna Bernstein with the Farman 192, at Le Bourget in March 1930, at the time of her first attempt to break the women's endurance record. She had to cut this flight short when one of the fuel tank valves could not be opened. (André Allibert, J. Moulin collection)

Léna Bernstein in discussion with her mechanic Guitton in front of her Farman F.231, around 1930. (André Allibert, J. Moulin collection)

from an accident that could have had tragic consequences.

A former war pilot provided her with a new plane, a Farman F.236.[2] That year (1932), she finally obtained French citizenship and started to make preparations for a Middle-East flight from Biskra to Baghdad. The authorities, however, would not allow her to leave Istres fully loaded. In a fit of pique, Léna Bernstein gave up on the idea of going for the distance record over a straight course and returned to Paris, though not for long, as she soon headed off for Algiers and the Biskra, where her plane, damaged in a tornado, was awaiting her. She was said to be exhausted and at the end of her tether. On 3 June, she took a taxi out into the desert then sent the driver away...Champagne and pills did the rest. Two days later her lifeless body was discovered in the sands.

1. The distance record for a third category light plane had been held since 5 October 1928 by the Czech Vicherek who had flown from Prague to Bednodem'janovsk, a distance of 2,011km.
2. The Farman 236 was a single-seater derivative of the F.230 with an increased wingspan.

Amy Johnson didn't mind getting her hands dirty. Her mechanical skills would prove to be extremely useful. (Bettmann/Corbis)

A girl named 'Johnnie': Amy Johnson-Mollison
(1903-1941)

'Johnnie' at Stag Lane on 10 January 1930, shortly after she had gained her mechanic's qualification. (Michael Nicolson/Corbis)

Described as 'an exceptionally tough young woman', Léna Bernstein remained aloft for 35hr 46min in her Farman. (ROL)

MISS AMY JOHNSON. O.B.E.

On 5 May 1930, Amy Johnson poses for the photographers just before her flight to Australia. (DR)

'I have seen Mrs Mollison only at the cinema. I admire her long, Florentine features, the grace of her smile, her simplicity. Everyone who has seen her close up has praised her beauty and is amazed that such an apparently fragile exterior could conceal so much strength and energy'. These words were penned by Madeleine Poulaine in the aeronautical weekly *Les Ailes*.[1] She went on: 'Mrs Mollison has accomplished a feat from which many others, even brave men, would have recoiled'.

It must be said that when she set out on her historic journey to Australia, the young Briton had shown remarkable courage. At the age of 27, she had decided to beat the record held by Bert Hinkler. Marked out for a career as a lawyer, she was the eldest of three daughters of the wealthy owner of 'Jason' a Hull-based fish merchant. She had received a good education, including studying at Sheffield University. While working as a secretary at a City law firm, at a salary of £5 a week, she had been obsessed by the desire to fly, but had had to put her name down on a long waiting list before being able to get into the London Aero Club. Yet Amy had not shown any particular aptitude for flying. Stubborn, she had persisted and begun to get interested in the flying machines themselves, to the point where she considered going for a mechanic's certificate. Little by little, following conversations with Jack Humphreys, the chief mechanic, and Captain Baker, one of the instructors, the seed of an idea had been sown to attempt a long flight, so why not Australia?

With the flying and mechanic's lessons becoming a full-time occupation, Amy left her job and fell back on paternal assistance to support her needs. Determined and tireless, she picked up the masculine nickname of 'Johnnie'. In late 1929, she gained her mechanic's qualification and a pilot's B licence (which permitted her to fly commercially). It was at this time that she announced her intention to fly to Australia... to be met with complete indifference. Sponsors, too, were impossible to find and she raised just £25. Once again, her father came to the

rescue and helped her to buy a Gipsy Moth, a plane with which she was very familiar. She christened it *Jason*, as the least she could do. It was then that her luck turned. She had written to Sir Sefton Brancker, the Director of Civil Aviation, who, struck by her enthusiasm, promised to help. This upturn in her fortunes had arrived at just the right moment.

Amy threw herself wholeheartedly into the preparations for her flight. In the cramped cockpit of her plane that she called 'the village shop', she stacked tools, spare parts, a fuel tank, clothes etc. A spare propeller was attached to the side of the plane. She took off on 5 May 1930 and disappeared into the fog. She had 12 stages ahead of her. She covered the early ones without much difficulty, even gaining a little on Hinkler's record, a fact that stirred the media's interest. But near Baghdad, caught in a violent sandstorm, the plane was so battered that it nearly crashed. However, Amy managed to land and then had to wait a few hours before being able to take off again. Unfortunately, *Jason's* landing gear broke in two on coming down at Baghdad. It was quickly repaired and Amy was able to set off again the following morning. At Bandar Abbas, the landing gear gave way once more, but it was again repaired and with two days in hand over Hinkler's time, Amy landed in Karachi. But fate seemed to be conspiring against her. With a strong easterly wind, she soon found herself running short of fuel and she was forced to land at Jhansi in the Punjab. Bad luck continued to dog her: arriving at Rangoon, Amy mistook her landing spot and *Jason* ended up in a ditch, with its propeller broken. After Bangkok, she had to face a tropical storm, but this was nothing compared with the crowd of hundreds of excited Malaysians waiting for her at Singora, through which she had to part a way.

The most perilous part of the journey to reach Port Darwin was still to come. The adventure turned into a nightmare. Arriving in Java, *Jason* was again seriously damaged, and patched up with plaster, it took off again for Surabaya where the propeller had to be replaced. All this time, the press was making the most of Johnnie's flight. After crossing the Timor Sea, she finally landed at Port Darwin in front of a jubilant crowd. She had covered some 19,110km in less than 20 days, and although she had not beaten Hinkler's record, the press and the public behaved as if she had.

Passing through Le Bourget in her De Havilland DH-80 Puss Moth, Amy Johnson is photographed shaking hands with an unidentified person. (André Allibert, J. Moulin collection)

Amy Johnson with her friend Amelia Earhart in the summer of 1933. Earhart's disappearance came as a great shock. (Bettmann/Corbis)

In 'Lindy's' shadow: Anne Morrow-Lindbergh (1906-2001)

With her becoming the celebrity of the moment, the media fell over themselves to get to her. There is no doubt that the charm of her personality made her attractive to the public. With receptions and interviews one after another, she allowed it all to go to her head. This achievement was the precursor of a series of long-distance flights, the first of which took place in July 1931 when she flew from London to Tokyo at the controls of a D.H.80A Puss Moth in 80 hours. In July 1932, she married Jim Mollison, who was also a pilot.[2] He shared Amy's ambitions and had the same competitive spirit. Again, the press was avid to report their idyll. Four months after her marriage, Amy broke her husband's record for the return flight to the Cape. Later, in June 1933, they crossed the Atlantic together in the D.H.84 Dragon Seafarer but, running short of fuel, they had to make an emergency landing at Bridgeport, short of their destination, and were slightly injured in the ensuing crash. In October 1934, the couple made a 22-hour flight to Karachi in a splendid twin-engined D.H.88 Comet Black Magic. Then, in May 1936, Amy undertook a solo return flight to the Cape in 4 days 6hr 45min.

Unfortunately, success began to evade the British aviatrix. The marriage was in a bad way and Amelia Earhart's disappearance was a terrible blow. Amy took a break from record setting. She became a ferry pilot at Portsmouth, while also taking part in a few motor races.[3] On the declaration of war, Amy Johnson joined the ranks of the ATA, ferrying new aircraft to their aerodromes. It was while she was delivering a twin-engined Airspeed Oxford[4] from Prestwick to Kidlington in Oxfordshire on 4 January 1941 that she met her death when her plane ran out of fuel and she parachuted into the icy waters of the Thames estuary. All the efforts made to rescue her failed.

1. In Les Ailes *12th January 1933.*
2. *In July 1931, James Allan Mollison (1905-1959) had completed a flight from London to Australia in 8 days 21hr.*
3. *The Paris-Vichy-Saint-Raphaël Rally in a Talbot-Lago in 1938; RAC in a Bentley in 1939.*
4. *To be exact, Airspeed Oxford Mk. II, registered as V3540.*

Anne Morrow-Lindbergh and her husband on a practice flight at Roosevelt, Long Island, in 1929. (AAHS)

The Lindbergh couple on one of their numerous air trips. (J. Underwood collection)

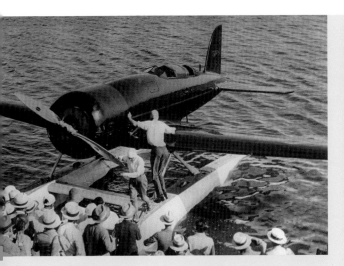

Built in October-November 1929, the Lindberghs' Lockheed Sirius was converted into a seaplane in early 1931. The couple are seen here preparing to depart on its second trip in July 1933. (Lockheed)

Anne Morrow-Lindbergh photographed at Nanking in August 1931. (DR)

During their trip to Germany in July 1936, Anne and Charles Lindbergh were invited to Hermann Göring's villa in Berlin. (J. Underwood collection)

Anne Morrow met Charles Lindbergh when he paid a visit to her father, Dwight Morrow, at that time the United States Ambassador to Mexico. Captivated by this pilot of international fame and won over by the plane rides he gave her, Anne married Charles quietly on 27 May 1929. She wasted no time in learning to fly and navigate, becoming the first American woman to take a glider-pilot's licence (see p. 84). At this time, the couple were in the habit of making most of their journeys by plane and the press was quick to dub them 'the first couple of the skies'.

On Easter Sunday 1930, Charles and Anne took off from Glendale, California, aboard an orange and black Lockheed Sirius[1] with the intention of beating the record for the crossing of the United States, which they achieved by linking the two coasts in 14hr 45min 32sec. Anne, having been the co-pilot and navigator, was effectively considered as the women's record holder for the crossing. The following year, Charles, who was a technical adviser for Pan American Airways, set up a study trip of potential air routes in the North Pacific. Anne was co-pilot of the Sirius for the trip, which lasted from July to October 1931. The plane was fitted with floats for this purpose. Having flown across Canada, Alaska, Japan and China, they landed at Nanking where they offered their assistance to victims of the floods. Unfortunately, the Sirius fell into the Yangtze at Hankow on 2 October and had to be sent back to the United States, while the couple returned by boat. Anne Morrow-Lindbergh would later tell the story of this first trip in her book *North to the Orient.*

On 1 March 1932 occurred the drama that everyone knows about, with the kidnapping of the baby Charles Lindbergh, whose body was to be found on 12 May, just a few kilometres from the family house. Seeing his wife in such a state of depression, Charles decided to plan a second reconnaissance trip on behalf of Pan American. Starting on 9 July 1933, at Flushing Bay, New York, it would end six months later, on 6 December, taking them via Nova Scotia, Newfoundland, Labrador, Greenland, Iceland, Denmark, Sweden, Finland, Russia, Estonia, Norway, Britain, France, the Netherlands, Switzerland, Spain, Portugal, the Azores, Cape Verde, Gambia, Brazil and Santa Dominica, a

distance of 48,000km over four continents. It was the last significant aerial exploit undertaken by Lindbergh and his wife.

Henceforth, Anne Morrow-Lindbergh would devote herself to writing and published several successful novels.[2] Otherwise, in the immediate pre-war years, she lent her support to her husband's non-interventionist stance. After suffering several heart attacks in the early 1990s, she passed away on 7 February 2001.

1. This was a Lockheed Sirius Model 8, no. 140, registered as NR211. It was powered by a Pratt and Whitney Wasp engine, no. 2099, and later by a Wright Cyclone, no. 13461 that Lindbergh bought for $17,825.
2. Among these were: Listen! The Wind (1938), The Wave of the Future (1940), The Steep Ascent (1944), Gift from the Sea (1955), The Unicorn and Other Poems (1956), Dear Beloved (1962), Earth Shine (1969).

Anne and Charles posing in front of their Lockheed Sirius before setting out on their transcontinental flight in April 1930. (J. Underwood collection)

Marga von Etzdorf at Aspern with her bright-yellow Junkers A50. (Wienbibliothek)

'Kiek in die Welt': Marga von Etzdorf

(1907-1933)

The bronze bust of Marga von Etzdorf, displayed in the Berlin Techniksches Museum. (A Pelletier)

Born into the family of a Prussian officer, and orphaned at the age of four, Marga von Etzdorf was 19 when she learned to fly. She gained her licence in 1927 and she became so enthusiastic about flying that she decided to train as an airline pilot. She succeeded in being hired as a co-pilot on a Junkers F13 at Deutsche Lufthansa (DLH), though she was obliged to keep her identity secret from the passengers.[1] 'This little game of hide-and-seek was made much easier, she said, because the F13's open cockpit compelled the pilots to wear a fur coat, thick boots and a cap.'[2] In 1929, her contract with DLH came to an end. However, she managed to find six months of work with a Hamburg aviation company and, at the same time, obtain her glider pilot's licence, which allowed her to take part in the Wasserkuppe 10th Gliding Championships.

In April 1930, Marga acquired a new Junkers A50[3] naming it *Kiek in die Welt* (discovering the world) and intending to use it to undertake long-distance flights. The following August, she made a flight from Berlin to Constantinople, then, in November, flew to the Canaries via Basle, Lyon, Madrid and Rabat. It was on the return leg that she encountered problems. Because of poor weather conditions, she was forced to make an emergency landing at Catania in Sicily. The little plane was badly damaged, obliging Marga to get back to Germany by boat and train. After these two probing flights, she began to make preparations for a long-distance flight to one of the most prized destinations of the time, Tokyo. Taking off in her Junkers Junior on 18 August 1931, she reached Japan in 11 days, having stopped off at Königsberg, Moscow, Kazan, Sverdlovsk, Kurgan, Omsk, Irkutsk, Verkhneudinsk, Chita, Harbin, Mukden, Seoul, Osaka and finally, Tokyo, where she received a triumphant reception. She realised at this point how, when she was abroad, she could play the role of 'ambassador of Germany'. But luck was not with her: during her return to Berlin, she crashed near Bangkok after engine trouble. The Junkers was turned into a heap of scrap metal and Marga suffered numerous bruises and injuries.

These two accidents made the search for sponsors for future expeditions that much more difficult. However, in 1933, after months of searching, Marga managed to persuade the Klemm Company to put an aircraft at her disposal.[4] This time, her objective was to reach Australia. On 27 May 1933, she took off from Berlin-Staaken, heading south. Misjudging her landing, she again badly damaged her plane. Badly shaken by this third crash, she asked for a period of rest in some isolated spot. What happened next resounded like a thunderclap. Marga von Etzdorf had committed suicide!

Marga von Etzdorf (left) with three other German aviatrixes, Thea Rasche (middle), Antonie Straßmann and Elly Beinhorn (right). (DR)

According to the official account, with her pride wounded and her career as a pilot compromised forever, the German aviatrix had chosen to take her own life. Another version, based on a later investigation by the Foreign Ministry, cast a quite different light on the affair. Being seriously short of money, Marga von Etzdorf had got herself mixed up in arms trafficking. She intended to take advantage of her various stopovers to make contacts and negotiate the sale of Schmeisser sub-machine guns. After an unexpected landing at an aerodrome under French control, she risked being discovered and arrested. Rather than face the dishonour, she had made the choice to end her life by shooting herself with a Schmeisser she had brought with

her. In Germany, the news of her death caused consternation and, on Hitler's orders, she was given a state funeral.

1. Since 1924, women had been excluded from having a career as a professional pilot in civil aviation.
2. Quoted by Marga von Etzdorf in her book: Kiek in die Welt.
3. This plane was a Junkers A50ce Junior with manufacturer's no. 3519 and registered as D1811.
4. A Klemm KL32.x.

Ready for any test: Maryse Hilsz

(1901-1946)

The best-known portrait of Maryse Hilsz, which was taken in about 1937. Her determination is expressed clearly here. (DR, H. Hazewinkel collection)

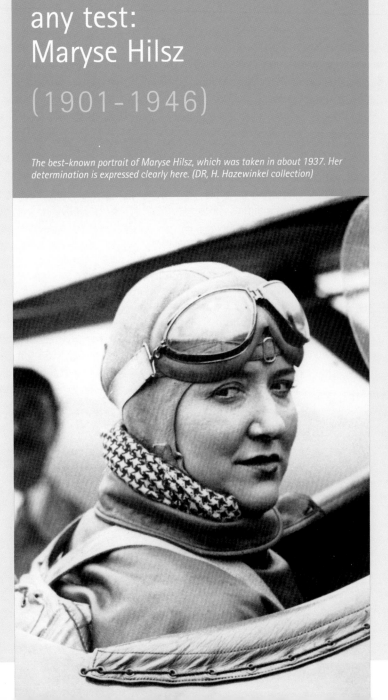

Maryse Hilsz sitting on her Morane-Saulnier AR.35C monoplane, no. 49 (F-AJBO) that she acquired in May 1929. (André Allibert, J. Moulin coll)

Born into a family of humble background, who had left Alsace so as to remain French, Maryse Hilsz began her working life as an apprentice milliner in the Paris suburbs at the age of 13. Soon, the sight of aeroplanes criss-crossing the sky aroused in her an enthusiasm for flying. She was barely 23 when she made her maiden flight at Le Bourget and, six months later, she made her first parachute jump at an amateur competition, in which she came first. To finance her pilot's training, Maryse Hilsz became a professional parachutist. After three years, she had built up a total of 122 jumps and managed to get together the sum required for her coveted licence and the purchase of a Morane-Saulnier AR.35C monoplane. Towards the end of June 1929, she started to get her hand in by planning five trips to European cities, though she actually did only two of them, to Croydon and Amsterdam.

On 12 November 1930 at 10.30am, after completing various official formalities, she took off from Villacoublay on her first long-distance flight, to Saigon. Despite appalling weather conditions, she was in Belgrade by 14 November, Baghdad by 19 November, Karachi by 20 November, Calcutta on 21 November and Rangoon on 25 November, where she had her fuel tank repaired. On 4 December, she landed in Bangkok and on the 5th she was, finally, in Saigon. It had taken her 25 days, or 92hr 31min of flying time. It was a first in women's aviation. Six days later, she began the return flight

Maryse Hilsz's second aircraft was the Morane Moth no. 1 (F-AJOE) that she bought in May 1930. It was, in fact, the first French-built De Havilland Moth, whose characteristically shaped fin is visible here. (André Allibert, J. Moulin collection)

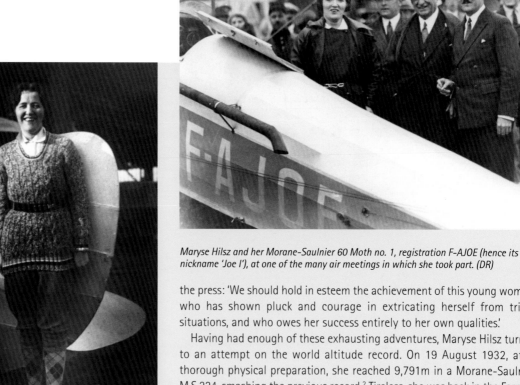

Maryse Hilsz and her Morane-Saulnier 60 Moth no. 1, registration F-AJOE (hence its nickname 'Joe I'), at one of the many air meetings in which she took part. (DR)

along the same route, but numerous setbacks slowed her progress. It wasn't until 7 February 1931 that she reached Paris, exactly three months after setting out and having travelled 24,000km. She had clearly demonstrated not only her abilities as a pilot and navigator, but above all, her physical stamina. This was the start of a 15-year career that would be punctuated with exploits of all kinds.

On 31 January 1932 at 12.55pm, after a year of preparation, Maryse Hilsz set off again, this time flying a Farman 291 monoplane. Accompanied by Dronne, a mechanic, she intended this time to undertake an expedition to Madagascar sponsored by the Air Ministry. Yet again, she had to suffer terrible weather conditions and mechanical problems at Niamey. The 12,000km journey was completed in two months, with the plane touching down in Antananarivo on 31 March.[1] The return flight, which was not a bed of roses either, ended at Le Bourget on 7 May. The feat was not ignored by

the press: 'We should hold in esteem the achievement of this young woman, who has shown pluck and courage in extricating herself from tricky situations, and who owes her success entirely to her own qualities.'

Having had enough of these exhausting adventures, Maryse Hilsz turned to an attempt on the world altitude record. On 19 August 1932, after thorough physical preparation, she reached 9,791m in a Morane-Saulnier M.S.224, smashing the previous record.[2] Tireless, she was back in the Farman 291, setting off from Le Bourget with the mechanic Lemaire for a Paris–Tokyo flight. The journey took just 15 days and she reached the Japanese capital on 16 April. The return took 20 (from 23 April to 14 May 1933). It was a kind of compensation for her problems on the earlier trips. Far from resting on her laurels, she set out again for the Far East at the beginning of the next year, flying a Breguet Br.330R2 provided for her by the Air Ministry. She arrived in Tokyo on 6 March 1934 and left again on 20 March. This time, the flight from Tokyo to Paris took just eight days and three hours: an unprecedented feat!

On 17 June 1934, she made another attempt on the world altitude record, bringing it up to 11,289m. But another aviatrix had her eyes on the record. This was the Italian, Carina Negrone (see p. 79), who took it up to 12,043m. Cut to the quick and determined to take back the record, Maryse took off from Villacoublay on 23 June 1936 at 5.11am, at the controls of a Potez 506 with a 900hp Gnome and Rhône 14Krsd engine.[3] She touched down at 6.22am, having climbed to 14,309m in 36 minutes. To record the altitude, Maryse Hilsz had used a new type of barograph, which registered the temperature and the time as well as the height. The lowest temperature she

Maryse Hilsz and the mechanic Dronne with the Farman 291 no. 7265. 1, christened 'Joe II'. (P. Gaillard collection)

18 February 1931: Maryse Hilsz attending a reception at the Aéro-Club de France with, on her right, the British flyer Mildred Bruce and, on her left, the Air Minister Dumesnil and Maryse Bastié. (ROL)

had recorded, for example, was -51°C at 10,000m. Foreseeing such temperatures, she had worn a fleece-lined, electrically heated suit, as well as an oxygen mask.

Maryse Hilsz now became a spokesperson for the Air Ministry and campaigned for the future of French aviation, giving speech after speech, criticising, among other things, the obsolescence of much of the equipment. 'While I have been able to undertake many great journeys during my career, I have also been able, I hope, to promote the cause of aviation' she said at the time.[4] Meanwhile, she took the second Hélène Boucher Cup flying a Caudron Super Rafale and made preparations for an assault on the speed record over a closed circuit that had been set by Hélène Boucher (see p. 144). On 19 December 1936, she narrowly escaped death over the Etang de l'Estorac,[5] when she was thrown out of her Caudron C-460 as it was hit by a gust of wind. Injured and obliged to convalesce, she planned an expedition to Bassora in Iraq, with the aim of beating the women's distance record. Terrible weather forced her to land at Alexandria and she had a change of heart. She decided to set off again immediately, but this time to attempt the Paris–Saigon record, which she achieved in 92hr 31min, beating the previous record by 6hr 21min.[6]

In December 1938, she failed in a new attempt to establish a distance record for multi-seat light aircraft, but when she was in Dakar, she met the other Maryse, Maryse Bastié (see p. 78) and the two women decided to do a publicity tour using three Caudron Simouns. Unfortunately, war broke out before the plan could come to fruition. Maryse Hilsz then became a ferry pilot for the Amiot Company and she was in Toulouse when the armistice was signed. She left for the United States with the intention of meeting Jacqueline Cochran, but nothing much came of this. She returned home, where she joined the 'Buckmaster' resistance group, using a clothes shop as a front for her activities. In September 1944, given the rank of pilot officer, she flew VIPs on behalf of GLAM, the ministerial air liaison group. It was while flying a Siebel 204 belonging to this group that she met her death in a crash on 30 January 1946, in the Bourg-en-Bresse region.

Maryse Hilsz on her arrival in Tokyo on 6 March 1934, after her flight in the Breguet Br.330R2 Joe III. (DR)

1. After a navigational error, M. Hilsz landed at Fianarantsoa, short of Antananarivo-Ivato.
2. The record had been held since 14 February 1932 by the American Ruth Nichols, with 6,074m.
3. This aircraft was derived from the Potez 50A2, with the wing surface increased by 14m² and the span by more than 2m. To avoid icing, the leading edges of the wings had been coated with a mixture of glycerine and oil.
4. Quoted in the programme of the 6th Air Fair at Vincennes, May 1934.
5. Between Fos-sur-Mer and Les Salins du Midi.
6. The record, of 98hr 52min, had been held by André Japy.

Maryse Hilsz and Dronne, her mechanic, at Le Bourget in January 1932. (ROL)

Le Bourget on 3 February 1938: Maryse Hilsz and her mechanic being welcomed by Commander Girardot (airport director) and Colonel Lepetit (Air Ministry representative) after their Paris–Saigon flight. (SAFARA)

Maryse Hilsz gets ready to take the altitude record, Villacoublay, 17 June 1934. (WWP)

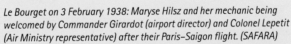

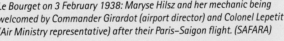

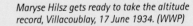

On her return to Britain aboard the liner RMS Queen Mary Beryl Markham was greeted at Southampton by the mayor, Councillor Saunders. (IPPS)

The African queen: Beryl Markham

(1902-1986)

Beryl Markham led a tumultuous life that was the subject of several books, including her autobiography, West with the Night, published in 1942. (DR)

A friend of Karen Blixen and daughter of a horse breeder, Beryl Markham was born in Ashwell on 26 October 1902, but had lived in East Africa[1] from a very early age. Her mother, Clara Clutterbuck, soon returned to England with her son, leaving Beryl and her father Charles to look after the farm he'd bought at Njoro, 100km from Nairobi. Here, the young Beryl learned to speak several local languages, such as Swahili, Nandi and Masai and developed a passion for horses to such an extent that by the age of 18 she had gained a race-horse training diploma.

Sadly, the following year, her father was to lose all his money as well as the farm. He left Kenya to seek a new life in Peru, leaving Beryl, at the age of 19, on her own. She was setting out on an adventure with just a horse and two saddlebags to her name. The only woman in the macho world of horse breeders, she nevertheless managed to assert herself and created a first-rate stud farm, which caused her to be known locally as the 'memsahib wa farasi' (the horse mistress). Beryl then met a wealthy young Englishman by the name of Mansfield Markham[2] and in 1927 she married him, after separating from her first husband, John Purves, whom she had married in 1919. The couple returned to England where Beryl gave birth to a boy on 27 February 1929. This union proved barely durable, Beryl having a fleeting affair with the Duke of Gloucester.

Shortly afterwards, Beryl Markham went back to Africa on her own. Once there, she met Denys Finch Hatton with whom she fell hopelessly in love. This big-game hunter and retired pilot soon took her up in his plane. For Beryl, the flight was a revelation. She decided to take flying lessons, but soon afterwards, Denys Finch Hatton was killed in an accident. But this harsh blow did little to crush the young woman's determination. In just a few months, she gained her licence and set out on a career as a bush pilot, carrying medicines, food, passengers and mail into the remotest areas, flying an Avro Avian biplane.[3] Another part of her flying activities was to locate big game for safaris, notably for Bror von Blixen (called 'Blix'), the husband of Karen Blixen the novelist, whom she befriended.

In Europe, the Mollison couple were much in the news for their aerial exploits. For Beryl, it seemed as if it was now or never to make an impression. On 24 April 1932, though she had barely been flying for a year, she set out to reach England flying solo in a plane that had no radio or navigational instruments. After many difficulties, she arrived in London 23 days later on 17 May.

That summer, she went to the King's Cup Races with Tom Campbell Black (with whom she had fallen in love). Here, Tom was to introduce her to Antoine de Saint-Exupéry.

She was now determined to achieve one of the flying exploits that so excited the press and paid out such large financial rewards. After considering an expedition to South Africa with Tom, she opted for a solo Atlantic crossing, from east to west,[4] London to New York. With this in mind, she borrowed a Vega Gull with a 200hp engine, christened The Messenger and had it fitted with reserve fuel tanks, giving it a range of 6,000km. It did, however, have a radio. The weather was gloomy and windy when Beryl Markham took off from Abingdon in the late afternoon of Friday 4 September 1936. That evening, she was spotted over Ireland and, at 4.35am the following day she was seen approaching Newfoundland. Then she disappeared. It was through a telephone call that it was learnt that a plane had crashed in a peat bog at Baleine Cove in Nova Scotia, not far from Cape Breton. She was unhurt but somewhat disappointed not to have reached New York, still 1,200km away. She had,

Beryl Markham poses, cigarette in hand, in front of the Percival Vega Gull with a single 200hp De Havilland Gipsy Six engine. It was one of four that were sold in Kenya. (TPA)

Beryl Markham waves to the crowd of 5,000 people waiting for her in New York. Note the two wristwatches she is wearing, one set at London time, the other New York. (John Underwood collection)

On arrival in London, on 28 September 1936, Beryl Markham went in an open car from Waterloo station to the Savoy Hotel, where a reception had been organised in her honour. (IPPS)

nonetheless, crossed the Atlantic in a flying time of 24hr 30min. The press made much of the flight, which Beryl deemed a success.

On returning to England, Beryl was amazed to find she was famous. She was to remain there some years and had no plans for any further aerial exploits, especially after her friend Tom Campbell Black was killed in an air race to South Africa. In 1939, she left for the United States and settled in California, where there was the possibility that a film of her adventures might be made, but nothing came of it. In 1940, Beryl Markham again met Antoine de Saint-Exupéry, who strongly urged her to write a book about her life. The following year, she met Raoul Schumacher, a frustrated author who helped her to get going on writing the book. He later claimed to be its true, sole author. Entitled *West with the Night*, it was published in 1942

and met with a degree of success. After writing a number of short stories for publications such as *Collier's Magazine* and the *Saturday Evening Post*, Beryl and Raoul split up. She returned to Kenya in 1952 where she successfully went back to raising racehorses. She died in Nairobi in 1986, aged 84.

1. In present-day Kenya.
2. Mansfield Markham had formerly worked for the Foreign Office and had emigrated to East Africa to breed horses.
3. The aircraft had a DH Gipsy 120hp engine and was registered as G-ABEA. She had bought it for £600 from Wilson Airways and it was re-registered as VP-KAN.
4. This was a first for a woman, as Amelia Earhart had made a west-east crossing, making use of the prevailing winds.

Globe-trotter in the clouds: Elly Beinhorn
(1907-2007)

Berlin-Staaken aerodrome on Sunday 26 June 1932, and a small silver plane has just come to rest in front of the hangars. It has flown from Bremerhaven. The young woman who climbs out of the cockpit is called Elly Beinhorn. She has just completed a seven-month trip around the world. The left side of her plane – a Klemm L 26aV – is covered in the flags of all the 26 countries she has, not without tribulations, crossed.

Elly Beinhorn had long wanted to achieve this feat, ever since the day when some friends had taken her to a lecture by the aviator Hermann Köhl.[1] She had been fascinated by his tales of long-distance flights, and that very day she had decided that she would learn to fly, to the great displeasure of her parents. The daughter of rich industrial magnate, Henry Beinhorn, Elly was born on 30 April 1907 in Hanover and had the benefit of a small nest egg from an inheritance. Taking this money, she had left for Berlin in the autumn of 1928, renting a room at Spandau and beginning

Elly Beinhorn at the controls of the all-red Heinkel He 64 in which she made demonstration flights after she was unable to take part in the third European Air Tour. (V. Koos collection)

her training at the Staaken aerodrome under the instruction of Otto Thomsen. She soon gained her private pilot's qualification and not long afterwards added her aerobatics licence.

In September 1929, Elly Beinhorn bought a second-hand BFW M.23b and, each weekend, did aerobatics with it before a stunned audience. She hoped that by doing this she would earn enough money to finance the long-distance flights she was so keen to undertake. An opportunity soon arose. Elly was able to obtain the position of photojournalist on a German scientific expedition to Portuguese Guinea.[2] On 4 January 1931, she left Berlin flying a Klemm L 25 monoplane and followed the coast of Africa as far as Guinea. On the way back, she decided to save time by cutting across the Sahara. She would come to regret it. A fuel leak forced her to come down in the middle of the desert. With the help of the Tuaregs, she managed to get to Timbuktu. Klemm sent her a replacement plane, enabling her to get back to Germany in April 1931.

These wanderings had pushed Elly Beinhorn into the limelight, with some journalists making use of her to feed their nationalist notions: 'This is what makes our hearts beat, when we shake the hand of someone like her. It is our hope that such youth will one day break the ties that bind the fatherland.'

On 4 December 1931, at the controls of a Klemm L 26aV, she set off again, this time eastwards, with India and Bali as the destinations. Stage followed stage[3] and, bar two forced landings, the flight passed off relatively easily. Not wanting to take the same route back to Germany, she decided to carry on to Australia, thus becoming, after Amy Johnson, the second woman to have made the flight solo. She reached Port Darwin on 22 March 1932. After having her plane sent to Panama via New Zealand, she set out for South America, crossed the Andes and reached Bahia in Brazil, from where her plane, after being dismantled, was sent back to Europe by boat. Elly completed her trip around the world with a final flight from Bremerhaven to Berlin, arriving there on 26 July. The achievement gained her the Hindenburg Cup and 10,000 Marks, a welcome sum in view of the debts she

Elly Beinhorn financed her aerial journeys by producing and selling illustrated reports of them. The well-known Leica company used the opportunity for publicity purposes. (Leica)

had accumulated. In 1932, Elly had registered for the third Aerial Tour of Europe (Europa Rundflug), flying a single-engined Heinkel He 64, but at the last moment she had to give up her plane to Fritz Morzik.[4] Following this, Ernst Heinkel designed an aircraft especially for her second long-distance expedition. The plane was designated He 71b and remained the only one of its type.[5] This second African expedition began on 4 April 1933 and took her

Elly Beinhorn waves to the people who have come to greet her arrival at Berlin-Staaken, on 26 June 1932 (V. Koos collection)

Elly Beinhorn with the He 64 (D-2304) she was supposed to fly in the third European Air Tour in 1932. Just visible is her name painted behind the spinner. (V. Koos collection)

The Messerschmitt Bf 108 Taifun, made famous by Elly Beinhorn, was powered by a 250hp (186kW) Hirth HM 8U engine driving a two-bladed, fixed-pitch propeller – later changed to a three-bladed propeller. (J. Underwood collection)

successively to Cairo, the Cape, Libreville in Gabon, Saint-Louis in Senegal, Casablanca and Tunis. She arrived back at Berlin-Tempelhof on 27 July after covering no less than 28,000km.

In 1934, Elly flew out to America in a Klemm Kl 32 with a 160hp engine. She flew from Panama to Mexico City, followed by Los Angeles, New York and finally Miami, where she and her plane boarded a ship bound for Europe, arriving back there on 13 January 1935.

These achievements saw Elly Beinhorn awarded the coveted Harmon Trophy in two successive years (1934 and 1935). Her fame steadily grew. On 13 August 1935, she again made the front pages by crossing two continents in the same day. Starting from Gleiwitz, she flew to Constantinople then back to Berlin, covering 3,570km in 13hr 30min of flying time. For this exploit she used the new Messerschmitt Bf 108A, christening it Taifun (Typhoon), a name that the manufacturer decided to retain. All these flights were interspersed with propaganda events (receptions, interviews, speeches etc) orchestrated by the Foreign Ministry and with Elly in the role of ambassador for the new Germany.

On 13 July 1936, the famous aviatrix married the no-less celebrated racing driver, Bernd Rosemeyer (they were to have a son together, but Rosemeyer was killed in an accident on 28 January 1938). She continued to pile up new achievements, this time linking three continents in the same day. Piloting the Taifun, she took off from Berlin-Tempelhof on 2 August 1936 at 2.00am, and flew via Constantinople, Damascus, Cairo and Budapest and back to Berlin, having covered 3,750km in less than 24 hours.

Far from being satisfied with this, in early 1937 she put her name down for the International Oases Tour, but in the event did not take part. A tireless globetrotter, in spring 1939, she set herself a new long-distance objective: Japan. Unfortunately, the Sino-Japanese War and the worsening situation in Europe cut this attempt short. Although she had reached Bangkok, she decided to retrace her steps.

Such an internationally known celebrity couldn't fail to interest the Nazi propaganda machine. Though courted by the leading lights of the Third Reich and personally invited to functions by Hitler and Göring, Elly Beinhorn managed to remain aloof from the political domain throughout the war. In 1942, she married Dr Karl Wittmann and for a number of years made no further flights.

For her round-the-world flight, Elly Beinhorn used this little Klemm L 26 monoplane with a 120hp Argus engine. The flags of the 26 countries she passed through and the names of the 50-odd stopping points have been painted on the left side of the fuselage. (H.P. Dabrowski collection)

When peace returned, she settled in Switzerland where, after regaining her pilot's licence, she flew a Piper Cub. With this plane, she undertook her third African expedition, in 1952, flying from Colombier in Switzerland to Benghazi, via Rome, Tunis and Tripoli. During these years, she continued to win fame, taking part in various competitions, including the Deutschlandflug, which she won in 1956, the 13th Powder Puff Derby, between Lawrence and Spokane in 1959 and the International Alpine Rally, where she came first in the women's section (1963). Awarded a gold medal in 1970 by the Bavarian Aerial Sporting Association and receiving a

Warnemünde aerodrome, 1933: Ernst Heinkel kisses Elly Beinhorn's hand before she takes off on a demonstration flight in the Heinkel He 71, registration D-2390. (V. Koos collection)

Elly Beinhorn congratulates her husband, the racing driver, Bernd Rosemeyer, after his victory in a race at Pescara, in 1937. (Audi A.G.)

diploma[6] from the FAI in 1987, Elly Beinhorn died in her 101st year, on 28 November 2007.

1. Hermann Köhl, along with Ehrenfried von Hünefeld and James C. Fitzmaurice, had achieved the first flight across the North Atlantic from east to west on 12 and 13 April 1928, flying a Junkers W33.
2. Now known as Guinea-Bissau. The expedition, led by Hugo Bernatzik and Prof. Struck, aimed to explore the Bijagos Archipelago.
3. Elly Beinhorn made stops at the following places: Budapest, Sofia, Constantinople, Aleppo, Baghdad, Bushir, Djask, Karachi, Delhi, Allahabad, Calcutta, Akyab, Rangoon, Bangkok, Victoria Point, Singapore, Batavia, Surabaya, Bima, Kupang, Port Darwin, Newcastle Waters, Cloncurry, Longreach, Charleville, Brisbane, Sydney, Panama, Cali, Guyaquil, Trujillo, Lima, Arica, Mendoza, Buenos Aires, Rio de Janeiro, Bahia, Bremerhaven and Berlin.
4. The deal done with Messerschmitt had left Fritz Morzik (the winner of the two previous competitions) without a plane. The decision was made to give him Elly Beinhorn's plane.
5. The Heinkel He 71b was wrecked in a crash at Friedrichshafen, on 13 August 1934.
6. The Tissandier Diploma.

Elly Beinhorn would die aged 100, on 28 November 2007. She voluntarily surrendered her pilot's licence in 1979 and ended her days quietly near Munich. (DR)

'The girl who beat all the men': Jean Batten

(1909-1982)

Jean Batten in 1934. Her beauty only enhanced her fame. (DR)

Jean Batten poses for the Associated Press photographer at Hatfield, on 9 November 1935, 48 hours before her departure for South America. (AP. H. Hazewinkel collection)

Acquiring a second-hand De Havilland Gipsy Moth[1] with the help of an aero-club friend, she decided to set off, but she had to make three attempts at it before success came her way. On 16 April 1933, she had to give up at Karachi after an engine failure and, on 21 April 1934, running short of fuel, she crashed onto a radio station in Rome. Just a month later, between 8 and 23 May, she managed to complete the flight from Lympne to Darwin.

Following this memorable flight, Jean had several more significant achievements, among which were: a flight to Brazil and Argentina in a Percival Gull 6 with a Gipsy Six engine[2] between 11 and 13 November 1935, a record flight from England to New Zealand between 5 and 16 October 1936, covering 22,886km in 11 days, 45 minutes and including the dangerous crossing of the Tasman Sea. Her arrival in Auckland took place in a frenzy. Even before her plane had been sighted, a 6,000-strong crowd had gathered on the grass at the aerodrome and nearly 2,000 cars had filled the car parking spaces. As soon

'-12 o'clock: have eaten – should see land soon.
-12.20: no land in sight.
-12.30: should be seeing land now. – Wonder if there'll be enough fuel.'

The hand that feverishly wrote these few words was Jean Batten's, the New Zealand aviatrix. It was Wednesday 23 May 1934. Flying her Gipsy Moth, the young woman was approaching the Australian coast, near the end of a 17,000km journey.

'-12.45: Hurray! Land! Hurray! It must be about 50km away.'

It was 13.30 when the little biplane's wheels made contact with the ground, 14 days 22hr 30min after taking off from the runway at Croydon, having shortened by more than four days the record set by Amy Johnson (see p. 100). The headline the next day in the *Daily Express* read: 'The girl who beat all the men.' But who was this aviatrix who was to become one of the stars of inter-war aviation?

Jean Gardner Batten was born in Rotorua, New Zealand, on 15 September 1909. Her father, a dentist, had hoped she would make a career as a pianist, but Jean, having read about Bert Hinkler's exploits, had been gripped by a sudden passion for flying. She soon sold her piano and, using the money from this, took flying lessons, gaining her licence on 5 December 1930. She explained the excitement she felt after first solo flight: 'As my little biplane left the ground, I felt an immense wave of happiness wash over me and joy flowed through my veins, like an elixir.' Her aim was simple: to beat the time record between England and Australia.

A smiling Jean Batten on her arrival at Croydon on 29 April 1935 after her flight from Australia to England. The journey had taken her from Darwin to Lympne with stops at Sydney, Bourke, Longreach, Winton, Cloncurry, Camooweal, Newcastle Waters, Darwin, Kupang, Lombok, Surabaya, Batavia, Singapore, Alor Star, Victoria Point, Rangoon, Akyab, Calcutta, Allahabad, Jhansi, Jodhpur, Karachi, Jask, Basra, Baghdad, Damascus, Cyprus, Athens, Foggia, Rome, Marseille, Lyon, Dijon, Abbeville, and Croydon. (Mundopress, H. Hazewinkel collection)

Jean Batten on her arrival in Auckland on 16 October 1936, having successfully completed the first direct England–New Zealand flight. (L. White/A. Turnbull Library)

condescension: 'Jean, you are a naughty girl. You deserve a spanking for giving us such an anxious time.'[4]

In February 1937, Jean Batten received the Royal Aero Club's highest distinction, the Britannia Trophy. The sun shone on her. Everyone admired her. In 1938, she wrote her autobiography before she was even 30, calling it simply *My Life*. Though full of charm, Jean Batten lived a solitary life and to those journalists who couldn't resist asking about her love life, she invariably replied: 'I have only one love and that's my plane.'

As suddenly as it had appeared, Jean Batten's name went missing from the front pages and she began a nomadic life with her mother, Helen, moving from one country to another leaving no address. She was gradually forgotten until 1969 when, at the age of 60, she made a spectacular reappearance, rejuvenated by a face-lift and with her hair dyed black. She gave interviews and appeared at aeronautical events, yet this new spell in the limelight did not last. In 1982, she left for Majorca and for the next five years completely disappeared. This behaviour led the documentary maker Ian Mackersey to compare her to Greta Garbo, and he decided to go in search of her. After painstaking enquiries, he discovered that the aviatrix had died in Palma on 22 November 1982 after being bitten by a dog.

1. DH-60, registered as G-AALG. In the 1934 flights, Jean Batten used a different Gipsy Moth, registered as G-AARB.
2. Percival Gull 6, registered as G-APDR (see p. 184).
3. In The Garbo of the Skies, Ian Mackersey, p. 248.
4. In Les Ailes, 22 October 1936, p. 8.

as she had touched down, the crowd broke through the mounted-police security barrier. Smiling for the cameras, despite her tiredness, she casually said to her father who was there to meet her: 'It's good to be back home.'[3] The mayor of Auckland congratulated her, though not without a degree of

The Count de Montigny, president of the Moroccan Aero Club (right) welcomed Jean Batten when she visited Casablanca on 11 November 1935. (IPP, H. Hazewinkel collection)

The Percival Gull used by Jean Batten was a 200hp De Havilland Gipsy Six-powered monoplane with a relatively comfortable cabin. (DR)

13 November 1935: Jean Batten takes a break in her hotel room in Buenos Aires. (IPP, H. Hazewinkel collection)

Jean Batten and her Percival Gull Six at Amsterdam-Schipol, on 9 August 1939. (NV Polygoon, H. Hazewinkel collection)

Alderman Saunders, the mayor of Southampton, congratulates Jean Batten who has just disembarked from the liner Asturias that has brought her back from South America. (IPP, H. Hazewinkel collection)

The 'Lioness':
Elisabeth Lion
(1904-1988)

Elisabeth Lion with her Caudron Aiglon at Tunis-El Aouina on 23 May 1938. (GPPA)

'Elisabeth Lion has done better than Mrs Earhart,' was the headline in the weekly *Les Ailes* on 19 May 1938, and it followed up with: 'It is women who, this week, have relit the flame of sporting aviation.' Indeed, a few days previously, on 13 May, the French aviatrix had taken the women's distance record, held since 25 August 1932 by Amelia Earhart with 3,939km, up to 4,063km. Her performance owed nothing to luck; it was, on the contrary, the outcome of some methodical preparation, to which the Frenchwoman was no stranger.

By this time, Elisabeth Lion was no longer an unknown figure in the aviation world. Born in the Ardennes region, into a middle-class family, she had been gripped by a sudden overwhelming passion for flying after her maiden flight at Guyancourt. Calm, organised and determined, she gained her pilot's licence in 1934, at the age of 30. In July 1935, she acquired a Caudron Aiglon[1] and got noticed by flying it on a Paris–Marseille–Bordeaux–Paris circuit that she completed on 9 April 1936 at an average speed of 180kph. Fame came on the following 5 July, when she came second in the overall classification in the Angers Twelve Hours race, and first in the women's section. With the bit now

between her teeth, she entered the Tour of the East, where she came fourth after covering 1,483km in her Caudron Aiglon.

On 27 December 1937, still flying the same plane, she beat the women's altitude record, climbing to 6,410m, to which she added, a few days later, the multi-seater altitude record (5,811m) and the record for aircraft of 2 litres engine capacity (4,372m). On 8 April 1938, having already done a non-stop tour of France in a little over 10 hours, Elisabeth Lion completed a non-stop Paris–Tunis–Paris flight, covering 3,500km in 18hr 10min. Leaving Le Bourget at 2.00am, she banked over Tunis at 10.02am and headed back to Le Bourget, landing there at 8.10pm. After such a performance, the women's world distance record was within her grasp. She duly broke it on Friday 13 May (was this superstition?), still flying her own Caudron, whose Renault Bengali engine delivered a mere 100hp compared with the 450hp of Amelia Earhart's Lockheed Vega. As an 'old hand' she had meticulously prepared all the details of her flight, including obtaining permission to use foreign airspace. She covered in one go the 4,063km from Istres to Abadan in Iran, taking some 21 hours. In doing this, she not only took the women's distance record, but also the distance record for second-category single seaters with between 4 and 6.5 litres engine capacity.[2] But records are made to be beaten, and a day later, Andrée Dupeyron added 250km to it.

With Soviet aviatrixes having smashed the world distance record with 5,948km (see p. 80), Elizabeth Lion and her compatriots, Andrée Dupeyron and Maryse Hilsz began preparations to take back the record for France. But the Air Ministry would not condone the attempt: In November 1938, it banned aircraft from taking off heavily laden with fuel and judged the Caudron Aiglon to exceed the limit by 250kg. Thus the record suddenly became unattainable. Needless to say, this decision was hardly to the aviatrix's liking, and she responded: 'I know perfectly well how to assess the risks of a particular performance or expedition that I have planned... My current plane has known characteristics and all I ask is to be allowed to take my chance, facing risks that I have weighed carefully.'[3]

The ministry was unbending and Elisabeth Lion was forced to abandon the project that meant so much to her. She had to be satisfied with a non-stop Paris–Dakar flight on 2 June 1939. Although she covered the 4,200km in 21hr 20min, the flight was not a record.

At the end of the war, in late 1944, Elisabeth Lion was among the 13 aviatrixes who presented themselves at Châteauroux for a training course, with the intention of joining the Air Force. It was at this time that Maryse Hilsz nicknamed her 'the lioness'. This experiment lasted for just a year, ending abruptly with the departure of the Air Minister, Charles Tillon. Elisabeth Lion returned to civilian life. She was 43 years old. At this point, she entered obscurity and little is known about her subsequent aeronautical activities.

---

1. A Caudron Aiglon no. 7035/19, registered as F-ANSK.
2. Up to this point the record had been held by Andrée Dupeyron with 1,678km.
3. Les Ailes, 1 December 1938.

Helen Richey in the early 1940s, before going to England to help strengthen the ATA. (McKeesport Heritage Center)

Window dressing only...: Helen Richey

(1909-1947)

Aviatrixes were often used more for their promotional value than their qualities as pilots. Here, Bobbi Trout (left) and Ruth Elder (right) do their duty and look pretty at the launch of Pickwick Airways on 29 March 1929. (AAHS/M.L. Bailey collection)

For a woman wanting to make a career in commercial aviation, the road was full of pitfalls. Helen Richey, who achieved fame as the first female airline pilot in the world, was to learn this to her cost. But the woman who was quite happy to call herself a tomboy was not lacking in fighting spirit. Born in McKeesport, Pennsylvania, she had had no hesitation in running away at the age of 12 to join a circus. When she had finished her studies, she considered a career in education, but soon abandoned this idea. It was only after landing at Cleveland aerodrome and being assailed by reporters that Helen Richey was gripped by a certain fascination with aviation. She was just 20 when she obtained her private pilot's licence and her father marked the event by buying her a plane! She then decided she wanted to be an airline pilot, a career that was inconceivable for a woman at this time. While waiting for an opportunity to present itself, she went in for aerobatics and competition flying, establishing a degree of fame in the field.[1]

In 1934, she won the Women's National Air Meet, a race in which Frances Marsalis met her death. Deeply affected by the loss of her friend, Helen Richey decided to try her hand in a less dangerous activity: being an airline pilot. She offered her services to various different airlines. The chairman of Central Airlines realised the publicity value of having a woman among his pilots. It was in this way that, on 31 December 1934, Helen Richey became the first woman to pilot a plane on a regular civil route, namely Washington to Detroit.[2] Much to her displeasure, she quickly realised that the whole thing was nothing more than a publicity stunt. She spent most of her time in public relations activities and actually flew very little. Furthermore, the company's male pilots were not happy with her being hired, and took every opportunity to let her know it. Even the aviation authorities were not averse to harassing her, going as far as to ban her from flying in bad weather.

Not wishing to be merely a 'fair-weather pilot', Helen Richey resigned, having completed just a dozen commercial flights in the space of ten months. This did not stop her from continuing to fly. In 1941, having accumulated 10,000 flying hours, she became the first fully certified flying instructress. The following year she led the contingent of American aviatrixes who went to England to strengthen the ranks of the ATA (see p. 125), later returning to the United States to join the WASPs, ferrying mostly bomber aircraft for a period of 16 months. As was the experience of so many other WASPs, the return to civilian life proved difficult for Helen Richey. Out of work, with no means of support and depressed, she ended her life on 7 January 1947.

1. Helen Richey came third in the race for the 1932 Amelia Earhart Trophy. In 1933, she was Frances Marsalis's co-pilot for the latter's endurance record.
2. The plane used was a Ford Tri-Motor.

The first women airline pilots

Year	Country	Pilot	Company
1928	Netherlands	Lady Heath	KLM (1st co-pilot)
1929	Germany	Marga von Etzdorf	Deutsche Lufthansa (co-pilot)
1934	United States	Helen Richey	Central Airlines (1st pilot)
1974	France	Danielle Décuré	Air France
1974	Canada	Christine Davy	Conair
1987	Great Britain	Lynn Barton	British Airways
2010	Japan	Ari Fuji	Japan Air Lines

Aviation couples

Sometimes it takes two to be adventurous. While the Lindberghs (see p. 102) and the Mollisons (see p. 101) unquestionably had the highest media profile in the history of aviation, they were not the only couples. Here are a few other examples.

In 1926, Clema and Jim Granger were running a flying school in Santa Monica, California, as well as being agents for Swallow aircraft. Jim, who had taught Clema to fly, was killed flying his Keith Rider racer in 1934 while he was practising for the London–Melbourne race. Clema took part in a number of races, particularly the 1931 and 1932 National Air Races.

In January 1928, Gladys and Lloyd O'Donnell opened a flying school in Long Beach, California. Gladys, who had learned to fly in 1927, distingui-shed herself in various races and notably came second in her category in the first Women's Air Derby in August 1929. Lloyd developed a method

The entire O'Donnell family: next to Gladys are her husband Lloyd and her two children, Lorrain May (left) and James Lloyd Jr. (right). (DR)

In 1912, the W.A. Davis couple learned to fly on a dual-control Curtiss Pusher at the flying school established by Glenn H. Curtiss in San Diego. (Curtiss Museum)

At Lympne (Kent) on 1 February 1933, Amy Johnson kisses her husband Jim Mollison before her South American flight. (Evening Standard/Getty Images)

The Lindberghs made the headlines not only for their flying exploits but also for the infamous kidnapping of their 20-month-old baby. They are pictured here, on 13 September 1929, in front of a Lockheed Vega. (Library of Congress)

Claire Fahy was one of the participants in the 1929 Women's Air Derby. She is seen here with her husband Herbert, known as 'Herb' (right). (DR)

of towing gliders that was used in the Second World War.

Representatives for the Buhl Pacific Aircraft Company, Bob and Margaret Blair ran charter flights out of Culver City from 1928 and taught a number of film stars to fly, including Clark Gable, James Stewart and Henry Fonda.

The Fahy couple both had a tragic end. Claire was killed at Tonopah, Nevada, on 19 December 1930, when the engine of her Waco Taperwing cut out suddenly on take-off. Her husband, Herbert had been killed a few months earlier, on 25 April 1930, during a demonstration flight of a Lockheed Sirius at Roscommon in Michigan.

In 1932, the pair of Bill Lancaster and Chubbie Miller hit the headlines when Bill was accused of having killed Haden Clarke, a young writer whom Chubbie had tasked with writing her biography. In prison for three and a half months before being cleared, Bill found himself discredited in

Among aviation couples, the woman often played the public relations role. Clarence Chamberlin and his wife pose in front of the Lockheed Altair Miss Stratosphere – She's The Tops, in which he planned to cross the Atlantic. (Wide World Photos)

The pairing of the British William W.N. Lancaster and the Australian Jessie M. Miller was more talked about in the sensationalist press than their flying exploits. Here they are seen in the Avro Avian III Red Rose as they prepare to leave for Australia. (IPS)

the United States and left for England with Chubbie, planning to make a record flight to South Africa in the hope of restoring his reputation. On 11 April, he took off in an Avro Avian heading for South Africa, but never made it, disappearing without trace in the Gao region (his plane was not discovered until 1962).

In 2006, Rob and Beth Makros, both Northrop T-38 instructors, were the first couple to become the crew of a B-2 Spirit stealth bomber in 509th Bomb Wing at Whiteman AFB in Missouri. (USAF)

Among the 916 female pilots in the US Army
Air Force on 20 December 1944 was Elizabeth
L Gardner of Rockford, Michigan. (USAF)

Dutrieu, Harriet Quimby, Katherine Stinson, Blanche Scott, Ruth Law, Bessie Coleman, Adrienne Bolland, Florence Klingensmith, Laura Ingalls, Liesel Bach, Lady Heath, Lady Mary Bailey, Louise Thaden, Thea Rasche, Ruth Rowland Nichols, Elinor Smith, Ruth Elder, Carina Negrone, Paulina Denisovna Ossipenko, Hanna Reitsch, Marcelle Choisnet, Maryse Bastié, Léna Bernstein, Amy Johnson-Mollison, Anne Morrow-Lindbergh, Marga Von Etzdorf, Maryse Hilsz, Beryl Markham, Elly Beinhorn, Jean Batten, Elisabeth Lion, Helen Richey, Eugénie M. Shakhovskaya, Cecil W. "Teddy" Kenyon, Pauline Gower, Nancy Harkness Love, Maria Ivanovna Dolina, Amélia Earhart, Hélène Boucher, Jacqueline Cochran, Jacqueline Auriol, Eileen Marie Collins, Anna Walker, Ellen Church, Clara Adams, Harriet Quimby, Marjorie Stinson, Mrs Eyman, Fay Gillis, Virginia Waibel, Eleanor Blevins, Aniwegi Boudinot, Helen Clifford, Janett Moffett, Bernetta Miller, Ruth Fontes, Jeanne Pallier, Blossom Miles, Emily Schaeffer, Raymonde de Laroche, Amelie Beese, Hélène Dutrieu, Harriet Quimby, Katherine Stinson, Blanche Scott, Ruth Law, Bessie Coleman, Adrienne Bolland, Florence Klingensmith, Laura Ingalls, Liesel Bach, Lady Heath, Lady Mary Bailey, Louise Thaden, Thea Rasche, Ruth Rowland Nichols, Elinor Smith, Ruth Elder, Carina Negrone, Paulina Denisovna Ossipenko, Hanna Reitsch, Marcelle Choisnet, Maryse Bastié, Léna Bernstein, Amy Johnson-Mollison, Anne Morrow-Lindbergh, Marga Von Etzdorf, Maryse Hilsz, Beryl Markham, Elly Beinhorn, Jean Batten, Elisabeth Lion, Helen Richey, Cecil W. "Teddy" Kenyon, Pauline Gower, Nancy Harkness Love, Maria Ivanovna Dolina, Amélia Earhart, Hélène Boucher, Jacqueline Cochran, Jacqueline Auriol, Eileen Marie Collins, A...

The fighting women

We have seen how women often encountered scepticism and sexist behaviour from their male counterparts, and this was generally even more evident in the military field. In Britain, the introduction of women into military aviation dates back to 3 March 1918 with the creation of the Women's Royal Air Force (WRAF), two thirds of whose numbers came from two pre-existing organisations: the WAAC (Women's Army Auxiliary Corps) and the WRNS (Women's Royal Naval Service). In the United States, Ruth Law tried to join up, but although she was able to wear the uniform, this was only on recruitment tours, not as a pilot.

In France, the attempt by women to actively participate in the war effort met with a categorical refusal from the military authorities. From 1914, several members of Stella (see p. 25) formed the Patriotic Union of French Aviatrixes. Marie Marvingt and Jeanne Herveu tried unsuccessfully to set up an air ambulance unit for wounded soldiers.

The first mention of the involvement of women in military aviation comes from Russia when, on the outbreak of war in 1914, Princess Eugenie M. Shakovskaya (see p. 132) made a personal request to the Tsar

Ruth Law was the only American woman authorised to wear a pilot's uniform, though only for non-military missions. She is seen here at Camp McClellan in 1918, surrounded by members of the 29th Division. (NA)

to be allowed to fly for her country. She was posted to the First Air Squadron as a reconnaissance pilot. A few others followed her and, three years later, women were officially authorised to join the army.

During the inter-war years, other aviatrixes joined fighting units. The Japanese Shigeno Kibe, having obtained her licence at the age of 22 from the Munesota flying school in Tsurumi, joined the forces of the Chinese general, Chang Tso Lin.[1] Supported by the Japanese, this warlord had proclaimed himself Grand Marshall of the Military Government of the Republic of China. In the same period, the daughter of the Chinese General Ju, Maupia Ju, learned to fly with an American instructor, becoming the only Chinese military aviatrix.

In Turkey, Sabiha Gökçen is renowned for having carried out combat missions before the Second World War, bombing Kurdish rebels in the 1937 revolt. She was christened the 'Amazon of the Skies' by the press and continued her career into the 1960s (see p. 81).

The exploits of Russian military aviatrixes in the inter-war period are not especially well known. The fact remains that in 1941, when the Germans invaded, Stalin ordered the formation of a female flying group, whose organisation and command were entrusted to Marina Mikhailovna Raslova, who was known for having beaten several records between the wars (see p. 78) and for having campaigned for women to be allowed to join the ranks of the military. This group, based in Engels on the Volga River, comprised three regiments: the 567th IAP (Istrebitel'naya Aviatsionnaya Polk, or Fighter Aviation Regiment), equipped with Yakovlev Yak-1 fighters (later provided with Yak-7s and Yak-9s), the 587th BAP (Bombardirovochnaya Aviatsionnaya Polk, or Bomber Aviation Regiment), equipped with twin-engined Petlyakov Pe-2s, and the 588th NBAP (Nochoy Bombardirovochnaya Aviatsionnaya Polk, or Night Bomber Aviation Regiment), equipped with the small Polikarpov Po.2 biplanes.

A recruitment poster for the Women's Royal Air Force (WRAF). (DR)

Shigeno Kibe was a Japanese aviatrix who fought in Manchuria for a Chinese warlord. She is pictured here climbing aboard a Nakajima biplane. (Bettmann/Corbis)

Mamayeva Bezmenova, of the 244th Bomber Regiment, puts on her parachute before setting out on a mission in her Douglas A-20 Boston. (DR)

Evdokia D. Berchanskaya, commander of the 46th Night Bomber Regiment (former 588th Regiment) briefs her pilots on a forthcoming mission. (DR)

Katya Krasnokutskaya in front of one of the Polikarpov biplanes that made life so difficult for the Germans. (DR)

Rufina Sergeyevna Gasheva (left) and Natalya Federovna Meklin (right) stand in front of the 46th Regiment's Polikarpovs, on 23 February 1945, just after they had been made Heroes of the Soviet Union. Natalya F. Meklin (1922-2005) carried out a total of 982 missions during the war. (DR)

Leaning on the tailplane of a Yak-1, Lydya Litvyak (left), Yekaterina Budanova (centre) and Maria Kuznetsova (right) make preparations for a mission over the Stalingrad sector. (DR)

Many Soviet aviatrixes were posted to men's regiments. Seen here are Sergeant Olia D. Dobrova (lower left) and mechanics (left to right, Macha, Valia, Tania and Nadia) from the 487th IAP (fighter regiment), operating in the Kursk sector, on 29 July 1943. (DR)

The 586th IAP chalked up its first victory when, on 24 September 1942, Valeyra Khomyakova shot down a German Junkers Ju 88 over Saratov. Shortly afterwards, the regiment and its three squadrons moved into the Stalingrad sector. The first squadron, commanded by Raisa Belyayeva, saw its pilots transferred to various men's regiments to compensate for their losses. In this way, Yekaterina V. Budanova, Maria Kuznetsova and Lydya V. Litvyak found themselves assigned to the 73rd IAP. The three women lost no time in demonstrating their manoeuvring abilities and their determination in combat. On her third sortie, L. Litvyak, working with her group leader, shot down a Ju 88. In total, the pilots of the 586th IAP chalked up 38 kills while posted to the Stalingrad sector. The regiment next prepared to take part in the Soviet offensive on the Voronezh front launched on 1 August 1943. Wounded on 22 March after being attacked by Messerschmitt Me 109s, Lydya Litvyak was sent back from the front line before later returning to action. She steadily built up her record of victories until 1 August 1943 when she, her flanker Victor Tabunov and nine other Yak-1 pilots got into a skirmish with a pack of 40-odd Me 109s. Lydya Litvyak failed to return home.[2]

However, the most talked about regiment was unquestionably the 588th NBAP, which throughout the war specialised in harassing German troops. Operating at night, in appalling conditions, these intrepid women's units were nicknamed Nachthexen (night witches) by the Germans, a sobriquet soon adopted by the Soviets themselves (Nochnaya Vedma). In the course of the war, these women carried out some 23,000 sorties and dropped more than 3,000 tonnes of bombs; 31 of them were killed in action and 23 were made Heroes of the Soviet Union.[3]

Besides these women's squadrons, numerous other aviatrixes flew in male units, sometimes even as commanders. One such was Valentina Grisodubova who commanded a long-range bomber group comprising 300 men. It is estimated that a total of around 600 aviatrixes served in the Soviet Air Force.

With 12 aerial victories in 138 operational missions, Lydya Litvyak was the top ace among Soviet aviatrixes. The portrait expresses her determination well. (DR)

Soviet women pilots' tallies

Name	Regiment	Kills	Missions	HSU*	Comments
Lydya Vladimirovna Litvyak	296th 73rd IAP	12	138	5 May 1990	Killed 1 Aug 1943
Ekaterina Vasilevna Boudanova	296th IAP	11			Killed 19 Jul 1943
Klavdiya Yakovlevna Fomichiova	587th BAP	11		18 Aug 1945	Died 5 Oct 1958
Klavdiya Pankratova	586th IAP	4			
Raïssa N. Sournachevskaïa	586th IAP	3 or 4	104		
Maria Ivanovna Dolina	587th BAP	3	72	18 Aug 1945	
Raïssa Belyayeva	586th IAP	3			Killed 19 Jul 1943
Antonina Lebedeva	653rd 65th IAP	3			
Olga Nikolaevna Yamshchikova	586th IAP	3			
Galina P. Bourdina	586th IAP	3 or 1	152		
Tamara Pamyatnika	586th IAP	2 or 4			Killed 3 Aug 1943
Valentina M. Lisitsina	586th IAP	2	160		
Ekatarina Ivanovna Zelenko	135th IAP	2		5 May 1990	Killed 12 Sep 1941
Klavdiya Blinova	586th IAP	1			
Valeriya Ivanovna Khomyakova	586th IAP	1			Killed 5 Oct 1942
Klavdiya Nechayeva	434th IAP	1			Killed 17 Sep 1942
Taya Smirnova	586th IAP	1			
Zina Solomatina	586th IAP	1			
Olga Yakovleva	586th IAP	1			
Maria Batrakova	586th IAP	1			Killed

* Hero of the Soviet Union.

During the Second World War, several countries mobilised their women flyers to assist with ambulance flights without actually integrating them into the armed forces. Romania was an exception to this. Before the outbreak of war, aviatrixes were asked to go on manoeuvres with the army, to carry mail and carry out liaison missions. Having shown their effectiveness, in 1940 Marina Strirbel, who served with the Military Air Ambulance Group on the eastern front and in the Crimea, formed female flyers into the 108th Air Ambulance Squadron. Operating in the combat zone, the group's Potez 65s, RWD-13s and General Aircraft ST-25s were relentlessly attacked by the Germans.

In Britain, the decision to form a women's section of the ATA (Air Transport Auxiliary) was the cause of much controversy. This organisation was set up just before war broke out, so as to make use of civil pilots in the ferrying of new aircraft to operational airfields. The war of the sexes raged in the columns of the aeronautical press, but despite all this, on 1

The first British ATA pilots at Hatfield aerodrome. Pauline Gower is second from the left. (IWM)

January 1940, 30 men and eight women made up the first contingent of the ATA (Winifred Crossley, Margaret Cunnison, Margaret Fairweather, Mona Friedlander, Joan Hughes, Gabrielle Patterson, Rosemary Rees and Marion Wilberforce). A ninth aviatrix, Pauline Gower, took command of the Women Pilots' Section based at Hatfield (see p. 135).

In the early days, the role of women flyers was confined to the ferrying of Tiger Moth biplanes, but when a shortage of male pilots was felt more sharply, they were given the job of flying ever larger and more powerful planes. Thus it was that 11 of the 168 women flying in the ATA were qualified to pilot four-engined bombers. Over the whole war, the

Miss J. Broad, an ATA instructor, gives advice to a male pupil before a flight in a twin-engined Airspeed Oxford. (IWM)

ATA ferried around 300 and 9,000 new planes and 14 women pilots lost their lives in crashes. Among these was Amy Johnson, who was lost over the Thames estuary while ferrying a twin-engined Airspeed Oxford (see p. 100).

In other parts of Europe, women who wanted to have the opportunity to serve their country in this way had, without exception, to struggle to be accepted by men. In France, women were employed to ferry requisitioned planes, but this was not to last and they were asked to 'go home and knit for [their] country'. Nevertheless, a small number persisted and, in 1940, an emergency decree was passed, allowing women to join the army. The decision was taken in such haste and with so little publicity that, initially, only one woman offered her services: Claire Roman. On 27 May 1940, with Maryse Hilsz, Maryse Bastié and Paulette Bray-Bouquet, these volunteers became 'Auxiliary Women Air Pilots', taken on at the rank of pilot officer, but remained allocated to ferrying duties. In 1945, the French government, represented by Charles Tillon, then Air Minister, formed a womens' military pilots' group. No fewer than 13 women offered their services, including Maryse Bastié, Maryse Hilsz, Elisabeth Boselli, Elisabeth Lion and Anne-Marie Imbrecq. After training at Châteauroux and Tours, all were accepted. Maryse Bastié was attached to the GMMTA and Maryse Hilsz to the GLAM. Five others were admitted to the Kasba-Tadla retraining school in Algeria to be trained to fly light twin-engined aircraft and a second group of six women began their training at Châteauroux. This experiment ended in November 1945 with the departure of Charles Tillon, and in July 1946, the recruitment of women into the Air Force ended.

In Germany, few women pilots had contributed to the war effort and those who did remained more or less unknown, with the exception of Hanna Reitsch, who was of international renown in the gliding field (see p. 87). Since the beginning of the war, female flyers had trained to become ferry pilots for the paramilitary NSFK (National-Socialist Flying Corps). This organisation also put aviatrixes in charge of maintenance centres. By the end of the war, at least five women pilots were ferrying planes for the Luftwaffe: Liesel Bach (see p. 44), Lieselotte Georgi, Thea Knorr, Lisl Schwab and Beate Uhse.[4] Two others were test pilots working for manufacturers: Hanna Reitsch and Melitta Schiller von Stauffenberg. At this time, the NSFK also recruited around 60 women to serve as gliding

On 16 September 1944, Maureen Dunlop, one of ATA's ferrying pilots, prepares to get on board a Fairey Barracuda torpedo plane. (Getty Images)

supervisors with a view to their possible use by the Luftwaffe, but the war came to an end before the project got off the ground. Generally speaking, while the Kriegsmarine and the Wehrmacht made little use of women personnel, it was quite different for the Luftwaffe who, in March 1945, planned to recruit 50,000 women to replace 112,000 men as mechanics.

In the United Kingdom by 1941, the shortage of pilots was beginning to be a real problem, to the point where American and Canadian pilots

During the war Lisl Schwab (1906-1967) made more than 3,000 military flights in many different types of aircraft, including Messerschmitt Me 109s and Focke-Wulf Fw 190s. (DR)

Promoted to the rank of flight lieutenant in October 1944, Beate Uhse was allocated to the 1st Uberführungsgeschwader (1st ferrying squadron), based at Berlin-Staaken. (Beate Uhse AG, via P.Selinger)

The WAFS: from theory to practice

WAFS operations began slowly. Initially because there was a shortage of women pilots, but later because, as with any new project, some of the practical aspects had not been foreseen. Returning to base after delivering a plane was one of these. Because of their civilian and female status, they were not allowed to hitch a lift on army planes. They therefore had to make use of civilian transport to get back to the second Ferrying Group (FG) base at New Castle, Delaware. Nonetheless, the second FG did sometimes provide an aircraft to fly them back. Even at New Castle, they were not permitted to make use of an army aircraft with more than one seat without the express authorisation of the Group commander. The reason for taking such draconian measures was to ensure that there was minimal contact between the WAFS and male personnel at the base. This was not to say that there was a lack of trust in the personnel, but rather to 'quash any rumours that journalists would readily seize on if there was even the slightest incident'. That, at any rate, was the official position. As Helen Snap later said: 'It was as if we were in a girls' boarding school, but even so, we still found ways to meet up.'

were taking on the job of helping to ferry planes across the Atlantic. At this stage, the United States had not entered the war and pilots there were recruited to fly for the ATA. Among them were 25 women brought together by Jacqueline Cochran (see p. 147), who had already tried, unsuccessfully, to establish an organisation of American aviatrixes. On her return to the United States, she learned that another pilot by the name of Nancy Love was in the process of setting up just such a group (the WAFS). The two women had diametrically opposite approaches. While Cochran advocated training hundreds of pilots from scratch, Love suggested using the lesser numbers of good, already-trained pilots who would therefore be more immediately available. Even among the chiefs of staff, opinion was divided: there were pro-Cochrans and pro-Loves. But the United States would soon enter the war and the ferrying of new aircraft began to pose a problem. On 11 June 1942, Ferrying Command requested the use of women pilots.

On 1 September 1942, nine months after Pearl Harbor and three years after Jacqueline Cochran's original proposal, the decision was taken to use qualified female pilots to ferry trainer aircraft. A specific unit, the Women's Auxiliary Ferrying Squadron (WAFS) was set up with Nancy Love at its head. Stung by this, Jacqueline Cochran nevertheless gained authorisation to create the Women's Flying Training Detachment (WFTD) to train novices so that they could then join the WAFS. This separate structure was short-lived. On 5 August 1943, the general staff of the USAAF decided to bring all the aviatrixes into a single structure, the WASP (Women Airforce Service Pilots), directed by Jackie Cochran.

As might be expected, initially at least, the women received a lukewarm welcome. The main training base was at Avenger Field in Sweetwater, Texas. From the beginning, WASP pilots, who were known as 'Fifinellas',[5] were involved in all kinds of tasks, bar combat missions and transatlantic ferrying, flying 77 different types of aircraft from the smallest to the biggest (from the Piper Club to the B-29 Super Fortress). These varied missions included: ferrying, test flying and target towing. More than 25,000 women applied, but only 1,830 were taken on for training. One of these was Sarah Winston, who had started flying on a J-3 Cub at the age of 15 and had gained her licence a year later. Joining WASP in May 1943, she qualified on twin-engined B-25s. After the war, she had her

Jacqueline Cochran pins Isabel Fenton's pilot's wings to her shirt on 3 July 1943 at Avenger Field, Texas. (USAF)

A gymnastics session for a new contingent of WASPs outside the barracks at Avenger Field, Texas, 23 August 1944. (USAF)

The WASPs in figures

Breakdown of the WASPs in the USAAF on 20 December 1944	
USAAF Headquarters	1*
Training Command	620
Air Training Command	141
1st Air Force	16
2nd Air Force	80
4th Air Force	37
Weather Wing	11
Proving Ground Command	6
Air Technical Service Command	3
Troop Carrier Command	1
TOTAL	916
*Jacqueline Cochran	

those who had flown with the ATA joined up so that they could continue flying. But with the advent of jet aircraft, maintaining a reserve of pilots trained on piston-engined planes no longer made sense. Only a few women were able to survive in this environment, such as Diana Barnato

own P-51 Mustang, competing with it in the National Air Races.

Despite all this, WASPs did not achieve military status and were treated as civilian personnel. It was not until 1977 that Congress decided that they were to be recognised for their role in the war by granting them military status and the privileges due to former combatants. On 10 March 2010, 70 years after its creation, WASP's pilots were honoured with the Congressional Gold Medal at a ceremony in the Capitol, attended by around 200 former WASPs.

Things were no better across the Atlantic. The ATA was disbanded in 1945. Women harboured the illusion that their experience would allow them to get jobs as commercial pilots. But it was not to be. They again had to face discrimination and were refused jobs simply because they were women, even when some of them may well have been better qualified for the post they were applying for than some of the men.

The emergence of jet aircraft was a further brake on women's future in military aviation. Countries that had already included women in their military aviation changed their policy and decided that, in view of family and social considerations, they could not support the lengthy and costly training required to train women on jets. The Royal Air Force Volunteer Reserve (RAFVR) had opened its doors to women in 1948 and many of

Barbara Jane Erikson sitting at the controls of a P-51A Mustang and Evelyn Sharp of the 6th Ferry Group at Long Beach in early 1943. Evelyn Sharp would later be killed when her P-38 Lightning crashed. (USAF)

Going through the pre-flight checklist on a Curtiss P-40 are Betty Jane Bachman (left) and Betty Whilow (right). (G. Grod collection)

Walker, who had been the first woman to cross the Channel at the controls of a Spitfire. On the 26th August 1963, this granddaughter of a South African diamond merchant was the first British woman pilot to break the sound barrier in an English Electric Lightning fighter.

The post-war conflicts gave little opportunity to aviatrixes. Just one woman flew for the military during the Korean War, carrying out liaison and communications missions. In 1949, President Syngman Rhee decided to polish the image of the new republic by creating a squadron of attractive female pilots to travel around the world. Kim Kyung Oh was one of these aerial ambassadors attached to the Republic of Korea Air Force. In truth, she was the only one to have completed her training.[6]

In France, after the break in the recruitment of women into the Air Force in 1946, Elisabeth Boselli was readmitted in 1953 as a press attaché to the minister's military office. She was granted a special dispensation to fly jet planes and managed to break several world records, including the speed record of 746kph over a fixed, 1,000km circuit on 26 January 1955, the distance record over a fixed circuit with 1,839km on 21 February 1955, and the distance record over a straight course with 2,331km on 1 March 1955.[7] She also served in Algeria, where she carried out 335 missions, of which 254 were related to 'keeping the peace'.

On the other side of the globe, in Indochina, two women in the medical corps had been involved in aerial missions. The first Frenchwoman to qualify as a helicopter pilot, Flight Lieutenant/Medical Officer Valérie

Andrée had learned to fly in the 1930s, before going on to become a neurosurgeon. Joining the army in 1949, she was posted to a paratroop unit in Indochina. While there, she had realised the need for a helicopter capability for rescuing pilots who had been shot down. Having gained her helicopter pilot's qualification in France, she returned to the Gia Lam base in Hanoi, from where she undertook 120 rescue missions and made 121 parachute jumps.[8] The other Frenchwoman, Suzanne Jannin, who was a dentist at the Haiphong military hospital, was authorised to fly Morane-Saulnier MS.500s with the ELA 52 aerial liaison squadron and flew 286 air ambulance and reconnaissance missions.

In the Near East, several women served in Israeli military aviation. In the early 1940s, Rachel Landau Markovski and Hava Diranska took part in dangerous missions carrying messages, arms and equipment. The first was captured several times by the British, but was released on each occasion. In 1953, Yael Rom[9] joined the 103rd squadron flying Douglas C-47s, and in October 1956, as a reservist, she was called up to take part in the airborne operations during the Suez Crisis and in air ambulance flights.

In the United States, after the passing of the 1972 Equal Rights Amendment and under lobbying pressure, the US Navy opened up pilot training to women in early 1973. An initial contingent of eight women was selected to follow the training programme beginning in the following spring. Six of them received their pilot's wings and, in 1975,

Elisabeth Boselli learned to fly on Lockheed T-33A jets at Meknès, subsequently receiving authorisation to attempt a series of records on SNCASE Mistral fighters. (SHAA)

President Barack Obama signs the act awarding the Congressional Medal to the WASPs. The scene is taking place in the Oval Office at the White House, in the presence of Lt. Col. Nicole Malachowski (visible on the far right), who was instrumental in promoting this measure. (USAF)

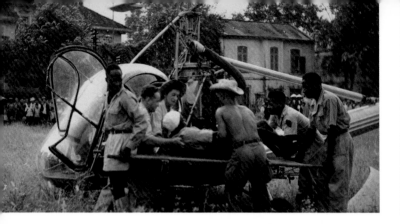

Tonkin, 1952: Valérie André evacuates a casualty in a Hiller helicopter. (ECPA)

Israeli Yael Rom flanked by two other student pilots. (S. Aloni collection)

the Chief of Naval Operations (CNO) gave authorisation for a second programme. The Army followed suit and, two years later, the Air Force recruited its first women trainee pilots. In 1977, the first group of 10 women completed their training on Northrop T-38As at Williams AFB, Arizona. This was just a first step as certain obstacles still remained: the type of mission and aircraft were still restricted by the regulations then in force. There was no question of women being able to get themselves behind the controls of warplanes and take part in wartime combat missions. The Secretary of State for Defense, Les Aspin, did not lift the ban until 1993.

Nowadays, women pilot all types of aircraft flown by the American military. However, just like other countries, until very recently, the United States did not permit women to carry out direct combat missions or missions that collocate with them. Nonetheless, American women have now been flying fighter aircraft for some years. The USAF has appointed its first test pilot, Captain Jacqueline Parker, a former T-38 and C-141 pilot, who was the first woman to qualify from the AFTPS based at Edwards AFB. The US Navy has trained women test pilots for a few years, the first one being Lt Cdr Colleen Nevius who received her wings in 1979 and became the first female member of the Test Pilots' Association.

Since the early 2000s, women have been at the controls of the most up-to-date and sophisticated warplanes ever built. Captain Jennifer Wilson, for example, was the first woman to pilot the B-2A Spirit stealth bomber, Captain Christina Szasz was the first to fly the F-117 Nighthawk stealth aircraft, and in November 2006, Captain Elizabeth A. Okoreeh-Baah became the first female Marines pilot to handle the MV-22 Osprey. Still more recently, in 2008, Captain Jammie Jamieson became the first

woman pilot on the Lockheed-Martin F-22 Raptor, flying with the 525th Fighter Squadron based at Elmendorf AFB, Alaska. Since then, the number of women in the USAF has continued to increase, with 683 women pilots at the end of 2010, although this represents only 4.5% of the total number of pilots.

In 1979, the Netherlands was the first European country to follow the United States' example when it admitted women to training. In 1986, they crossed an important threshold with the authorisation of training for combat missions. Since then, a growing number of countries have abolished the exclusion-from-combat rule. In Europe, Belgium, Norway and Sweden have done so, while across the Atlantic, Canada did the same in 1987, lifting all restrictions. In June 1988, the first two women were allocated to an operational fighter squadron: Captain Deanna Brasseur, 35 years old, and Captain Jane Foster, 28. Flying respectively since 1981 and 1984, they followed the five-month training course to fly CF-18 Hornets.

These were not simply empty gestures. The first American woman to carry out a wartime mission at the controls of a jet fighter aircraft was Lt Col. Martha McSally, in Iraq.[10] In the meantime, a helicopter pilot had paid with her life for her part in 'Operation Desert Storm', when Major

Valérie André at the controls of a Sikorsky H-34. (ECPA)

Lt. Col Martha McSally was the first woman in the US Air Force to fly in combat and to command an operational squadron. She is seen standing in front of a Fairchild A-10A Thunderbolt II, on 3 April 2006.

The first female military pilots

This selection of the first military jet plane pilots, allocated to operational units, shows how many countries have recently opened this avenue to women.

Year	Country	Name	Plane	Unit
1981	Canada	Deanna Brasseur	CF-18 Hornet	410 squadron
1986	Netherlands	Manja Blok	F-16	334 squadron
1992	Norway	Marianne Mjelde Knutsen	F-16	
1993	USA (USAF)	Sharon J. Preszler	F-16	
1994	USA (US Navy)	Kara Spears Hultgreen	F-14 Tomcat	VF-124
1994	Great Britain	Jo Salter	Tornado	617 squadron
1997	Belgium	Anne-Marie Jansen	F-16	349 squadron
1999	France	Caroline Aigle	Mirage 2000	EC 2/2
2001	Israel	Roni Zuckerman	F-16	
2002	Greece	Ioanna Hrisavgi	RF-4	110 Fighter Wing
2002	South Korea	Jong Mi Ha	F-16	20 Fighter Wing
2005	Denmark	Line Bonde	F-16	
2006	Italy	Stefania Irmici	Tornado	36 Stormo
2006	Germany	Ulrike Flender	Tornado	
2006	Pakistan	Saba Khan	F-16	
2006	Turkey	Asli Senol	F-16	162 squadron
2007	Morocco	Hanae Zarouali	F-16	
2007	Spain	Rosa Maria Garcia Malea	F/A-18 Hornet	ALA 15
2008	Eritrea	Haymanot Hailemariam	Su-27	
2009	South Africa	Catherine Labuschagne	Gripen	2 squadron
2010	Malaysia	Patricia Yapp	MiG-29	17 squadron

1. Chang Tso Lin 1873–1928, sometimes called Zhang Zuolin.
2. The spot where Lydya Litvyak's Yak-1 crashed was located only in 1989.
3. In February 1943, the 588th NBAP became the 46th Guards NBAP, then in October 1943, the 46th Taman Guards NBAP.
4. Beate Uhse Koestlin (East Prussia 1919-Switzerland 2001).
5. The origin of this name is unclear. It appears to have been painted on the trucks that took the trainees from their quarters in Houston to the airfield. Later, the name was applied to the commanding officer's plane, along with a symbol created by the Walt Disney Studios.
6. She flew Cessna L-19s until 1956.
7. These are records that stand for all categories, the women's records being in each case identical.
8. In 1976, Valérie André was promoted to air chief marshal and retired in 1981.
9. Born Yael Finkelstein, 1932–2006, qualified as a military pilot on 27 December 1951.
10. Martha McSally was also the first woman to command a fighter squadron, namely the 354th Fighter Squadron based at Davis Monthan AFB, Arizona.

Marie T. Rossi crashed while flying a CH-47 Chinook on 1 March 1991 in Saudi Arabia. She was 32 years old.

Perhaps less well known was the first victory in aerial combat won by a woman pilot flying a jet plane. On 26 February 2000, during the conflict between Ethiopia and Eritrea, Captain Aster Tolossa, piloting a Sukhoi Su-275, shot down an Eritrean MiG-29UB with two air-to-air missiles and bursts of 30mm cannon fire. In September 1997, in France, a young woman appropriately named Caroline Aigle ('aigle' meaning 'eagle' in French) joined the Ecole de l'Air and qualified as a fighter pilot on 28 May 1999. After a period with the EC 2/5 'Ile-de-France' fighter squadron to train on Mirage 2000s, she was allocated to the EC 2/2 'Côte d'Or' squadron. Sadly, she was struck down with a virulent cancer and died on 21 April 2007. Since then, other women have swelled the ranks of French Air Force fighter pilots, with seven as of 2007.

Lt. Cdr Rosemary Bryant Mariner was the first US Navy, carrier-borne fighter pilot. She is seen here at Point Mugu, on 24 April 1990, when she was chief of operations of VAQ-34 Squadron. (R.J. Francillon)

Captain Kim of the 332nd Air Expeditionary Wing, reviews the damage inflicted on her A-10 after it had been hit by enemy fire over Baghdad on 7 April 2003, during Operation 'Iraqi Freedom'. (USAF)

In many countries today, women fly combat aircraft. This is Patricia Yapp of the 17th Royal Malaysian Air Squadron, flying MiG-29s. (RAAF)

Eugenie M. Shakhovskaya posing in front of a Wright biplane at Johannisthal, near Berlin. (V. Koos collection)

The fighting princess: Eugenie M. Shakhovskaya

(1889-1920)

Eugenie M. Shakhovskaya and Vsevolod Abramovitch aboard a Wright biplane. (Library of Congress)

Lyubov Golanchikova, a former cabaret singer also known under the pseudonym of 'Molly Moret', was the third qualified Russian female pilot. She took the women's altitude record on 12 November 1912, climbing to 2,000m in a Fokker monoplane. Like Eugenie Shakhovskaya, she was a strong personality, and carried out reconnaissance missions for the Bolsheviks. (V. Koos collection)

From 1910, American, French and German aviators started to travel abroad to show off the qualities of their planes and their skills as pilots. Baroness de Laroche went to Russia in April 1910 and had many who emulated her among the wealthy young women there. On 22 August 1911, Lydia Zvereva, aged 21, was the first to qualify as a pilot, flying a Farman biplane at the Gatchina flying school. On 3 October Eudocie V. Anatra followed her and opened a flying school the following year. Among her pupils was Princess Eugenie Mikhailovna Shakhovskaya, supposedly a cousin of Tsar Nicholas II, who was born in St Petersburg in 1889. She began her training with the instructor Vladimir Lebedev, before going to Germany where she continued her lessons with Vsevolod Abramovitch, the chief pilot for the Wright subsidiary in Germany. Eugenie gained her pilot's licence on 16 August 1912, flying a Wright biplane at the Johannisthal airfield near Berlin. When war broke out in September between Italy and Turkey, she offered her services to the Italian government, but was turned down. She then returned to St Petersburg to demonstrate the Wright to the Russian military and built a sound reputation as a plucky flyer. However, she was soon back at Johannisthal where she taught flying alongside Abramovitch with whom she had fallen in love. Unfortunately, on the morning of 11 April 1913, an engine failure on the Wright they were both flying caused the plane to lose power and crash. Abramovitch was seriously injured and died the following day. Eugenie escaped with a few bruises and a broken nose.

Little is known of what happened to Eugenie Shakhovskaya in the ensuing years. The story varies according to the sources. Some claim that she gave up on flying as she felt a guilty responsibility for the accident and married a German officer in 1918 (whom she later left). According to other sources, she started to fly again in the spring of 1914 in the Tsarist army. As an officer in the first Air Squadron, she may have undertaken reconnaissance and artillery range-finding missions. During one of these, it is alleged that she was wounded by enemy fire, subsequently being decorated by the Tsar with the Order of St George military medal. Known for being the first female combat pilot in the world, Eugenie Shakhovskaya led a military career that remains rather unclear and the information we have needs to be treated with some caution. It is said she had many liaisons with officers from her unit. Accused of having supplied the enemy with information and tried to cross over to enemy lines, she was accused of high treason and condemned to the firing squad. Nicholas II commuted her sentence to lifetime in a convent (she was at this point pregnant), from

which she was liberated by the Bolsheviks in 1917. She was then supposed to have worked for the secret police and was named responsible for executions in Kiev under the orders of General Tcheka. Addicted to drugs, in 1920 she was said to have killed one of her assistants while in a drug-induced delirium, before being shot herself.

Cat woman: Cecil W. 'Teddy' Kenyon

(1905-1979)

In the spring of 1930, Teddy Kenyon was crowned 'Miss America of the Air' and given a cup filled with $300-worth of gold coins. (SI)

Under the title of 'I tame Hellcats', Teddy Kenyon was the subject of a promotional comic strip in the Saturday Evening Post *on 10 June 1944. (DR)*

'Now, my little pussy cat, let's see how you bite...' words that appeared in the *Saturday Evening Post* on 10 June 1944. The 'pussy cat' in question was none other than the Grumman Hellcat fighter, one of the most powerful of its time, and its pilot was a woman by the name of Teddy Kenyon. She had achieved such celebrity that she had become the number one choice to advertise a well-known brand of cigarettes.

The daughter of Wholsey and Cecil Hopkins, Cecil W. Kenyon was born on 11 September 1905 at Dobbs Ferry, in New York State. She fell in love with a former American Airlines pilot and Grumman engineer named Theodore 'Ted' Kenyon and they were soon married. Going under the nickname of 'Teddy' she was gripped by a passion for flying, and was taught the basics by her brother-in-law, who had served in naval aviation. In 1929, with Teddy having accumulated a mere 10 hours or so flying, she had undertaken a flight from Boston to New York at the controls of a Travel Air biplane. That autumn, she gained her pilot's licence then joined the famous '99s'.

There she met Amelia Earhart and Louise Thaden, becoming friends with the latter.

With her Air Travel, Teddy had gained considerable experience and celebrity, being awarded the title of 'Miss America of the Air' in the spring of 1930, with prize money of $300.

In October 1933, she learnt by chance that the women's aerobatics championships would be taking place at Roosevelt Field. She hastily borrowed a friend's Waco biplane and arrived in the nick of time to take part. After three days of fierce competition, she took the $5,000-cash first prize and simultaneously beat the women's altitude record, albeit unofficially, with

5,335m. Speaking to a reporter from *The Globe*, she declared: 'I'm sure I could have gone even higher if I'd had oxygen, the right carburettor setting... and a pair of gloves.'

The money she won did not sit burning holes in her pockets. That same day, she bought an all-red Waco that proved to be an excellent investment. Ted Kenyon, who had set up his own company, decided to use the plane to test and develop various special on-board items of equipment, and Teddy took charge of all the test flights. It was also at this time that she got involved with films, acting as a double in two, still-well-known aviation films: *Hell's Angels* (1930) and *Tail Spin* (1938).

In 1942, Teddy became a Flight Officer in the Civil Air Patrol. Her first mission was to act as a plastron for the Sperry Corporation, which was developing an anti-aircraft gun at that time. She then took part in a number of sorties to flush out German submarines patrolling off the American coast. The following November, she joined Grumman, where she was given the job of carrying mail between the various plants, but she was soon getting training on piloting ship-borne Hellcats.

Her first flight in one of these planes was a memorable experience: 'One fine day, she recalled, Bud Gillies, who was in charge of testing and aerial operations at Bethpage, called us in and said: girls, starting next Monday you'll be paid by Grumman as test pilots on production aircraft!' With two other aviatrixes, Barbara K. Jayne and Elizabeth H. Hooker, Teddy was given the job of taking aircraft as they emerged from the plant, or green planes, as they were called. At a rate of several hours a day, the three women flew hundreds of Wildcats, Hellcats and other Avengers. Grumman made much publicity out of its trio of aviatrixes. Press conferences, photo shoots, publicity reports; nothing was ignored. The press soon had eyes only for Teddy Kenyon and her ever-present bright-red cap.

In a little less than three years, she amassed a good 1,000 flying hours, and

Teddy Kenyon in 1942 when she was flying a Taylorcraft in the Civil Air Patrol (CAP). This organisation's emblem can be seen on the plane's fuselage: a red propeller in a white triangle on a dark-blue disk. (SI)

these on flights that were far from easy, though major incidents were rare. On one occasion, she was to relate later, 'I noticed that I could move the stick only backwards or forwards. I climbed in the hope of getting high enough to make a parachute jump. But I couldn't come to terms with losing such a fine aircraft. So, I executed a wide turn using the rudder and lined myself up on the runway. I prayed to God for a perfect landing as the runway was full of emergency rescue vehicles. Fortunately, everything went well. We found out that the problem had been caused by a pin that had fallen out.'

The trio of Grumman pilots kit themselves up for another day of test flights. From left to right: Barbara Kibbee Jayne, Elizabeth H. Hooker and Teddy Kenyon. (Grumman HC)

Wearing her trademark bright red cap, Teddy Kenyon prepares to 'tame' a Grumman F6F Hellcat that has just emerged from the factory. (John Underwood collection)

The surrender of Japan brought this incredible period to an end. However, Teddy continued to fly on behalf of her husband. In 1953, the couple moved to Mitchell Hill Road, in Lyme, Connecticut, and continued flying Vultee B-13s and Piper Tripacers. Not satisfied, Teddy gained her helicopter pilot's qualification on 17 December 1959. In 1976, at the age of 71, she was still flying and even took part in an air race sponsored by the '99' Club, in New England. Her husband died in 1979 and she died on 13 December 1985 in Middletown Hospital. In accordance with her last wishes, her ashes were scattered in the clouds.

Pilot and spare-time poet: Pauline Gower

(1910-1947)

Pauline Gower at Hatfield as she prepares to deliver a De Havilland Tiger Moth biplane. (IWM)

One woman who was in at the start of the celebrated British female ferry pilots came from a fairly privileged background. Born in Tunbridge Wells in 1910, younger daughter of Conservative MP Sir Robert Gower, Pauline Mary de Peauly Gower underwent a conventional upper-middle class education at the Sacré-Cœur Convent School. After a bout of pneumonia and pleurisy when only 17, she narrowly escaped death and it left her much weakened. She decided not to let this stop her from leading a normal life and initially decided on a career as a violinist, but soon abandoned this idea. She then considered going into politics, but rejected this, too. It was at this time that she had her first flight, with Captain Hubert S. Broad, but what really affected her was Amy Johnson's historic flight. This exploit awakened in her an extraordinary fascination with aviation. She took flying lessons, unknown to her father, and showed a natural instinct for flying. Deciding to make a living from it, she wasted no time in gaining her pilot's licence, and then set up a small on-demand air transport business (Air Trips Ltd) with her friend Dorothy Spicer. She had just celebrated her 21st birthday, and to mark the occasion, her father – who had come round to the idea – had bought her a plane.[1] The business proved to be very profitable, later telling a BBC reporter who had come to interview her that she had carried around 30,000 passengers.[2] But this was not her only interest. Endowed with a fine turn of phrase, Pauline regularly contributed to women's magazines such as *Chatterbox* and *Girl's Own Paper* and, in 1934, she published a collection of poems entitled Piffling *Poems for Pilots*.

In 1938, as the skies over Europe were ever darkening, Pauline Gower was appointed to London's civil defence committee and posted to the Civil Air Guard (CAG) and also brought out a book devoted to women flyers: *Women with Wings*.[3] When war broke out, she decided to make use of her contacts in high places to propose, and obtain, the formation of a women's section in the ATA. Put in charge of the new organisation, she selected eight women from the CAG who all had over 500 hours' flying time on their record. Becoming a part of the ATA on 1 January 1940, the women came from a variety of backgrounds. There was a professional hockey player (Margaret Fairweather) and a ballet dancer (Rosemary Rees) to take just two. The little group soon attracted media attention and was the subject of a number of articles in the British press and cinema newsreels. The ATA's adventure was underway.

When the Battle of Britain started, Pauline Gower gained authorisation to recruit 10 further women and to choose from among her pilots the five best so that they could carry out training on bigger and faster planes than the little De Havilland Tiger Moth biplanes that had been allocated to them up to that point. However, they had to be patient, as it was not until February 1943 that the first of them was authorised to fly four-engined aircraft.[4] However, Pauline Gower flew less than the other ATA pilots. She was convinced that her role on the ground was more important than the one in the air. She placed her duty above everything else and, for her, credit for it came second.

In 1944, she married Wing Cdr Bill Fahie. Sadly, she died two years later, at the age of 36, a few months after her business partner Dorothy Spicer, and two days after having given birth to twins, Paul and Michael.

---

1. *Pauline Gower was thus the first British female commercial pilot and the third in the world.*
2. *Quoted by Giles Whittell in* Spitfire Women, *p. 54. This figure is, very likely, much exaggerated.*
3. *See Bibliography, p. 189.*
4. *The pilots selected were Lettice Curtis and Joan Hughes.*

Nancy Harkness Love and her first pupil, Betty Gillies, at the controls of a Fairchild PT-19A trainer. It was these two who attempted to ferry a Boeing B-17 to England in September 1943. (USAF)

Ferrying pilot with a mission: Nancy Harkness Love

(1914-1976)

Nancy Harkness Love played a major role in the formation of a ferrying unit in the US Army Air Force. (USAF)

'It didn't release in me a passion to fly, as it probably should have done,' explained Nancy Harkness after watching with her own eyes the arrival of Charles Lindbergh at Le Bourget. In that May of 1927, this young woman, born in Houghton, Michigan, was still a student and it was not until three years later that she became enthusiastic about flying and learned to fly, gaining her pilot's qualification in November 1930. In the autumn of 1931, she entered Vassar College, New York and kept up her flying not far away at Poughkeepsie. Two years later, she obtained her transport pilot's licence and left Vassar a few months afterwards to look for a job. She worked for a year in Boston selling and demonstrating aeroplanes, before finding a position with the Bureau of Air Commerce in 1935. It was at this time that she met Robert Love, marrying him on 11 January 1936. Together, they set up a company, Inter City Air Lines, based in Boston. Changing jobs again, she then became a test pilot for the Gwinn Aircar Company.

With the coming of the Second World War, even though her country had not yet taken up arms, she started to ferry military aircraft to the Canadian border. While Jacqueline Cochran was with Mrs Roosevelt laying out her plan to train some 650 qualified American aviatrixes with a view to their supporting the war effort, Nancy Harkness penned a letter, dated 21 May 1940, to Lt Col Robert Olds of the Air Corps general staff. 'I have managed,' she wrote, 'to compile a list of forty-nine women pilots whom I could describe as excellent...I would reckon that there might be about another fifteen I don't know about...the majority of them have around a thousand hours of flying, some more, and have flown many different types of aircraft.' On the list were names such as Ruth Nichols, Gladys O'Donnell, Louise Thaden and Bobbi Trout.

These ideas met with considerable resistance. After much prevarication, on 1 September 1942 Henry L. Stimson, Secretary of State for War, announced the creation of the Women's Auxiliary Ferrying Squadron, or WAFS, made up of 27 pilots under the command of Nancy Harkness Love. In September 1942, she became the first woman to fly a P-51 Mustang fighter. During September 1943, Nancy Love and Betty Gillies were on the tarmac preparing to take off from Newfoundland in a four-engined B-17 with the object of ferrying it

During her career as a pilot, Nancy Harkness Love flew 50 types of civil aircraft and 20 types of military planes. She is pictured here at the controls of a PT-19A basic trainer. (USAF)

Avenger Field, May 1943 as an instructor explains a manoeuvre to a group of student aviatrixes. Standing, from left to right: Nancy Harkness Love, Eileen Roach, Mary E. Engel, Isabel Madison, Virginia Malany, Virginia Hill and Ruth Underwood. (USAF)

across the Atlantic when Gen. Henry 'Hap' Arnold intervened and categorically forbade the mission.

On 5 August 1943, all the women pilots in the US Army Air Force were brought together in a single organisation – the WASP – with Jacqueline Cochran appointed as director and Nancy Harkness Love in charge of supervising the Ferrying Division. With the outcome of the war by that time foreseeable, WASP was disbanded on 20 December 1944, and Nancy Harkness Love, like all the other pilots, was sent home without further ado. She spent the rest of her life fighting to have the WASPs granted military status. She died of cancer on 22 October 1976, aged 62, in Sarasota, Florida, sadly not being able to witness President Jimmy Carter signing the decree, on 23 November 1977, which granted veteran status to former WASPs.

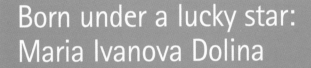

Born under a lucky star: Maria Ivanova Dolina

(Born in 1922)

Behind the happy smile is a determined fighter, Maria I. Dolina. She is seen here displaying her decorations (Order of Lenin, Order of the Red Flag and Order of the Great Patriotic War), standing in front of one of the Pe-2s of the 125th Guards Bomber Regiment of the 4th Bomber Division. The date is probably late 1945. (DR)

A native of Sharoka, near Omsk in Siberia, Maria Ivanova Dolina was the eldest of 10 children in a peasant family of Ukrainian origin. Her father had lost a foot in the Revolution and his infirmity obliged her to cut short her studies to go and work in a factory, though this did not prevent her from enrolling at a gliding club, where she soon showed promise. However, she was still too young to learn to fly powered aircraft, but thanks to a false declaration of her age by the director of her aero club, she was able to sign up with the flying school at Kherson, in Ukraine.

She was a supervisor at Dniepropetrovsk when war broke out. In the early period, she took part in the ferrying of planes then joined the Red Army. She was at the Engels academy from which she emerged with the rank of lieutenant in the reserve. She was posted, with the rank of pilot officer, to the 587th Dive-Bomber Regiment,[1] formed in the autumn of 1941[2] and flew three-seater, twin-engined Petlyakov Pe-2s. She carried out her first combat mission in the Stalingrad sector, then fought in the Caucasus and at the famous Battle of Kursk. On 2 June 1943, while she was preparing for an attack at Kuban in the Crimea, her plane was hit by flak and the port engine was damaged. After dropping her bombs, she turned for home, unescorted. She then came under attack from half a dozen German fighters. She defended herself as well as she could and her gunner Ivan Solenov succeeded in putting a Focke Wulf Fw 190 and a Messerschmitt Me 109 out of action. However, the Russian plane was on fire. Dolina nevertheless managed to land the burning plane near the front line. Hardly had Solenov managed to get Dolina and the navigator, Galina Dzhunkovskaya, out of the plane than it exploded. Wounded, but alive, Dolina spent a month in hospital before rejoining her unit.

Maria Dolina completed 72 bombing missions and was made a Hero of the Soviet Union on 18 August 1945. She had shot down three enemy planes in aerial combat and dropped 45 tonnes of bombs. She was one of the survivors from her unit, which had lost 42 of its pilots during the conflict, leading her to remark that she had 'been born under a lucky star'. After the war, she remained in military aviation and became second in command of the 125th Guards Bomber Regiment. On her retirement, she settled respectively at Siauliai (Lithuania), Riga (Latvia) and Kiev (Ukraine), becoming a freewoman of the latter city in 1995.

1. This regiment was later redesignated 125th Guards Bomber Regiment.
2. The regiment was formed by Marina Raskova, who was killed in an accident in January 1945.

The icon of icons, the American flyer Amelia Earhart has had more media coverage than any aviatrix in the history of aviation and has most certainly had more books published about her than anyone else. (DR)

The icons

When aviation was still in its golden age, the fame of certain aviatrixes took on such a magnitude that it does not seem an exaggeration to speak of them as icons of their times. Their names and their exploits travelled well beyond the boundaries of their own countries to anchor themselves indelibly in the collective memory. From among this handful of people, we have chosen four. Two of them, whose tragic ends when they were at the height of their fame were to cause universal shock, are Amelia Earhart and Hélène Boucher. The other two, whose chivalrous aeronautical jousting lit up the skies of the 1950s, are Jacqueline Auriol and Jacqueline Cochran. Several decades have passed since these exceptional flyers ceased to haunt the clouds – leaving their names and faces to fade inexorably.

The tragic adventure: Amelia Earhart

(1898-1937)

Amelia Earhart naming the TAT Company's first Ford 5-AT Trimotor City of New York, on 7 July 1929. (TAT)

Amelia Earhart in front of her Kinner Airster biplane with its 100hp Kinner engine. She named it The Yellow Canary. (DR)

By 1935, Amelia Earhart already had a number of achievements to her name, of which the most significant were her Atlantic crossings, once as the first female passenger and the other as the pilot. She was also at this time one of the leading lights of the feminist cause. Her numerous articles published in the magazine *Cosmopolitan* and her speeches were both calls to and encouragement for the benefit of American women. She considered herself no better or worse than anyone else. She simply had the will to cross the gulf separating the daily routine of household chores from the realisation of her desires. She had decided to do what she enjoyed doing – for the fun of it – as she would say.

Her feminist activities and her passion for flying led to her being taken on by the University of Purdue, Indiana, on 2 June 1935, to give lectures, act as an advisor to the female students and supervise the aeronautical department, as at the time, it was the only university to have its own aerodrome. The Purdue Foundation for Research set up an 'Amelia Earhart Fund' with the aim of buying an aircraft. Within a few weeks, the amount raised was sufficient to consider the purchase of a twin-engined aircraft. Amelia had set her heart on a Lockheed Electra. She also announced to her husband, the publisher George Palmer Putnam (known as G.P. or Gippy) that she had decided to undertake a journey around the world. It was true that this had twice been done before (in 1931 and 1935) by Wiley Post, but flying well north of the equator. Amelia, on the other hand, intended to follow the equator as closely as possible. The flight across the Pacific Ocean would necessitate using as staging points islands that were barely visible on the map. It was for this reason that she considered it vital to have the services of an experienced navigator, at least for the longest sections. Contact was made with Bradford Washburn, a navigation specialist, but he was unwilling to get involved with an enterprise where the risks were so great.

Amelia Earhart taking delivery of the Lockheed Vega she would use in 1932 for her solo Atlantic crossing. From left to right: A.E., unknown, Carl Squier, sales director at Lockheed and Lloyd Stearman, managing director. (Lockheed)

On 22 July 1936, A.E. as she was often known, visited the Lockheed plant in Burbank. On the plane that was due to be delivered to her on 24 July, the seating had been removed so that additional fuel tanks could be installed, taking the capacity up to 4,540 litres, enough for the Electra to be able to cover over 4,000km without refuelling. Numerous extra navigational instruments had also been installed and A.E. spent the next few weeks making familiarisation flights over the California coast. In August 1936, she went to New York to take part in the Bendix Trophy. During this event, the Electra encountered feed problems and Amelia and her co-pilot, Benny Howard, were forced to abandon the race. Though she was irritated by this contretemps, there was no reason for any drama and it was seen as part of the pre-flight preparation and testing.

Soon after this event, she recruited her team. Clarence Williams, from Los Angeles, was engaged to prepare the necessary maps. The technical adviser was none other than the famous Paul Mantz, who had worked before for 'Miss Lindy'. Finally, George Putnam was in charge of logistics. There were indeed many administrative problems to be overcome: organising the staging and refuelling points, emergency-landing areas etc. On 11 February 1937, A.E. met the press at the Barclay Hotel and introduced the person who was going to be the navigator: Captain Harry Manning. She told them: 'So there it is, I'm going to try to go around the world by plane. I shall follow the equator as closely as possible, from east to west, for about 40,000km.'

The radio equipment was Amelia's biggest worry. She had been able to obtain only a big 50-Watt receiver with a range of about 800km. She decided to press on regardless. By the beginning of March, everything was ready, but she had to wait a further two weeks for the weather conditions to improve. It was agreed that there would be four people on board for the first stage to Honolulu. Paul Mantz would act as co-pilot while Fred J.

Noonan would sit behind to help Manning. Mantz would be dropped off in Honolulu, Noonan in Howland and Manning in Brisbane.

On Wednesday 17 March 1937, Amelia decided to go. The flight to Honolulu went off without any problems. At 5.40am the next day, having covered 3,900km, the plane touched down on terra firma. The weather conditions were not ideal and they were unable to set off again straight away. The plane was taken to Luke airfield where there was a longer runway. At dawn on 19 March, the plane was taking off when it ground looped, the left wing touched the ground and the undercarriage gave way. Amelia was unshaken. She told the journalists who had come to question her: 'Nothing has happened to change my plans. I have more confidence than ever in my plane and I'm impatient to continue my flight.'

It wasn't until 19 May that the Electra was ready to set off again. But two months had passed by and the weather conditions had significantly changed. The original plans had to be revised, with it now looking better to fly from west to east. Manning was no longer available and would have to be replaced. The choice fell on Fred Noonan, but Jacqueline Cochran, Amelia's friend, considered him a poor navigator and suggested putting him to the test. She therefore took him out into the Pacific and gave him the task of finding the way back to Los Angeles. Noonan complied, but they reached the coast about halfway between San Francisco and Los Angeles. The error was substantial, but Amelia appeared to be not unduly concerned and continued with her preparations.

On 21 May 1937, the Electra was taken from Burbank to Oakland and, the following day, took off for Miami. The port engine caught fire, but fortunately, they were able to repair it overnight. The team began making their final preparations. It was at this point that Amelia decided to dispense with the 75m-long wire antenna in order to save weight. This decision may well have been fatal.

It was 5.56am on Wednesday 1 June when A.E. took off and headed south-east. The first two planned stops were San Juan, Puerto Rico, and Paramaribo, Suriname. The flight to Puerto Rico passed without incident, but they discovered that the take-off runway was under repair. In consequence, they had to take off with much less fuel on board and there was now no question of their being able to reach Paramaribo. By 2 June they had only got as far as Caripito, Venezuela. Paramaribo was reached on 3 June and, the following day, after a 2,150km flight, the Electra touched down at Fortaleza, on the north coast of Brazil.

After a rest day, A.E. and Noonan set off for Natal at 04.50 on 6 June. The following day, when the Electra took off, weather conditions were hardly favourable. For 3,000km, the two Americans had to face rain and a 30kph easterly wind. The equator was crossed at 6.45am. But a navigational error had brought the plane to St-Louis, Senegal, instead of Dakar as

12 January 1935: Amelia Earhart is acclaimed by the crowds on her arrival in Oakland at the end of her solo flight between Hawaii and California. (Hawaii Aviation)

Amelia takes a short break in one of the hangars at Burbank while preparing for one of her flights. (Lockheed)

Amelia in discussion with Wiley Post in Cleveland on 29 March 1935. In 1931, Wiley Post and Harold Gatty had completed a round-the-world trip in 8 days, 15hr 51min, in a Lockheed Vega. (H. Hazewinkel collection)

planned. The crossing of the South Atlantic had taken 13hr 12min. The following morning, the plane was taken to Dakar for a full service, and on 10 June, they began the flight across the continent of Africa. They took off for Mali just before 6am and reached Gao late in the evening. The next day, the Electra touched down at Fort-Lamy before noon, but as the wheels hit the runway, the left shock absorber gave way. The plane was not seriously damaged, but it had to be repaired. It was by then too late to hope for a long stage and they managed a further 1,000km, reaching Al Fashir, Sudan by that evening.

The Electra had eaten up the miles without complaint. On 13 June, it took off again towards Khartoum. Just the time to refill the tanks and it was off once more heading for Massaoua in Ethiopia. On Tuesday Amelia Earhart set a south-easterly course for Assab. Here, the runway was long and allowed them to take off fully loaded. This was just as well as the authorities had not given permission for them to land. Well before daylight had broken over Assab, they were on their way for a non-stop stage to Karachi.

With their arrival in India, half of their journey had been completed, but the toughest part was still to come. On 17 June, the Lockheed set off for Calcutta and throughout most of this 2,250km stretch, she could be seen from the ground. At 4.00pm she landed at Calcutta's Dum-Dum Airport. The ground here was soft, but despite the risks this posed, A.E. took off. The objective was Rangoon, in Burma, with a service stop at Akyab. Shortly after they'd left Akyab, the rain came on harder than ever and Amelia had to face a veritable cloudburst. Two hours later, she had returned to Akyab. The weather station predicted no improvement for…three months. For A.E. this was inconceivable. She decided to try again the next day.

On 19 June, the take-off and the journey to Rangoon went without any trouble, although a deluge in Rangoon surprised them. The following day, calmer weather allowed them to get to Bangkok. Then they were off again and, after a six-hour flight, the Electra was touching down in Singapore. Early on the morning of 22 June, the plane took to the air again, heading for Java. For the third time since the start of the expedition, the equator was crossed. Following its arrival in Bandung, the plane was serviced. On 24 June at 3.45am, the engines were started, but immediately one of the instruments indicated a problem. They had to make repairs and the take-off did not take place until 2.00pm. There was now no question of reaching Australia before nightfall and the two Americans decided to go as far as Surabaya only. Unfortunately, the repairs had to be redone and Amelia was obliged to turn back to Bandung. It took two days to complete the repairs and the Electra didn't set out for Port Darwin until 27 June. Amelia had underestimated the effect of the shortening days and by the time they arrived at Koepang, it was already too late for them to think of carrying on. The next day, they crossed the Timor Sea and arrived in Port Darwin where they jettisoned the parachutes to save weight. There then followed a 7hr 43min flight to Lae, in New Guinea. Beyond lay the Pacific…

On Thursday 1 July 1937, they were ready for the longest leg of the journey: Lae-Howland, a distance of 4,200km. The Electra had been filled with 4,500 litres of fuel. The wind was blowing across the runway and threatening clouds were building on the horizon. Fred Noonan couldn't manage to regulate his chronometers. The departure was delayed until the following day. By 10.00am the wind was still blowing hard but Amelia managed to get airborne. The flight over the ocean presented some risks. The Electra's radio had a range of just 800km, so Amelia would be able to indicate her position only when she got within that distance of Howland,

A caricature of Amelia Earhart that appeared in the aeronautical press in 1937. (DR)

A smiling Amelia Earhart not long before setting out on her round-the-world journey. (Lockheed)

Amelia Earhart at United Airport in 1935 with a roll of maps as she was getting ready to take part in the Bendix Trophy race. (Dusty W. Carter)

Amelia talking to Paul Mantz with the Lockheed 10 Electra under construction in the background. (Lockheed)

A.E. with Fred Noonan, whose navigational errors proved fatal. (Dusty W. Carter)

where a US Navy Coastguard cutter, the *Itasca* was waiting. At Howland, a high-frequency direction finder had been installed, but Amelia was unaware of this. To put it another way, over a distance of around 3,700km, she was going to have to trust in Fred Noonan's navigation.

At 5.20pm, Amelia communicated her position to Lae. At 12.04am the *Itasca* sent out a first signal to guide them in, followed by regular weather bulletins. The Electra was not picked up until 2.45am, but the message was incomprehensible. A further message was received an hour later: 'Overcast. Will listen on hour and half hour on 3105'. The *Itasca* then received nothing more for three long hours. At 6.45am Amelia was heard: 'Please take a bearing on us and report in half an hour. I will make noise in microphone – about 100 miles out'. At 7.42am, the Electra was heard again: 'We must be on you but cannot see you but gas is running low; been unable reach you by radio; we are flying at altitude 1,000 feet'.

At 7.58am Amelia still could not hear the *Itasca*: 'We are circling but cannot hear you; go ahead on 7500 either now or on the schedule time on half hour'. Finally, at 8.00am, she picked up a signal from the ship: 'We received your signals but unable to get a minimum. Please take bearing on us and answer 3105 with voice'.

At 8.33am, the *Itasca* signalled: 'Will you please come in and answer on 3105. We are transmitting constantly on 7500. We do not hear you on 3105. Please answer on 3105. Go ahead'. Then a few moments later: 'Answer on 3105 with phone. How are signals coming in? Go ahead'.

At 8.45am, Amelia's voice was heard for the last time: 'We are on the line of position 157-337. Will repeat this message on 6210 KCS. We are running north and south'. The *Itasca* acknowledged reception but the receiver remained silent. The ship kept repeating its calls until 10.00am, without any response. It became clear that Amelia Earhart and Fred Noonan were lost. The information given in the 8.45am message was insufficient

to narrow down the search area. For 16 days significant resources were devoted to searching tens of thousands of square kilometres of ocean, but all the efforts were in vain. Miss Lindy was not to be found.

And here the adventure would appear to end, were it not for the results of research published in 1985, which threw new light on the mystery in tragic fashion. The American, Vincent Loomis, having spent several years investigating both American and Japanese archives, appears to have been able to reconstruct what actually happened on that fateful 2 July 1937.

The first discovery was that Amelia Earhart decided to change her flight plan at the last minute. She took the decision to fly over an intermediate reference point, namely Nauru Island. Unfortunately for her, a north-easterly wind imperceptibly blew her off course, so that when she transmitted, at 19.12 GMT: 'We must be on you but cannot see you', she was in fact nearly 250km to the north-west of Howland. Seeing her fuel running low, she decided to retrace her steps and head for the Gilbert Islands. Taking account of her incorrect position, she would actually have been heading for the Marshall Islands. She would have crash-landed the Electra on the coral-reef atoll of Mili. Unfortunately for the two Americans, the Marshall Islands were at this time under Japanese control and military installations were under construction. Amelia and Fred were arrested by the Japanese and taken, successively, to Jaluit, Truk and Saipan.

On Saipan, the Japanese headquarters in the Pacific, the two of them were interned at the Garapan prison in particularly harsh sanitary conditions and with poor food. They would soon have succumbed to dysentery. Fred was the first to crack. One day, at the end of his tether, he threw a bowl of soup into the face of one of his captors and was immediately taken out and executed. Amelia survived until around mid-1938 until, weakened by disease, she died.

These sad events were taking place at the very same time that the

Amelia in conversation with her husband and coach George Palmer Putnam. The others are Paul Mantz (left) and Harry Manning (centre). (Dusty W. Carter)

Japanese claimed to be assisting the search with several ships that, it was later discovered, never left their moorings.

'The French girl': Hélène Boucher
(1908–1934)

In a photograph taken around February 1933, Hélène Boucher, on the threshold of a promising career, expresses the pleasure she takes in flying. (DR)

Hélène Boucher at Le Bourget on her return from Baghdad, on 13 February 1933. The aircraft, still with its British registration, is an Avro 616 Avian IVM with a 115hp Hermes engine. (GPPA)

Amelia Earhart's records

22 November 1929, in a Lockheed Vega, women's speed record: 296.330kph.

25 June 1930, in a Lockheed Vega, women's speed record over 100km closed circuit, no payload: 281.409kph; with 500kg payload: 275.844kph.

5 July 1930, in a Lockheed Vega, women's world speed record over 3km: 291.482kph.

7 April 1931, in a Pitcairn, altitude record for an autogyro: 5,613m.

12–13 July 1932, in a Lockheed Vega, women's record for Los Angeles–Newark: 19hr 15min of which 17hr 59min 40sec was actual flying time.

24–25 August 1932, in a Lockheed Vega, women's world distance record in a straight line, Los Angeles–Newark: 3,939km.

7–8 July 1933, in a Lockheed Vega, women's transcontinental record Los Angeles–Newark: 17hr 7min 30sec.

19–20 April 1935, in a Lockheed Vega, Los Angeles–Mexico City speed record: 13hr 33min.

8 May 1935, in a Lockheed Vega, Mexico City–Los Angeles speed record: 14hr 19min.

It is Tuesday 4 December 1934. Flying low, an aircraft from the Etampes patrol drops a wreath of white carnations over the funeral procession that has just entered the little cemetery of Yermenonville, a final homage to the great flyer who has recently been lost: Hélène Boucher. She is just 26.

The Friday before, 30 November, the young woman had eaten at the Grand Palais restaurant, where the XIV Aeronautical Show had been taking place since 17 November, an exhibition that commemorated her success and the records she had broken that summer. She had left the table in a hurry to go to Guyancourt for a training flight, essentially to do a final practice with her plane[1] ready for the exhibition flying scheduled for the following day. There was a layer of mist over the airfield, but she had decided to take off anyway and, after a short flight, she had begun her approach. Coming in too fast and overshooting, she had decided to abort the landing and go around for a second attempt. Flaps lowered, she again approached, but this time too short and, realising her error, she opened the throttle wide. Caught by the sudden application of power from the 120hp engine, the plane flipped onto its back and crashed into the ground. The whole country was thrown into dismay by the death of the young aviatrix.

The funeral took place at the church of St-Louis des Invalides attended by numerous dignitaries from the Air Force and the field of aeronautics (including Adrienne Bolland and Maryse Bastié). But she was accompanied to her final resting place in the village where she spent her childhood by her friends from the world of flying, of whom the most noted was Michel Détroyat.

The daughter of an architect, Hélène Boucher was born on 23 May 1908. While she was at school, she had struck up a friendship with Dolly van Dongen, the daughter of the painter. She had learnt English and piano and had shown some inclination for dressmaking. At one point, it appeared that her future was already mapped out. She had joined a fashion house in the Rue St Honoré where she had been a great success among the Anglo-Saxon clientele. Yet fate had other things in store. On the bus that daily took her home, she had got to know a pilot. Behind her sensible outward appearance, there had long been hidden a lover of strong sensations. She had managed to persuade the pilot to take her up in a plane, making her maiden flight on 4 June 1930. In March 1931, with enthusiasm trumping reason, she had left the capital for the flying school at Mont-de-Marsan. After 17hr 50min of flying, she had gained her pilot's licence.

Driven by an all-consuming passion, she had, in January 1932, managed to scrape together enough money to go to England and buy a little De Havilland Gipsy Moth biplane,[2] which allowed her to practise navigation and take her first steps in aerobatics. With an engine of barely 85hp, this second-hand plane soon proved to be inadequate. Six months later, she had sold it and bought another English biplane, an Avro Avian,[3] taking possession of it on 18 July, just in time to enter the Cannes-Deauville race, but engine trouble had intervened to put an end to this first foray into aeronautical competition.

With persistence being not the least of her qualities, Hélène Boucher had got her plane back in working order and, on the advice of her friends Paul Codos and Henri Robida, had thrown herself into organising a 'big expedition'. On Monday 13 February 1933, after a first abortive attempt (6 February), she had taken off for Saigon at the controls of her Avian, now christened *Foire de Paris*. She had reached Pisa the same day and on the 14th she was in Naples, which she left again on the 17th, heading for Athens. By 20, she had arrived in Aleppo, Syria. Thanks to engine trouble (a leak had appeared in the oil sump), she had been forced to land at Ramadi on the 21st, instead of Baghdad as planned. She had been obliged to wait there for days while the necessary spare parts were sent out. On 29 April, having given up on reaching Indochina, she arrived back at Le Bourget. This costly failure had led her to sell the plane in order to pay back some of the money that had been invested in the flight and to allow her to take part in meets.

Clearly, this was not what she had hoped for. And what really nagged at Hélène Boucher were speed records. Here, luck played its part. On 2 July 1933 the manufacturer Pierre Mauboussin took her on to fly a two-seater 60hp M.120/32[4] in the first 'Douze Heures d'Angers', a competition organised by the Aéro-Club de l'Ouest. It was open to aircraft that were 'at least two-seater' and offered 100,000F in prize money. Hélène Boucher had teamed up with Edmée Jacob (the future Edmée Jarlaud) for the competition. Two other women had also entered the race: Alek Plunian, who

In the field of aerobatics, Hélène Boucher had no hesitation in measuring herself against the great champions of the discipline, such as Liesel Bach. (V. Koos collection)

Hélène Boucher at the time of the Paris–Saigon attempt that she was forced to abandon at Baghdad. (GPPA)

Hélène Boucher with Michel Détroyat at the 1934 Brussels Meeting. He was the one who taught her all the finer points of haute école aerobatics. (Int. Photo Press, H. Hazewinkel collection)

An idealised studio portrait of Hélène Boucher, her eyes lifted towards the sky. (GPPA)

This photograph of the wreck of the Caudron C.430 Rafale, F-AMVB, gives an idea of the violence of the crash on 30 November 1934. (GPPA)

her in preference to Maryse Hilsz (see p. 105) and hired her as a contracted pilot.

In July the following year, Hélène Boucher had again entered the 'Douze Heures' in which, this time, ten teams were pitted against each other, three of which were female: Viviane Elder and P. Gautier in a Farman 400, Madeleine Charnaux and Yvonne Jourjon in a Miles Hawk, and herself and Marie-Louise Becker in a Caudron C.530 Rafale.[6] She had been the first to take off, at 6.00am. Over the first three hours, she had held her lead, slipping temporarily to third before finally taking second spot from the ninth hour onwards. Covering 2,821km at an average speed of 235.1kph, she had completed 70 circuits of the course, just two fewer than the winner, Yves Lacombe. In addition, the four Caudron C.530s that had been entered occupied the first four places. As a bonus, Hélène had also taken the world speed record and the women's speed record over 1,000km with 254.327kph.

To confirm her skills as a racing pilot, she had subsequently headed to Istres in search of further records, using the well-known C.450 marked with the number 13 that René Caudron had entrusted her with.[7] Within a few days, she had broken several records, including the all-categories speed record, which had made her a star in the firmament of aviation. France finally had its heroine, with her name on the front pages. She embodied a 'certain idea of France', and had come to be known as 'the French girl', but on 30 November 1934, she had her appointment with destiny.

---

1. A Caudron C.430 Rafale, also known as 'Grand Sport', no. 2/6886, registered as F-AMVB, with a 120hp Renault 4Pdi engine.
2. A De Havilland DH-60G Gipsy Moth, no. 1175, registered as F-AJKM, later sold to Charles Navarre.
3. An Avro 616 Avian IVM, no. 491, built in 1931, registered as G-ABIE, owned by S. Jackson. Powered by a 115hp ADC Cirrus Hermes II engine, it was fitted with a 415-litre reserve fuel tank.
4. A Mauboussin M.120/32, no. 109, registered as F-AMOZ, with a 60hp Salmson 9Adr engine.
5. Mae Haizlip, in a Buhl Pup, had broken the women's altitude record on 13 June 1931, at Saint Clair, Michigan, with 5,516m.
6. A Caudron C.530 Rafale, with a 140hp Renault 4Pei engine.
7. Commonly known as no. 13, the Caudron C.450's official no. was 6910.

was teamed with Maurice Finat in a Farman 359, and Mme Lefebvre, teamed with her husband in a Farman 231. On the day, Hélène Boucher had not performed brilliantly, coming in at only 14th out of the 17 competitors who started, and a long way behind the winner, after covering only 1,645.864km at an average speed of 137.155kph. But the main thing was that she had finished and, better still, had begun to make her mark in the aviation world through getting noticed by Michel Détroyat, the French pilot of the time. It would not be long before she was learning aerobatics with him at the Morane School in Villacoublay.

That summer, Hélène Boucher had broken her first record. Flying a Mauboussin-Peyret Zodiac, on 2 August 1933, she had taken the American Mae Haizlip's altitude record for second-category aircraft that had been held since 13 July 1931.[5] On Sunday 8 October, at the Villacoublay meet, and in front of thousands of spectators, she had shown her mastery in confronting the German aerobatics champion Vera von Bissing. The following year, on 29 April, at Vincennes, she had crossed swords with no less a person than the world champion, Liesel Bach (see p. 44).

Little by little, Hélène Boucher had built a reputation as an outstanding pilot: driven, enthusiastic, determined, and a regular at meetings. Détroyat and various other friends had such faith in her that, on 12 June 1934, they succeeded in getting her a test flight with Caudron, where she had got to know Marcel Riffard. Initially hesitant, Pierre Caudron had eventually chosen

Hélène Boucher's records

2 August 1933, in a Mauboussin-Peyret Zodiac, the women's international altitude record: 5,900m (previously held by Mae Haizlip).

1 July 1934, in a Caudron C.530 Rafale, world light plane speed record over a 1,000km closed circuit: 2,821km at 240kph.

8 July 1934, in a Caudron C.530 Rafale, women's speed record for a two-seater light plane over 1,000km: 254.327kph.

8 August 1934, in a Caudron C.450, women's speed record over 100km: 412.371kph (previously held by Amelia Earhart).

8 August 1934, in a Caudron C.450, all-category speed record over 1,000km: 409.184kph (previously held by Maurice Arnoux).

10 August 1934, in a Caudron C.450, women's speed record over 3km: 428.223kph (previously held by Mae Haizlip).

11 August 1934, in a Caudron C.450, women's speed record over 3km: 445.028kph.

'Faster and faster!': Jacqueline Cochran

(1906-1980)

During her career, Jacqueline Cochran flew many types of aircraft. She is pictured here in the cockpit of a Curtiss P-40. (USAF)

Jacqueline Cochran in front of the Northrop T-38 Talon in which she broke seven records in 1961, including the women's speed record over 100km, with 1,262.188kph. (USAF)

'In my mike, I read out the figures from the mach indicator so that Chuck could hear me on his radio. Mach 0.97...0.98...0.99...Mach 1.0...1.01.'[1] It was 18 May 1953 and the American Jacqueline Cochran was the first aviatrix to break the sound barrier flying a jet aircraft.

Who could have dreamt that this woman would have had such an exceptional career? Certainly, nothing predisposed her to this. Born in Muscogee, Florida, on 11 May 1906, Bessie Lee Pittman was the youngest in a family of five children.[2] Unable to follow her studies because of her parents' limited means, she decided to leave the family home and make her own way (it was somewhere around this point that she changed her name to Jacqueline Cochran). After beginning a nursing course, Jackie took her first job as a beautician in Pensacola. Changing jobs several times, she eventually found a position in New York in 1932 and began creating her own range of cosmetics. It was in the same year that, during a holiday in Florida, she met the millionaire, Floyd B. Odlum who, captivated by the young woman, encouraged her to learn to fly so that she could travel around the country selling her products on a bigger scale. She took his advice. Full of enthusiasm, she soon obtained her licence and then acquired a second-hand Travel Air biplane to practise on.

In the autumn of 1934, feeling sufficiently confident, and with Odlum's financial support, Jackie decided to take part in the famous London to Melbourne race, at the controls of the Northrop Gamma she had just bought.[3] Despite the great care with which she prepared for this competition, mechanical problems with the Gamma, causing a crash, forced her to change planes at the last minute and use a Gee Bee QED, but this also broke down, taking her no further than Budapest. The setback did not in any way discourage her. The next year, she entered the Bendix Trophy race, flying her Gamma, but was obliged to withdraw after technical problems. Persistent, she was back again in 1937, this time at the controls of a Beech D-17W biplane and came third. However, it was 1938 before she gave a full account of herself, taking first place and the precious trophy. She had, in the meantime, married Floyd Odlum (in May 1936) and the couple had bought a huge ranch in Southern California.

As the situation inexorably worsened in Europe, Jacqueline Cochran suggested using qualified women pilots to ferry planes from the factories to their operational units. However, prejudice in the armed forces soon put a brake on this project's implementation. While she awaited a decision, Jackie crossed the Atlantic to see how the problem had been resolved in Britain. In fact, in August 1941, the British Aeronautical

Howard S. Welch, managing director of the Bendix Aviation Export Corporation, hands the Bendi Trophy to Jacqueline Cochran on 5 September 1938. (Bruno & Ass., H. Hazewinkel collection)

Jacqueline Cochran and Charles 'Chuck' Yeager at the time she broke the sound barrier. (USAF/AFFTC)

The woman who rode the thunder. Jacqueline Cochran and the Lockheed F-104G Super Starfighter in which she broke the women's speed record over a 15/25km course, with 2,300.234kph, on 11 May 1964. (Lockheed)

Commission asked her to recruit American aviatrixes to come and swell the ranks of the ATA. This she did in the spring of 1942, readying a first contingent of 25 women. At the same time, the idea of using aviatrixes was very slowly beginning to make some headway. An initial structure was set up in September 1942, then, in June 1943, all the aviatrixes were brought into a single organisation, the famous WASPs (see p. 126). Jacqueline Cochran was then appointed head of the group and remained there until its disbandment, before the end of the conflict, on 20 December 1944. For services rendered to the nation, she was awarded the DSM (Distinguished Service Medal).[4]

With the end of hostilities, Jacqueline Cochran left for the Far East as a correspondent for the magazine *Liberty*. She thus found herself aboard the battleship *Missouri* on the day of the Japanese surrender. She then returned to the United States, passing through China, Egypt, Italy, Germany and the Soviet Union.

In 1946, still driven by a hunger for flying, Jackie took part in the first post-war Bendix Trophy race, at the controls of a P-51C Mustang, and took second place. She was to compete again two years later, but this time came in only third. She then began a career in politics, with the intention

Jacqueline Cochran steps down from the Lockheed Jetstar named Scarlett O'Hara after her record Atlantic crossing on 22 April 1962. (Lockheed)

of standing for Congress, and in 1952 she supported Dwight D. Eisenhower's candidacy for the presidency. Simultaneously, she made her comeback in high-performance flying, with the aim of breaking not merely women's records, but overall records. Spurred on by the speed record that had recently been established by the Frenchwoman Jacqueline Auriol in a De Havilland Vampire jet fighter, Jackie Cochran asked the US Air Force for permission to use one of its North American F-86 Sabres, but the authorities turned her down categorically. In 1948, an opportunity presented itself. The Royal Canadian Air Force had recently decided to equip itself with Sabres constructed under licence by Canadair. Having managed to get taken on by the manufacturer as a test pilot, Jackie Cochran obtained authorisation to make use of a Sabre Mk 3 and, making good use of advice given by Charles 'Chuck' Yeager, she raised the world speed record over 100km to 1,049.610kph on 18 May 1953 (the record had been held up to that point by Colonel Fred J. Ascani). This achievement won her the FAI's (International Aeronautical Federation) gold medal. Keen for this record to be permanent, Jacqueline Cochran (who was vice-president of the FAI at the time) decided to abandon separate women's records as of 1 June 1953. However, she had not reckoned with Jacqueline Auriol's response, as she re-took the record on 31 May with 1,151kph. Now president of the FAI, Jacqueline Cochran, in a somewhat cynical volte-face, reinstated women's records, thus regaining it for herself. There followed a decade in which one or the other Jacqueline held the speed record in turn (see tables).

After the Canadair Sabre, Jackie Cochran made use of the new Northrop T-38A Talon jet trainer, taking the women's speed record up to 1,262.188kph, a record that was, of course, soon won back by Jacqueline Auriol. Not content with leaving things as they were, Jackie Cochran took as her next steed the Lockheed F-104 Starfighter. On 12 April 1963, she raised the speed record over 15-25km to 2,048.875kph and, a month later, the record over a 100km closed circuit to 1,937.5kph. When Jacqueline Auriol, in a Dassault Mirage IIIR, regained the record for France, the American took it as another affront. Returning to the Flight Test Center on 11 May 1964, she took the speed record over a 15/25km course to 2,300.234kph in a Super Starfighter F-104G. On 5 June 1964, she brought the duel to a close by breaking both the women's speed record over a 100km closed circuit with 2,095kph, and the record over a 500km closed circuit with 1,826kph.

In the meantime, she had other exploits to her name. Flying a Lockheed

Jacqueline Cochran and her co-pilot, Wesley Smith, in October 1934, just before leaving on the London–Melbourne Race. Their Gee Bee QED was damaged on landing at Bucharest after the flaps failed, and they decided to withdraw from the race. (DR)

Jacqueline Cochran in discussion with Alexander Prokofiev de Seversky, known as 'Sasha', in front of the plane in which she won the 1938 Bendix Trophy. (DR, H. Hazewinkel collection)

Jacqueline Cochran and General Henry 'Hap' Arnold, at Avenger Field, on 6 December 1944, at the time of the final intake of WASPs. (USAF)

Jetstar executive jet, she had become the first woman to pilot a jet across the Atlantic, linking New Orleans and Hanover in 13hr 40min and, in the process, taking 32 international records and 36 women's records.

1. In Les Etoiles de Midi, p.393 (France Empire, 1955).
2. J. Cochran's childhood is obscure. According to certain sources, she was an adopted orphan, and did not know her date of birth.
3. This was a Northrop Gamma 2G, no. 11, registered as NC13761, built in August 1934 and purchased by J. Cochran on 30 September 1934.
4. This was the first time that this decoration had been awarded to a woman.

Jacqueline Cochran's records

26 July 1937, in a Beechcraft Staggerwing, women's 1,000km speed record: 328.067kph.

28 July 1937, in a Beechcraft Staggerwing: 322.945kph.

21 September 1937, in a Seversky SEV, speed record over 3km: 470.264kph.

3 December 1937, in a Seversky SEV, New York–Miami speed record: 4hr 12min 27sec.

13 December 1937, in a Seversky SEV, speed record: 411.811kph.

3 September 1938, in a Seversky SEV, Burbank–Brooklyn speed record: 10hr 27min 55sec.

3–5 September 1938, in a Seversky SEV, women's record for west–east crossing of United States: 10hr 27min 55sec.

24 March 1939, in a Beechcraft Staggerwing, women's altitude record: 9,160m.

10 December 1947, in a P-51, women's speed record over 100km course: 755.668kph.

17 December 1947, in a P-51, women's speed record over a 3km course: 663.054kph.

22 May 1948, in a P-51, world speed record over 2,000km: 720.134kph.

24 May 1948, in a P-51, women's speed record over 1,000km course: 693.780kph.

29 October 1949, in a P-51, speed record over a 500km course: 703.12kph.

29 December 1949, in a P-51, speed record over a 500km course: 703,376kph.

9 April 1951, in a P-51, women's 15/25km speed record: 747.339kph.

18 May 1953, in an F-86, speed record over 100km: 1,049.610kph; first woman to break the sound barrier.

3 June 1953, in an F-86, women's speed record over 15km course: 1,087.068kph.

24 August 1961, in a Northrop T-38, speed record over a 15km course: 1,358.32kph.

31 August 1961, in a Northrop T-38, speed record over a 500km closed circuit: 1,095.41kph.

8 September 1961, in a Northrop T-38, speed record over a 1,000km closed circuit: 1,028.99kph.

15 September 1961, in a Northrop T-38, women's distance record over a closed circuit: 2,166.770km.

18 September 1961, in a Northrop T-38, women's distance record in a straight line: 2,401.780km.

12 October 1961, in a Northrop T-38, women's altitude record in horizontal flight: 16,841m.

6 December 1961, in a Northrop T-38, women's speed record over 100km: 1,262.188kph.

12 April 1963, in a Lockheed F-104G, women's 15/25km speed record: 2,048.875kph.

2 May 1963, in a Lockheed TF-104G, speed record over a 100km closed circuit: 1,937.5kph.

11 May 1964, in a Lockheed F-104G, women's 15/25km speed record: 2,300.234kph.

1 June 1964, in a Lockheed F-104G, women's speed record over a 100km course: 2,097.266kph.

3 June 1964, in a Lockheed F-104G, women's 500km speed record: 1,814.368kph.

5 June 1964, in a Lockheed F-104G, women's speed record over a 100km closed circuit: 2,095kph, and over a 500km closed circuit: 1,826kph.

'The fastest woman in the world': Jacqueline Auriol

(1917-2000)

After her records in the Vampire and the Mistral, Jacqueline Auriol turned to Marcel Dassault's early jet fighters; here she is in MD450 Ouragan no. 105. (Dassault)

Jacqueline Auriol standing in front of the Mystère IVN in which she broke the speed record on 21 May 1955. (CEV)

Marignane on Saturday 12 May 1951; Jacqueline Auriol has just smashed the women's world speed record. The first Frenchwoman to pilot a jet aircraft has just covered a 100km circuit at an average speed of 818.181kph. She has suddenly become 'the fastest woman in the world'. Even with the passing of time, it is hard to believe it. There was nothing in this woman's background that would have led anyone to think that she might become such an exceptional aviatrix.

The daughter of a timber importer, Jacqueline Douet first saw the light of day on 5 November 1917 at Challans in the Vendée. After studying at the Blanche-de-Castille Institute in Nantes, she was destined for an artistic career and prepared for entry to the Ecole du Louvre. In 1938, she broke off her studies to marry Paul Auriol, son of Vincent Auriol who would become President of the Republic a few years later. The sophisticated world of the Elysée soon bored her. She was barely 30 years old when she decided to learn to fly, rapidly becoming consumed with a passion for aeroplanes. In 1948, she obtained her tourist pilot's licence. Following this, she made a start on aerobatics and soon became known through her activities to the public at large (Algiers–Dakar and the Auxerre Meeting, 1949). Unfortunately, this was not to last. On 12 July 1949, the little seaplane she was in somersaulted as it came down in the Seine. By some miracle, Jacqueline Auriol escaped, but was badly injured and disfigured. She underwent 32 surgical operations on her face. A year's hospitalisation in France and numerous operations in the United States failed to dampen her will to live.

Flying became her raison d'être. To take her revenge on a fate that had treated her so badly, she took up flying again with renewed vigour. She now had just one aim: to become a test pilot; on the face of it, an insurmountable challenge in this exclusively masculine world. She gained additional qualifications, including a helicopter licence, but it was not enough. She would have to get herself noticed through some significant exploit. What better than the world speed record? Before the war, it had succeeded in making Hélène Boucher's name (see p. 144). Her aim was to take the women's speed record over 100km from her American namesake, Jacqueline Cochran, who had broken it flying a piston-engined aircraft at an average speed of 765.688kph. Jacqueline Auriol now decided to make an attempt with a jet plane. She went into training at Istres, then Marignane, first on a piston-engined plane then later with a jet. On 30 April she was given authorisation to fly a De Havilland Vampire fighter. After a few training flights, she was ready for the big day. On 12 May, strapped into the narrow cockpit of the little British fighter, she gained the

Less well known were the executive-jet records set by Jacqueline Auriol on 10 June 1965, in a Dassault Mystère 20. (Dassault)

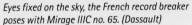

Eyes fixed on the sky, the French record breaker poses with Mirage IIIC no. 65. (Dassault)

It was in this Mirage IIIR that Jacqueline Auriol broke the 100km speed record with 2,038.7kph. (Dassault)

A discussion between test pilots: Jacqueline Auriol and René Bigand. (P. Gaillard collection)

coveted record for France with a speed of 818.181kph. In just 7min 20sec she covered the 100km course! This achievement won her the Harmon Trophy (see p. 186), the highest aeronautical distinction in the United States, receiving the trophy from Harry Truman in person.

Jacqueline Auriol now joined the narrow circle of test pilots and was admitted to the flight test centre at Brétigny-sur-Orge. The first thing she did was to improve on her own record, in December, with 855.92kph, winning her a second Harmon Trophy. Across the Atlantic, Jacqueline Cochran had no intention of letting things stand. An exciting long-distance duel now began between the two aviatrixes. On 19 May 1953, the American hit back with a speed of 1,050.182kph and then became the first woman to break the sound barrier. On 15 August 1953, Jacqueline Auriol became the first European woman to break the sound barrier, at the controls of a Dassault Mystère II. She was back, on the 31 May 1955, reaching 1,151kph in a Mystère IVN – a new world record![1] Cochran replied with 1,262kph, flying a Northrop T-38 (7 April 1961). Auriol riposted with 1,849.587kph, in June 1962, in a Mirage III. Cochran refused to let it stand there, flying a Lockheed Super Starfighter at 1,937.5kph in May 1963. Back came the Frenchwoman with 2,038.7kph. At this point, Jacqueline Auriol stopped and the last word went to Cochran who, on 1 June 1964, reached 2,097.266kph. The most extraordinary post-war duel had come to an end.

This did not stop Jacqueline Auriol from breaking one more record. In June 1965, as the Le Bourget Show was taking place, she flew a Mystère 20 executive jet at an average speed of 859kph. It was her last feat. Because of her age, she had to give up flying jets and finally took her retirement having flown a good 100 different types of aircraft. For all that, Jacqueline Auriol did not cut herself off from the world of aviation, devoting herself to promoting French aviation to which she had given her all and taken so much from. 'Live and fly', two verbs that sum up so well her career, were

used as the title of the memoirs that she published in 1968. Jacqueline Auriol died on 11 February 2000, at the age of 82. As Jacques Chirac said at her funeral service: 'Her name will forever be associated with the history of aviation and aeronautical research.'

1. From 1 June 1952, J. Cochran, at the time vice-president of the FAI, took the decision to abolish women's records (except for gliding records), leaving just a single category, taking no account of the sex of the holder. This rather crude decision assured her of the record in perpetuity.

Jacqueline Auriol's records

12 May 1951, in a D.H. Vampire, speed record over a 100km course: 818.181kph.

21 December 1952, in a SNCASE Mistral type 53, speed record over a 100km course: 855.92kph.

15 August 1953, in a Dassault Mystère IIC: the second aviatrix to break the sound barrier.

31 May 1955, in a Mystère IVN, women's 15/25km speed record: 1,151kph.

26 August 1959, in a Dassault Mirage III no. 01: first aviatrix to fly at more than Mach 2.

22 June 1962, in a Dassault Mirage IIIC, women's speed record over 100kph: 1,850.2kph.

14 June 1963, in a Dassault Mirage IIIR, speed record over 100km: 2,038.7kph.

10 June 1965, in a Mystère 20, speed records for executive jets: over a 1,000km closed circuit, 859.51kph, and over a 2,000km closed circuit, 819.13kph.

Assisted by the mechanics Bouillon and Gallière, Jacqueline Auriol gets out of the Mirage IIIC in which she jousted with Jacqueline Cochran. (CEV)

Jacqueline Auriol preparing for a flight in the Mirage IIIC no. 65 in which she beat the women's 100km speed record on 22 June 1962 with 1,850.2kph. (Dassault)

A native of the Yaroslavl region, Valentina Tereshkova began her career as a parachutist before joining the Soviet women's cosmonaut programme, along with three of her compatriots, in 1962. On her historic flight, she used the radio call sign 'Tchaika' (seagull). (DR)

Dutrieu, Harriet Quimby, Katherine Stinson, Blanche Scott, Ruth Law, Bessie Coleman, Adrienne Bolland, Florence Klingensmith, Laura Ingalls, Liesel Bach, Lady Heath, Lady Mary Bailey, Louise Thaden, Thea Rasche, Ruth Rowland Nichols, Elinor Smith, Ruth Elder, Carina Negrone, Paulina Denisovna Ossipenko, Hanna Reitsch, Marcelle Choisnet, Maryse Bastié, Léna Bernstein, Amy Johnson-Mollison, Anne Morrow-Lindbergh, Marga Von Etzdorf, Maryse Hilsz, Beryl Markham, Elly Beinhorn, Jean Batten, Elisabeth Lion, Helen Richey, Eugénie M. Shakhovskaya, Cecil W. "Teddy" Kenyon, Pauline Gower, Nancy Harkness Love, Maria Ivanovna Dolina, Amélia Earhart, Hélène Boucher, Jacqueline Cochran, Jacqueline Auriol, Eileen Marie Collins, Anna Walker, Ellen Church, Clara Adams, Harriet Quimby, Marjorie Stinson, Mrs Eyman, Fay Gillis, Virginia Waibel, Eleanor Blevins, Aniwegi Boudinot, Helen Clifford, Janett Moffett, Bernetta Miller, Ruth Fontes, Jeanne Pallier, Blossom Miles, Emily Schaeffer, Raymonde de Laroche, Amelie Beese, Hélène Dutrieu, Harriet Quimby, Katherine Stinson, Blanche Scott, Ruth Law, Bessie Coleman, Adrienne Bolland, Florence Klingensmith, Laura Ingalls, Liesel Bach, Lady Heath, Lady Mary Bailey, Louise Thaden, Thea Rasche, Ruth Rowland Nichols, Elinor Smith, Ruth Elder, Carina Negrone, Paulina Denisovna Ossipenko, Hanna Reitsch, Marcelle Choisnet, Maryse Bastié, Léna Bernstein, Amy Johnson-Mollison, Anne Morrow-Lindbergh, Marga Von Etzdorf, Maryse Hilsz, Beryl Markham, Elly Beinhorn, Jean Batten, Elisabeth Lion, Helen Eugénie Teddy Kenyon, Pauline Gower, Nancy Harkness Love, Maria Ivanovna Dolina, Amelia Earhart, Hélène Boucher, Jacqueline Cochran

Recent times

On Sunday 16 June 1963, on board *Vostok 6*, the Russian Valentina Tereshkova became the first woman to go into space, orbiting our planet 48 times. A new era was opening for our high-flying women. In its titanic struggle with the United States, the Soviet Union was always keen to score propaganda victories and this had undeniably been one. Not that the Americans had failed to consider this. In the very early 1960s, 25 women had been selected and put through the same tests as the male astronauts in the Mercury programme. This group had been progressively whittled down to 13 candidates,[1] known under the acronym of FLAT (First Lady Astronaut Trainees). Out of the blue, just a few days before they were due to go to the Naval Aeronautical Center in Pensacola (Florida) they each received a telegram informing them that the training programme had been cancelled. Two of them, Jerrie Cobb and Janey Hart, were unwilling to accept this decision and campaigned to save the programme, but without success. In the event, not one of the FLATs would go into space.

Making the front pages across the world, Valentina Tereshkova spent 71 hours aboard her spacecraft, more than the total for all the Mercury astronauts combined! Nonetheless, it was almost a further 20 years before we would see another woman in space, in the form of Svetlana Savitskaya who, on 19 August 1982, docked her Soyuz with the orbiting Salyut 7 station. However, it was for her second spaceflight that the cosmonaut gained fame when, in July 1984, she became the first woman

After undergoing 87 psychological and physical tests, Jerrie Cobb was the first American woman to qualify as an astronaut. She is seen here next to a model of the Mercury capsule. (NASA)

Yelena Viktorova Kondakova was the first Russian female cosmonaut to fly on the space shuttle, on mission STS-84, from 15–24 May 1997. (NASA)

Claudie Haigneré, the first French astronaut, went into space on two occasions. The first was on Soyuz TM-24/TM-23 on a flight to the Mir station (17 August–2 September 1996). The second was on Soyuz TM-33/TM-32 on a visit to the International Space Station (20–31 October 2001). She is seen here wearing the Russian style of space suit. (ESA)

Kalpana Chawla, the first astronaut of Indian origin, was on the shuttle Columbia *when it exploded on re-entry, on 1 February 2003. (NASA)*

to do a 'spacewalk.'

In the meantime, NASA had designed the space shuttle and, in parallel, launched a major astronaut-training programme, which included a number of women. From among these, the astrophysicist Sally Ride became the first American woman to go into space, on the seventh shuttle mission (STS-7) that lifted off from launch pad 39 at the Kennedy Space Center, on Saturday 18 June 1983. On 5 October 1984, Kathryn D. Sullivan became the first American woman to carry out a 'spacewalk' during a mission, in which Sally Ride also took part (mission STS-41G).

In January 1986, the tragic accident with the *Challenger* shuttle had a great impact on morale. One woman, Judith Resnik, was among the unfortunate crew. In the ensuing years, American women, as well as some

from other countries, took part in both American and Russian space flights. Among these were the first British female astronaut, Helen P. Sharman (18–26 May 1991 on board Soyuz TM-12/TM-11), the first Canadian woman, Roberta Bondar (22 January 1992, on board mission STS-42) and the first Frenchwoman, Claudie Haigneré (17 August–2 September 1996, on board Soyuz TM-24 and TM-23) (see Appendix 7, p.187).

1985 marked a turning point in the story of women in space. On its 73rd mission, from 3 to 11 February, the shuttle had a woman pilot for the first time, in the person of Eileen M. Collins. It was thus she who

Sally K. Ride, the first American woman to go into space, aboard the Challenger shuttle (mission STS-7), on 18 June 1983. (NASA/GRIN)

The first contingent of American women trainee astronauts, from left to right: Margaret Rhea Seddon, Kathryn D. Sullivan, Judith A. Resnik, Sally K. Ride, Ann L. Fisher and Shannon W. Lucid. (NASA)

Peggy A. Whitson, the first woman to be appointed as NASA Science Officer on the International Space Station, where she stayed for 184 days, from 7 June to 7 December 2002 (flights STS-111/113). (NASA)

Anousheh Ansari, the first space tourist, took advantage of the Russian Space Agency's offer of a place on the Soyuz vessel. Setting out on 18 September 2006, she spent 10 days on the European Space Station. The cost of the trip was $20 million. (JSC)

Sunita L. Williams has, at the time of writing, made only one journey into space (STS-116/117, from 9 December 2006 to 22 June 2007) but, at 195 days, it is the longest ever undertaken by a woman. (NASA)

Marta Bohn-Meyer was one of only two women to have flown the famous Lockheed SR-71 Blackbird, at NASA's Dryden Flight Research Center, located at Edwards AFB in California. Sadly, she was killed on 18 September 2005, in a crash while flying a Giles G-300 aerobatics plane. She was 48 years old. (NASA)

of jet airliners and, indeed, warplanes (see Chapter 8, p. 120). On 7 April 1975, in France, Danielle Décuré, having already flown Mystère 20s for Europe Falcon Air Service, became the first female flight captain with Air France, on an Airbus A.320.

The very closed world of test pilots was beginning to open its doors and women such as Pamela Melroy (a future astronaut), Susan Still, Lori Tanner and Marta Bohn-Meyer (one of the two women qualified to fly the famous Lockheed SR-71 Blackbird) were to be a breeding ground for enriching the astronaut corps.

In the field of nostalgia there are the female warbirds pilots, including the inimitable Sue Parish and more recently Anna Walker (see p. 159) who since 2009 has been authorised to fly the Hawker Hurricane belonging to Warbirds of Great Britain. Suzanne 'Sue' Parish was a being apart in

guided the giant bird on its return to land in the final stages of the mission. Four years later, the same Eileen Collins was the mission commander (mission STS-93, 22 July 1999). On 16 January 2003, a tragic end once again awaited the crew of the shuttle *Columbia* whose destruction caused the death of Kalpana Chawla, an Indo-American on her second mission, and Laurel B. Clark, who was making her first space flight.

Since then, women have been present on nearly every shuttle flight; to such an extent that NASA no longer makes any specific announcement to that effect. The media hardly registered the longest time in space by a woman, when Sunita L. Williams spent 195 days in space in 2006-2007, nor when Barbara R. Morgan became the first woman teacher in space, on 8 August 2007 aboard mission STS-118. At the time of writing, no fewer than six of these female astronauts have five space missions apiece on their record (see Appendix 7, p. 187). Although shuttle missions have now ceased,[2] NASA continues to recruit new astronauts for future missions.

The last few years have been marked by the appearance of a new type of astronaut, the tourist. Dubbed the first 'space tourist', the American-Iranian Anousheh Ansari[3] is the managing director of Telecom Technologies Inc. In September 2006, she treated herself (for a mere $20 million) to a ride on the Russian Space Agency's 14th mission to the International Space Station (ISS), staying aboard for 10 days 21 hours. At the same time, back on Earth, other women were taking the controls

Joan Higginbotham poses proudly in front of one of NASA's Northrop T-38As. At the time of writing, she has journeyed just once into space, on 1 December 2006, accompanied by Sunita L. Williams. (NASA)

The first class of female USAF pilots on the completion of their training on two-seater Northrop T-38As at Williams AFB, Arizona. (USAF)

the world of aviation. She began flying lessons at the age of 19 and was only 21 when she tried to join the WASPs, but was rejected by Jacqueline Cochran as being too young. Amassing flying hours, she would not rest until she had joined the ranks of women pilots in the Air Force. She was not lacking in persistence and was finally accepted at the sixth attempt in 1944. Six months later the war was over and she was sent home. She soon became involved in the world of aircraft collecting and Frank Saunders restored a Curtiss P-40 fighter for her, painting it in pink.[4] Flying this plane, Sue Parish took part in countless air meetings over more than 20 years, including the legendary Oshkosh Show. In 1974, she swapped her P-40 for a Cessna Citation, 'this poor thing being unable to cope with anything more' as she put it.[5] In 1977, Sue and her husband founded the soon-to-be-famous Kalamazoo Air Zoo, which maintains numerous Second World War combat planes in working order.

On 9 June 1967, Ann Pellegreno, in a Lockheed 10A (registration no. N79237), took off from Oakland to repeat A.E.'s journey, arriving back in Oakland on 7 July (William Polhemus, navigator, and Leo Koepke, mechanic). In 1997, to commemorate the 60th anniversary of Amelia Earhart's failed circumnavigation attempt (see p. 140), Linda Finch, a 46-year-old businesswoman from San Antonio, Texas, repeated the flight. Leaving Oakland on 17 March 1997, she travelled some 45,600km at the controls of a Lockheed L-10E Electra and returned to land at her departure point on 28 May. It is difficult to make an accurate estimate of the number of women flyers in the world today, but if the FAA's

Linda Finch on her arrival at Le Bourget in 1997. She was flying a Lockheed L-10E Electra similar to that used by Amelia Earhart in 1937 on her ill-fated expedition. (Pierre Gaillard)

figures[6] are to be believed, there are around 37,000 female pilots in the United States, of which 5,600 are airline pilots. While this figure may sound impressive, it represents barely 5% of the total number of qualified pilots in a country where aviation is particularly developed.

With her pink Curtiss P-40 and her flowery hat, Sue Parish is unlikely to go unnoticed at air meetings. She is seen here signing autographs at the Madera (California) meeting on 7 August 1989. (A. Pelletier)

1. They were: Myrtle K. Cagle, Jerrie Cobb, Jan Dietrich, Marion Dietrich, Wally Funk, Sarah Gorelick, Janey Hart, Jean Hixson, Rhea Hurrle, Irene Leverton, Jerri Sloan, Gene N. Stombough and Bernice B. Trimble Steadman.
2. The space shuttle's final mission began on 2 May 2011.
3. Anousheh Ansari was born in Tehran in 1967 and emigrated to the United States in 1984, where she took American citizenship.
4. The colour of the sand in the Libyan desert.
5. In Aviation for Women, Sept-Oct 1999.
6. Statistics of the Federal Aviation Administration for 2009.

A new kind of aviatrix has recently made her appearance, in the form of drone pilots. Here, Major Tammy Barlette poses with one of 214th Reconnaissance Group's drones, at Davis-Monthan AFB. (USAF)

One idea in mind: Eileen Marie Collins

(Born in 1956)

On 15 May 1997, Eileen Marie Collins prepares to take part in a space mission aboard the Atlantis shuttle (mission STS-84). (NASA/KSC)

'I took out my pen and it floated in the air. I said to myself, that's it. I'm in space!'[1] This was 3 February 1995. The shuttle *Discovery* had lifted off from its launch pad on a new mission (STS-63). It was the first of the new Russian/American space programme. It included a rendezvous with the Russian Mir space station, putting one satellite into orbit and retrieving another. On board Discovery, six astronauts had taken their places, the one woman, Eileen Collins, being the pilot.

Eileen Marie Collins was the second American astronaut to go into space, after Sally Ride. Hailing from Elmira in New York State, she had caught the aviation bug at a very early age, spending hours sitting on the bonnet of her father's car watching planes taking off from the runway of the nearby aerodrome. Hence, as soon as she'd saved up enough money from her job in a pizzeria, she started taking flying lessons. She was 19 years old when she first climbed into a plane, with just one idea in mind: to become a professional pilot, or more precisely, a military pilot. By chance, her ambition coincided with the decision taken by the Navy (1974) and later the Air Force (1976) to open military aviation to women.

Eileen Collins entered Corning Community College, New York to add a mathematics diploma to her qualifications, a necessary step before joining the ROTC (Reserve Officer Training Corps). With that, she entered the University of Syracuse, leaving in 1978, with a string of qualifications in maths and economics. The long journey to fame was only just beginning. In January 1990, after a ruthless selection process, she became one of four women (out of 120 candidates) to get into the air training school at Vance Air Force Base, Oklahoma. There, she became the first female Air Force instructor. There followed three years (1983-1985) at Travis AFB, as the captain of a four-engined C-141 Starlifter jet aircraft, then four years as a maths teacher and instructor on Cessna T-41s at the Air Force Academy. Having amassed hundreds of hours flying time and gained several new diplomas, Eileen Collins was accepted into the holy of holies of American aviation, the Test Pilots' School at Edwards AFB, in California. It was there, in January 1990, that she was selected by NASA to become an astronaut.

She then had to submit to the testing, intensive, basic training undergone by all astronauts. However, before going aboard the shuttle, she had to hold a number of posts on the ground, designed to prepare her for her first space flight planned for early 1995. For this first flight on *Discovery* (mission STS-63, from 3 to 11 February 1995), Eileen Collins was allotted the role of shuttle pilot. This meant that she was responsible for guiding the huge spacecraft in its gliding flight back to Earth. For this mission, she was awarded the prestigious Harmon Trophy for that year, in recognition of an impressive aeronautical achievement.

The second mission, aboard the *Atlantis* (STS-84, from 15 to 24 May 1997), incorporated a rendezvous to resupply the Russian space station Mir. Collins was the commander on her third mission, aboard *Columbia* (STS-93, from 22 to 27 July 1999). This shuttle mission began somewhat badly: shortly after lift-off, two of the three engines failed. The shuttle escaped this dangerous situation thanks to its commander's complete calm, despite a further problem with a fuel leak causing the third engine to overheat. She concluded her career as an astronaut with a fourth mission, once again on board *Discovery* (STS-114, from 26 July to 9 August 2005), during which she docked the shuttle with the International Space Station. The mission lasted two weeks and covered 5.8 million kilometres.

On 30 October 2003, Colonel Eileen M. Collins has just arrived in a Northrop T-38A at the Kennedy Space Center, where she is due to take part in space-shuttle mission STS-114. (NASA/KSC)

When she left NASA in May 2006, Eileen Collins was 50 years old. She had flown 872 hours in space. Despite her fame, she had always kept her family life out of the public eye. Married to a pilot, whom she had met when they were both instructors in California, she is the mother of two children – a boy and a girl – who have always thought that 'all moms fly space shuttles.'

1. Quoted by Al Weisel in US Weekly.

The official portrait of Eileen M. Collins as the space shuttle's mission commander on STS-93. She is wearing the distinctive orange suit used by American astronauts. (NASA/GRIN)

Riding the 'hurricane': Anna Walker

(Born in 1962)

On Sunday 23 May 2010, a superb Hawker Hurricane[1] lined itself up on the grass runway at La Ferté-Alais and took off to the roar of its Rolls-Royce Merlin engine. At the controls was one of the rare female warbird pilots, Anna Walker. Probably the first woman to fly this kind of aircraft since the Second World War, Anna Walker was born in Brazil to an Anglo-Danish father and an Italo-Brazilian mother. From a young age, she had of necessity been involved in flying, thanks to the huge size of the country, in which the aeroplane was generally the most appropriate means of transport.

Following her three brothers, Anna was soon learning to fly; first gliders, then towing planes. She was then just 13. Obliged to wait because of her age until she could take her pilot's licence, she turned to go-karting, a sport that was flourishing at this time, though a few years later to suffer a decline thanks to the sudden withdrawal of its sponsors, forcing the young woman to end a promising career.

Working for the family firm, Anna travelled in Brazil and to the United States, arriving in Britain in 1984 to finish her education, which led to a job in international commerce and shipbuilding. In 1988, she took the opportunity to obtain her private pilot's qualification and joined the famous Tiger Club based at Redhill, where she started aerobatics training. The following year, while flying a De Havilland Tiger Moth, she was the victim of a crash, which resulted in the near-destruction of the precious

Along with Carolyn Grace, Anna Walker is one of only two female warbird pilots in Europe. (A. Bréand)

biplane. By way of 'apology' she bought another Tiger Moth a few weeks later and lent it to the club.

A year later, Anna decided to replace her limited-performance Tiger Moth with a rather friskier Bücker Jungmann[2] bought jointly with Peter Kynsey of the Historic Aircraft Collection (HAC). Flying this plane, she won her first aerobatics competition in 1992, followed by several others, giving her the opportunity to perform at air meetings.

Founder and chief pilot of the aeronautical company Skytricks, Anna Walker demonstrates vintage planes at meetings, the most recent at the time of writing being the HAC's Hawker Hurricane, on which she was given free rein in June 2009.

1. Hawker Hurricane Mark XII, number Z5140, registration G-HURI.
2. Bücker Bü 131, built under licence in Spain by CASA in 1954, registration G-BSAJ.

Anna Walker learned to fly gliders in Brazil at the age of 13. (A. Bréand)

Strapped into the tight cockpit of her Hurricane, Anna Walker prepares for take-off from the runway at La Ferté Alais, during the 2010 meeting. (A. Bréand)

Before Anna Walker got her hands on a Hurricane, the last women to fly these planes had been the ATA pilots in the Second World War. (A. Bréand)

Sarah M. Deal was the first helicopter pilot in the US Marine Corps. She is seen here standing next to a Bell TH-57 Sea Ranger from the Pensacola Navy base in Florida, in 1963. (USMC)

Flying a Bell Super Cobra, Captain Jessica M. Moore operated in Iraq during 2005, with the Marines' 167th Light Helicopter Squadron (HMLA-167). (USMC)

The 'Whirly Girls' make a name for themselves

For many years, Hanna Reitsch remained the only woman helicopter pilot, having flown the Focke-Achgelis since 1938. It wasn't until the end of the Second World War and the development of this kind of aircraft that another woman helicopter pilot appeared on the scene, in the shape of Ann Shaw Carter, who gained her licence in 1947. However, very few other women followed in her footsteps.

In spring 1955, the International Women Helicopter Pilots (Whirly Girls), which was founded by Jean Ross Howard, had just about a dozen members, including Dora J. Dougherty, who worked in the Bell Aircraft design office and, having flown only 34 hours on helicopters, broke in quick succession two world records: the altitude record with 5,915m and the straight-line distance record with 650km. The group soon began to grow and quickly reached 35 members. But this was just the beginning: by February 2007, there were no fewer than 1,455 women helicopter pilots from 43 countries. Today, there are women helicopter pilots in all the areas where this type of machine is used, from air-ambulance to combat helicopters via transport and air-sea rescue.

Left Lieutenant Terry J. Kindness flies an Aerospatiale HH-65 Dolphin from the Coast-Guard station at Port Angeles. (USCG)

Centre Born in 1971 at Seclin, Juliette Bouchez has been French helicopter champion eight times (1991, 1995-2001) flying Hughes 300s. (A. Bréand)

Right Jacqueline Auriol familiarising herself with one of the very first helicopters, the Bell 47D-1. (DR)

Dutrieu, Harriet Quimby, Katherine Stinson, Blanche Scott, Ruth Law, Bessie Coleman, Adrienne Bolland, Florence Klingensmith, Laura Ingalls, Liesel Bach, Lady Heath, Lady Mary Bailey, Louise Thaden, Thea Rasche, Ruth Rowland Nichols, Elinor Smith, Ruth Elder, Carina Negrone, Paulina Denisovna Ossipenko, Hanna Reitsch, Marcelle Choisnet, Maryse Bastié, Léna Bernstein, Amy Johnson-Mollison, Anne Morrow-Lindbergh, Marga Von Etzdorf, Maryse Hilsz, Beryl Markham, Elly Beinhorn, Jean Batten, Elisabeth Lion, Helen Richey, Eugénie M. Shakhovskaya, Cecil W. "Teddy" Kenyon, Pauline Gower, Nancy Harkness Love, Maria Ivanovna Dolina, Amélia Earhart, Hélène Boucher, Jacqueline Cochran, Jacqueline Auriol, Eileen Marie Collins, Anna Walker, Ellen Church, Clara Adams, Harriet Quimby, Marjorie Stinson, Mrs Eyman, Fay Gillis, Virginia Waibel, Eleanor Blevins, Aniwegi Boudinot, Helen Clifford, Janett Moffett, Bernetta Miller, Ruth Fontes, Jeanne Pallier, Blossom Miles, Emily Schaeffer, Raymonde de Laroche, Amelie Beese, Hélène Dutrieu, Harriet Quimby, Katherine Stinson, Blanche Scott, Ruth Law, Bessie Coleman, Adrienne Bolland, Florence Klingensmith, Laura Ingalls, Liesel Bach, Lady Heath, Lady Mary Bailey, Louise Thaden, Thea Rasche, Ruth Rowland Nichols, Elinor Smith, Ruth Elder, Carina Negrone, Paulina Denisovna Ossipenko, Hanna Reitsch, Marcelle Choisnet, Maryse Bastié, Léna Bernstein, Amy Johnson-Mollison, Anne Morrow-Lindbergh, Marga Von Etzdorf, Maryse Hilsz, Beryl Markham, Elly Beinhorn, Jean Batten, Elisabeth Lion, Helen Richey, Cecil W. "Teddy" Kenyon, Pauline Gower, Nancy Harkness Love, Maria Ivanovna Dolina, Amélia Earhart, Hélène Boucher, Jacqueline Cochran, Jacqueline Auriol, Eileen Marie Collins, Anna

And many others...

E. Lilian Todd was one of the first women to design an aeroplane. She is seen here, in 1908, showing one of her models at the Aeronautical Society's exhibition at Morris Park, New Jersey. However, none of Miss Todd's constructions ever managed to leave the ground. (LoC)

During the First World War and the 1920s, the aeronautical industry made considerable use of female labour, especially for the fabric covering, a task at which they excelled. Here, at Boeing's Seattle plant, workers are finishing the wing covering of an MB-3A fighter. (Boeing)

The contribution of women to the history of aviation is not restricted to the achievements of those who have made the front pages of the newspapers or who have astonished the public watching them at air shows. Many more women than this have played an important part in the great epic of aviation. Whether hostesses, workers, stuntwomen, engineers or company bosses, they have always been there – sometimes discreet – but always effective.

A worker at the Vega Aircraft Corporation in Burbank, California gives the glazed nose cone of a Boeing B-17F Flying Fortress a final polish, before it is delivered to an operational unit. (Lockheed)

Some women found their way into laboratories or design offices. One such was Pearl I. Young who, after outstanding results in physics, chemistry and mathematics, joined NACA in 1922, where she was sent to the Langley Research Center, under the direction of Henry J. E. Reid. During the 28 years she spent at Langley, she set up the service responsible for preparing and distributing research reports and official documents that contributed to establishing NACA's, and the NASA's image. (NASA)

During the Second World War, the aeronautical industry made use of female labour to ensure production of the phenomenal quantity of aircraft ordered by the belligerents. In the United States, the propaganda surrounding their contribution gave rise to the character of 'Rosie the Riveter'. Here, an unknown worker in the Vultee plant in Nashville, Tennessee, drills holes in the skin of an A-35 Vengeance bomber. (LoC)

Two employees of the Curtiss-Wright Corporation check the undercarriage of a C-46 Commando cargo plane. (USAF)

In the Second World War, many women were employed as mechanics with operational units, as seen here in a photograph showing two mechanics working on the engine of an Australian Curtiss P-40 fighter. (RAAF)

During the war, 'flying nurses' gave invaluable service, flying thousands of kilometres giving aid to wounded soldiers brought back from the front. Here, some of them are undergoing training at the Bowman Field air-ambulance school, in Kentucky. (USAF)

Aircraft and their pilots depend greatly on ground handling services. In times of conflict, they are even more crucial. In 1942, Eloise J. Ellis was the head of the Assembly and Repairs Department at the big Navy base at Corpus Christie, Texas. (LoC)

In April 1932, in the middle of the Great Depression, Walter Beech and his wife Olive Ann, whom he had married when he was managing the Travel Air Airplane Manufacturing Company, founded the Beech Aircraft Company, whose first model was the Beech 17R Staggerwing. When Walter Beech died in 1950, Olive Ann took over the firm, running it masterfully until 1968 when she took a well-deserved retirement. (Beech)

165

The first
air hostess:
Ellen Church

(1904–1965)

Boeing Air Transport's (BAT) first eight hostesses standing in front of a Boeing 80. Ellen Church is the third from the left. (Boeing)

To be a pilot had been Ellen Church's dream. The young nurse from Iowa had satisfied her passion for flying by taking lessons, and it was with the idea of becoming a pilot that she turned up in San Francisco, licence in hand, to see Steve Simpson, the representative of Boeing Air Transport (BAT). Unfortunately, the idea of women as airline pilots was still very far from most people's minds. Disappointed, but by no means discouraged, Ellen Church suggested another idea: why not have qualified nurses on board planes to look after passengers and help them overcome their fear? The notion appealed to Steve Simpson who saw it as good publicity and a way of attracting new customers. He quickly convinced senior management of its merits and by the spring of 1930 BAT had taken on eight nurses for a three-month trial period. It was thus on 15 May 1930 that Ellen Church became the world's first air hostess, as part of the crew of a Boeing 80 on the Oakland–Chicago route. It was a complete success and other airlines were quick to follow Boeing's lead.

At the time, the recruitment criteria for hostesses (or stewardesses, as they were then called) were very strict. In addition to being qualified nurses, candidates had to be single, less than 25 years old, weigh no more than 52kg and be no taller than 1.62m. As well as attending to sick passengers' needs, they had various other tasks such as loading the luggage, overseeing refuelling, checking tickets, cleaning the cabin and even helping ground crews push the planes into the hangars. For all this, they were paid $125 a month.

In the event, Ellen Church's career as an air hostess did not last long – a mere 18 months. After a car accident, she went on to complete her studies at the University of Minnesota and pursue her career as a nurse. She did not board a plane again until 1942 when she joined the Army Nurse Corps. With the return of peace, she settled in Terre Haute, Indiana and it was here that she died in 1965 after falling from a horse.

A special passenger: Clara Adams

(1884-1971)

Pilots are not the only ones in aviation to break records. Some passengers also get in on the act. One such was Clara Adams, a wealthy American widow who, throughout her life, did her best to collect aeronautical firsts, of all kinds. Born in 1884, in Cincinnati, Ohio, this granddaughter of Augusta von Hindenburg made her first flight in 1914 at Lake Eutis, Florida. In 1928, she was the first female who was a paying passenger to cross the Atlantic in the German airship *Graf Zeppelin*, a trip that cost a trifling $3,000! In 1931, she flew to Rio de Janeiro just to be the first female paying passenger in the huge Dornier Do X flying boat. In 1936, she was aboard the airship *Hindenburg* for its inaugural flight. The following year, she was among the passengers on the Boeing China Clipper flying boat for its first flight across the Pacific. The same year, she took part in the Boeing Hawaii Clipper's first regular flight to Hawaii. In 1936 alone, Clara Adams flew 43,000km. In 1939, she was the first female passenger to complete a round-the-world trip, in 16 days 19hr 8min 10sec. Finally, in 1940, she was on board the TWA Boeing Stratoliner on the occasion of its first trans-continental flight. The war put an end to the travels of this special passenger who, by the time of her death at the age of 87, had flown more than 240,000km.

In 1936, Clara Adams spent $3,000 to be among the passengers on the inaugural flight of the Hindenburg airship to the United States. (Curtiss Museum)

Dutrieu, Harriet Quimby, Katherine Stinson, Blanche Scott, Ruth Law, Bessie Coleman, Adrienne Bolland, Florence Klingensmith, Laura Ingalls, Liesel Bach, Lady Heath, Lady Mary Bailey, Louise Thaden, Thea Rasche, Ruth Rowland Nichols, Elinor Smith, Ruth Elder, Carina Negrone, Paulina Denisovna Ossipenko, Hanna Reitsch, Marcelle Choisnet, Maryse Bastié, Léna Bernstein, Amy Johnson-Mollison, Anne Morrow-Lindbergh, Marga Von Etzdorf, Maryse Hilsz, Beryl Markham, Elly Beinhorn, Jean Batten, Elisabeth Lion, Helen Richey, Eugénie M. Shakhovskaya, Cecil W. "Teddy" Kenyon, Pauline Gower, Nancy Harkness Love, Maria Ivanovna Dolina, Amélia Earhart, Hélène Boucher, Jacqueline Cochran, Jacqueline Auriol, Eileen Marie Collins, Anna Walker, Ellen Church, Clara Adams, Harriet Quimby, Marjorie Stinson, Mrs Eyman, Fay Gillis, Virginia Waibel, Eleanor Blevins, Aniwegi Boudinot, Helen Clifford, Janett Moffett, Bernetta Miller, Ruth Fontes, Jeanne Pallier, Blossom Miles, Emily Schaeffer, Raymonde de Laroche, Amelie Beese, Hélène Dutrieu, Harriet Quimby, Katherine Stinson, Blanche Scott, Ruth Law, Bessie Coleman, Adrienne Bolland, Florence Klingensmith, Laura Ingalls, Liesel Bach, Lady Heath, Lady Mary Bailey, Louise Thaden, Thea Rasche, Ruth Rowland Nichols, Elinor Smith, Ruth Elder, Carina Negrone, Paulina Denisovna Ossipenko, Hanna Reitsch, Marcelle Choisnet, Maryse Bastié, Léna Bernstein, Amy Johnson-Von Beinhorn, Batten, Elisabeth Lion, Helen Richey, Eugénie M. Shakhovskaya, Cecil W. Teddy Nancy Harkness Love, Maria Ivanovna Dolina, Amelia Earhart, Hélène Boucher, Jacqueline Cochran, Jacqueline Auriol, Eileen Marie Collins, Anna

So many forgotten faces...

Beyond the dozen or so aviatrixes who achieved a degree of fame, there were hundreds of others who lived in more or less complete obscurity. Nonetheless, these women had their role to play in the history of aviation. Today, just a few scattered photographs remain as testimony to their existence...

Fay Gillis who spent a large part of her career in Russia. (NASM)

Mrs Eyman and 'Laddie Boy', in 1918.

Aniwegi Boudinot. (LoC)

Bernetta Miller in front of a Blériot XI from John Moisant's Hempstead Plains flying school on Long Island. (LoC)

Janett Moffett, daughter of the well-known admiral, learned to fly in 1923, with Lt. Rittenhouse as her instructor. (LoC)

Virginia Waibel at the controls of a rather showily decorated aircraft. (LoC)

Emily Schaeffer, accompanied by Geo Burgess, before going up in a Curtiss Jenny. (LoC)

The French aviatrix Jeanne Pallier who became a qualified pilot on 3 August 1912. (DR)

The British flyer Ruth Fontes and her brother Luis, with her Miles Hawk at the 1935 King's Cup Race. (H. Hazewinkel collection)

The English aviatrix Blossom Miles, pilot, designer, aerodynamicist and co-director with her husband, F.G. Miles, of Phillips and Powis Aircraft Ltd. (H. Hazewinkel collection)

Appendices

Aviatrixes in flying competitions 1926-2010

Women competed in numerous flying contests, some of which were exclusive to them. The main ones are listed here with the names of the aviatrixes, the types of plane used, as well as the positions and performances.

I – French competitions

Tour de France – 3,700km – Organiser: Le Journal & l'Union des pilotes civils de France

Date	Aviatrix	Plane	Reg.	No.	Posn.	Performance
25/4-10/5/1931	Maryse Hilsz	Moth-Morane	F-AJOE	-	8th	139.680 km/h
	Maryse Bastié	Caudron 230	F-ALOF	-	24th	114.840 km/h
21-30/7/1933	Alek Plunian	Farman 359	F-ALMK	9	disqualified	-

Les Douze Heures d'Angers – 40 km triangular circuit – Organiser: Aéro-Club de l'Ouest

Date	Aviatrix	Plane	Reg.	N°	Posn.	Performance
2/7/1933	Finat/Alek Plunian	Farman 359	F-ALMK	16	2nd	2,385 km
	Hélène Boucher/Jacob	Mauboussin M.120	-	3	14th	1,645 km
8/7/1934	Hélène Boucher	Caudron 530	-	-	2nd	2,821 km
	Viviane Elder	Farman 402	F-AMTF	-	7th	2,051 km
	Madeleine Charnaux	Miles Hawk	F-AMZW	-	8th	2,023 km
7/7/1935	Marthe de Lacombe	Maillet 20	F-ANQY	1	6th	2,624 km
	Geneviève du Manoir	Caudron Aiglon	F-ANSH	14	7th	2,306 km
	Viviane Elder	Caudron Aiglon	F-ANVN	8	9th	-
	Madeleine Charnaux	Caudron Aiglon	F-ANAR	10	withdrew	
5/7/1936	Élisabeth Lion (cat. 8 litres)	Caudron Aiglon	F-ANSK	83	2nd	1,070 km
	Suzanne Pelissier* (cat. 2 litres)	Gaucher 40T	F-AOZY	18	6th	593 km
	Andrée Dupeyron (cat. 8 litres)	Caudron Aiglon	F-ANSI	85	abandoned	-

Teamed with Barrelli.

Circuit de l'Est – Vittel – Organiser: ACF & various aero-clubs

Date	Aviatrix	Plane	Reg.	N°	Posn.	Performance
16/8/1937	Élisabeth Lion	Caudron Aiglon	F-ANSK	13	4th	1,483 km
	Francine Tuefferd	Caudron Aiglon	F-AOKX	3	abandoned	-
	Andrée Dupeyron	Caudron Aiglon	F-ANSI	1	withdrew	-
	Elisabeth-Louise Spitzer	Percival Gull Four	F-AQLZ	12	withdrew	-

Coupe Hélène Boucher – Buc-Cannes (694km) – Organisers: ACF & Aéro-Club de Cannes

Date	Aviatrix	Plane	Reg.	N°	Posn.	Performance
31/8/1935	Maryse Hilsz	Breguet 27-4	F-ANHM		1st	277.263 km/h
	Claire Roman	Maillet-Lignel 21	F-AODA		2nd	251.403 km/h
	Béatrice MacDonald	Miles Hawk Major	G-ADAB		3rd	213.606 km/h
	Yvonne Jourjon	Maillet 20	F-ANQY		4th	209.359 km/h
	Andrée Dupeyron	Caudron Aiglon	F-ANSI		abandoned	-
	Mlle de Franqueville	Caudron Aiglon	F-ANZR		abandoned	-
	Marthe de la Combe	Caudron Simoun	F-...		abandoned	-
29/8/1936	Maryse Hilsz	Caudron-Renault 680-5	F-ANAM		1st	366.760 km/h
	Claire Roman	Maillet-Lignel 21	F-AODA		2nd	268.325 km/h
	Yvonne Jourjon	Maillet-Lignel 20	F-ANQY		3rd	232.530 km/h
	Geneviève du Manoir	Caudron Aiglon	F-ANSH		4th	210.668 km/h
	Andrée Dupeyron	Caudron Aiglon	F-ANSI		5th	207.079 km/h
	Élisabeth Lion	Caudron Aiglon	F-ANSK		6th	185.700 km/h

Rallye international féminin – Destination: Deauville – Organiser: ACF

Date	Aviatrix	Plane	Reg.	N°	Posn.	Performance
24-25/7/1953	Janette Poujade	Nord 1203 Norécrin	F-BBKD		1st	75.9 pts
	Berthe Lorrette	Nord 1203 Norécrin			2nd	69.6 pts
	Marcelle Dormois	Minicab			3rd	61.2 pts
	Mlle Mourgeon	Minicab			4th	55 pts
	Andrée Dupeyron	SIPA 91			5th	53.1 pts
	Jacqueline Herbinière	SIPA 901 Minicab			6th	43.4 pts
	Micheline Tessier	Nord 1203 Norécrin			7th	42.1 pts
	Yvonne Jourjon	Ercoupe			8th	41.8 pts
	Mme Arnaud	Piper Family			9th	33 pts
	Mlle Hansen (DK)	KZ-VII			10th	24.5 pts
	Mme Van Hulsen-Doesie (NL)	Ercoupe			11th	19 pts
	Mme Newmark	Taylorcraft			12th	3.4 pts
	Mme Kries (NL)	Fairchild			13th	2.9 pts
	Lily Irvine (G.-B.)	D.H.89 Dragon			14th	1.792 pt
	Mlle Denise	Nord 1203 Norécrin			15th	1.692 pt
24/7/1954	Marie-Gabrielle Nicolas	Nord 1203 Norécrin	F-BEBN		1st	62.86 pts
	Marcelle Dormois	Minicab			2nd	52.50 pts
	Mlle Mourgeon	Minicab			3rd	46.98 pts
	Mlle Muller	Minicab			4th	30.12 pts
	Jacqueline Moucaud	Minicab			5th	21.90 pts
	Mme Kries (NL)	Fairchild			6th	12.92 pts
	Françoise Feuillet	Percival Proctor			7th	7.21 pts
	Mme Arnaud	Piper Pacer			8th	4.45 pts
	Mlle Denise	SIPA 901			9th	3.92 pts
	Lily Irvine (G.-B.)	D.H.89 Dragon			10th	0.90 pt
9/1955	Marie-Gabrielle Nicolas				1st	-

Reg.: civil registration. - No: race number. - Posn.: unless otherwise indicated, this is the position in the overall classification. - Performance: time, distance, average speed or number of points.

II – British Competitions

Nottingham Meeting

Date	Aviatrix	Plane	Reg.	No.	Posn.	Performance
23-28/7/1927	S.C. Eliott-Lynn	D.H.60 Moth	G-EBMV	9	1st	-
	Lady Bailey	D.H.60 Moth	G-EBPU	3	2nd	-
	Miss O'Brien	D.H.60 Moth	G-EBLI	28	3rd	-
	Miss Poppy Short	Avro Avian II	G-EBRS	8	abandoned	-

King's Cup Race – Organiser: Royal Aero Club

Date	Aviatrix	Plane	Reg.	Nº	Posn.	Performance
30/7/1927	S.C. Eliott-Lynn	Avro Avian II	G-EBRS	8	abandoned	-
	Lady M. Bailey	D.H.60 Moth	G-EBPU	3	abandoned	-
21/7/1928	Winifred E. Spooner	D.H.60 Moth	G-EBOT	37	3rd	16hr 0min 33sec
5/7/1929	Winifred E. Spooner	D.H.60G Gipsy Moth	G-AAAL	32	5th	16hr 36min 50sec
	Lois Butler	D.H.60G Coupé Moth	G-AACL	35	14th	17hr 17min 34sec
	Lady Bailey	D.H.60G Coupé Moth	G-AAEE	6	21st	18hr 30min 16sec
5/7/1930	Winifred S. Brown	Avro Avian III	G-EBVZ	55	1st	165.24 km/h
	Winifred E. Spooner	Southern Martlet	G-AAYZ	65	14th	201.93 km/h
	C. M. Young	D.H.60G Gipsy Moth	G-ABA	49	30th	159.77 km/h
	Lady Bailey	D.H.60 Moth	G-AAEE	123	53rd	162.83 km/h
	Diana C. Guest	D.H.80A Puss Moth	G-AAZP	186	abandoned	-
	F.M. Wood	D.H.60G Gipsy Moth	G-AAGI	99	withdrew	-
	Lois Butler	D.H.80A Puss Moth	G-AAXL	-	-	-
25/7/1931	F.J. Crossley	D.H.60G Gipsy Moth	G-AAKC	6	20th	143.60 km/h
	Diana C. Guest	D.H.60G Gipsy Moth	G-ABHM	26	abandoned	-
	Winifred S. Brown	Avro Avian Sport	G-ABED	32	abandoned	-
	Lady Bailey	D.H.80A Puss Moth	G-AAYA	39	abandoned	-
9/7/1932	Winifred E. Spooner	D.H.60G Gipsy Moth	G-AAYL	6	15th	183.02 km/h
	Winifred S. Brown	Avro Avian Sport	G-ABED	16	21st	189.06 km/h
8/7/1933	Lois Butler	D.H.85 Leopard Moth	G-ACHB	24	6th	218.98 km/h
15/7/1934	G. Patterson	Miles M.2 Hawk	G-ACIZ	41	abandoned	-
6-7/9/1935	Ruth Fontes	Miles M.2U Hawk	G-ADOD	7	abandoned	-
	Elise Battye	Miles M.2H Hawk Major	G-ADLA	29	abandoned	-
10-11/7/1936	Mrs J.A. Mollison	B.A. Eagle 2	G-ACRG	25	abandoned	-
10/9/1937	Miss L. Dillon	Percival Vega Gull	G-AEYD	13	unplaced	-
30/7/1949	Miss R.M. Sharpe	Miles M.28 Mercury IV	G-AGVX	8	unplaced	-
	E. Lettice Curtis	Percival Proctor II	G-ALIS	11	unplaced	-
17/6/1950	Mrs M.M. Rendall	D.H.89A Rapide	G-ALBB	25	abandoned	-
	Lady Sherborne	Percival Vega Gull	G-AFBC	30	28th	244.57 km/h
	Miss R.M. Sharpe	S. Spitfire F. Mk.VB	G-AISU	40	abandoned	*
19/6/1954	Miss Freydis M. Leaf	Hawk Major	G-ACYO	45	3rd	222.04 km/h
14/7/1957	Miss Aurey A. Windle	D.H.82	G-AOAA	-	22nd	172.16 km/h
	Margo A. McKelllar	D.H.82	G-ANZZ	-	25th	177.79 km/h
11/7/1959	Margo A. McKellar	Turbulent	G-APBZ	-	8th	147.22 km/h
8-9/7/1960	Gillian M. Cazalet	D.H.82	G-ANPK	24	12th	176.18 km/h
	Sheila Scott	Jackaroo	G-APAM	52	19th	162.51 km/h
15/7/1961	Sheila Scott	-			20th	171.36 km/h
18/8/1962	Sheila Scott	Cessna 175	G-ARFL	91	15th	230.48 km/h
5/8/1963	Sheila Scott	Jodel DR.1050	G-ARUH	52	4th	205.95 km/h
1/8/1964	Margo A. McKellar	Turbulent	G-ARZM	-	10th	165.40 km/h
	Sheila Scott	Cessna 172B	G-ARMO	-	13th	213.19 km/h
	Beryl Sanders	Turbulent	G-ARRZ	-	15th	160.90 km/h
	Adèle Park	Bölkow 207	G-ASAW	-	abandoned	-
21/8/1965	Christine E. Hughes	Condor	G-ASEU	-	-	-
13/8/1966	Margo A. McKellar	D.H.82	G-ANDA	-	-	-
	Christine E. Hughes	Chipmunk 22	G-AOTG	-	-	-
	Sheila Scott	Piper Comanche 260B	G-ATOY	-	-	-
19/8/1967	Sheila Scott	Piper Comanche 260B	G-ATOY	-	-	-
	Margo A. McKellar	Condor	G-AVKM	-	-	-
24/8/1968	Gwen A. Smith	Condor	G-ASEU	-	-	-
	Sheila Scott	Piper Comanche 260B	G-ATOY	-	-	-
12/7/1969	Sheila Scott	Piper Comanche 260B	G-ATOY	-	-	-

During the race, Miss R.M. Sharpe broke the women's speed record over 100km with 519.37kph.

Grosvenor Challenge Cup – Lympne – 120 km

Date	Aviatrix	Plane	Reg.	No.	Posn.	Performance
18/9/1926	S.C. Eliott-Lynn	D.H.60 Moth	G-EBKT	-	-	-
30/7/1927	S.C. Eliott-Lynn	Avro Avian II	G-EBRS	8	-	-
	S.C. Eliott-Lynn	D.H.60 Moth	G-EBKT	9	-	-

Folkestone Aero Trophy Race

Date	Aviatrix	Plane	Reg.	No.	Posn.	Performance
5/8/1939	Mona R.V.E. Friedlander	Miles M.3B Falcon Six	-	-	8th	251.8 km/h

National Air Races – Organiser: Royal Aero Club

Date	Aviatrix	Plane	Reg.	No.	Posn.	Performance
29/7/1949	Miss R.M. Sharpe	Miles M.28 Mercury 4	G-AGVX	8	-	-
	E. Lettice Curtis (3)	Percival Proctor 3	G-ALIS	11	5th	236.92 km/h
	E. Lettice Curtis	Ercoupe L15	-	-	11th	181.01 km/h
6/1950	Miss M.M. Rendall	D.H.89A Rapide	G-ALBB	25	withdrew	-
	Lady Sherborne	Vega Gull	G-AFBC	30	28th	244.57 km/h
	Miss R.M. Sharpe	S. Spitfire F. Mk.VB	G-AISU	40	withdrew	-
23/07/1951*	E. Lettice Curtis (7)	Wicko G.M.1	G-AFJB	-	-	-
	Zita Irwin	Percival Proctor 5	G-AJET	-	-	-
	Mrs Y.M. Grace	Taylorcraft Plus D	G-AHKO	-	-	-
20/6/1953	Miss F.M. Leaf (1)	Hawk Major	G-ACYO	-	10th	205.95 km/h

Date	Aviatrix	Plane	Reg.	No.	Posn.	Performance
30/4/1955	Miss F.M. Leaf (6)	Tipsy Tr.1	G-AFWT	3	1st	152.86 km/h
21/7/1956	Miss A. Windle (4)	Miles W. Straight	-	-	6th	188.25 km/h
3/6/1960	Janet L. Ferguson (5)	Turbulent	G-APMZ	-	13th	136.76 km/h
	Joan H. Short (5)	Turbulent	G-APIZ	-	12th	135.96 km/h
	Margo A. McKellar (5)	Turbulent	G-APBZ	-	5th	145.61 km/h
9/7/1966	Anneliese Pinto	Turbulent	G-ARZM	-	-	-
	Margo A. McKellar	D.H.82	G-ANDA	-	-	-
	Christine E. Hughes	Chipmunk 22	G-AOTG	-	-	-
	Sheila Scott	Piper Comanche 260B	G-ATOY	-	-	-
23/8/1968	Gwen A. Smith	Condor	G-ASEU	-	-	-

Contest cancelled because of bad weather.

(1) Norton-Griffiths Challenge Trophy; (2) RAC International Trophy; (3) Siddeley Challenge Trophy; (4) Goodyear Trophy; (5) Orange Cup; (6) Grosvenor Cup; (7) Bristol Air Race.

Daily Express International Air Race – Organiser: *Daily Express*

Date	Aviatrix	Plane	Reg.	No.	Posn.	Performance
16/9/1950	Miss J.L.A. Hughes	Fairchild 24W-41A	G-AJAT	-	13th	-
	E. Lettice Curtis	Wicko G.M.1	G-AFJB	39	39th	-
	Zita Irwin	Percival Proctor 5	G-AIET	-	46th	-
	Miss R.M. Sharpe	D.H.89A Rapide	G-AKVU	-	56th	-
22/9/1951	E. Lettice Curtis	Wicko G.M.1	G-AFJB	-	-	-
	Zita Irwin	Percival Proctor 5	G-AIET	-	-	-
	Mrs J.H. Ashton	Hawk Trainer Mk.3	G-AKMN	-	-	-
	Mrs Y.M. Grace	Taylorcraft Plus D	G-AHKO	-	-	-
2/8/1952	Mrs Y.M. Grace	Taylorcraft Plus D	G-AHKO	-	-	-
	E. Lettice Curtis	Wicko G.M.1	G-AFJB	-	-	-
	Zita Irwin	Percival Proctor 5	G-AIET	-	-	-

British 99s Air Racing Challenge Trophy – Organiser: British Section of American 99s

Date	Aviatrix	Plane	Reg.	No.	Posn.	Performance
12/6/1965	Sheila Scott	Piper Comanche 250	G-	-	1st	291 km/h
	Christine Hughes	Rollason Condor	G-	-	2nd	193 km/h
	Diana Barnato-Walker	Auster Alpine	G-	-	3rd	193 km/h
	Margo McKellar	Druine Turbulent	G-	-	4th	159 m/h

England to Australia Commemorative Air Race – Organiser: BP

Date	Aviatrix	Plane	Reg.	No.	Posn.	Performance
18/12/1969	Sheila Scott	Piper Comanche 260B	G-ATOY	99	-	264hr 3min
	M.H. Kentley (1)	Money M20F	VH-ERX	-	-	-
	D.E. Dunster (2)	Piper Comanche 260	G-ATNV	-	-	-
	J. Irwin (3)	Beech V35 Bonanza	9J-REF	-	-	-
	S.A.Jones (4)	Beagle Pup 150	G-AXMX	-	abandoned	-

(1) Teamed with: P. Kentley.
(2) Team members: G.J. Dunster, I.F. Peradon, M. Glinski.
(3) Teamed with O.J. Irwin.
(4) Teamed with R.H. Britton.

III – German competitions

Deutschlandflug – 2,156km – Organiser: German Aero Club

Date	Aviatrix	Plane	Reg.	No.	Posn.	Performance
11-16/8/1931	Liesel Bach	Klemm	D-...	-	4th	5hr 26min 30sec
	Elly Beinhorn	Klemm	D-...	-	14th	6hr 1min 30sec
August 1932	Elly Beinhorn	Heinkel He 64	D-2304	C6	-	did not take part
22/6/1956	Elly Beinhorn	Piper L-4	CH-	-	2nd	-
20/6/1957	Irmgard Müller	Piper J3C	-	-	1st	-
20-23/6/1963	Edith Neuer	Piper Pa-22	-	-	-	975 pts
25-28/6/1975	Edith Neuer	?	-	-	3rd	-
1985	Christiane Collin	M.S.880	D-EOBE	-	1st	-
1991	Christiane Maurer	M.S.880	D-EOBE	-	1st	-
1995	Edith Neuer	Cessna 172	D-ERPE	-	1st	-
1997	Edith Neuer	Cessna 172	D-ERPE	-	1st	-
2005	Corinna Fuchs	D.V.20	D-ELED	-	1st	-

IV – Dutch competition

Rotterdam Meeting

Date	Aviatrix	Plane	Reg.	No.	Posn.	Performance
20-22/7/1928	Lady Heath	D.H.60 Moth	G-EBZC	-	1st	176.5 pts
	Miss O'Brien	D.H.60 Moth	G-EBOS	-	7th	104.3 pts

V – Italian competition

1st European Tourist Plane Circuit – Orly – (5,942km) – Organiser: ACF

Date	Aviatrix	Plane	Reg.	No.	Posn.	Performance
1930	Winifred Spooner	D.H.60G Gipsy Moth	G-AALK	38	4th	24hr 48min 23sec

VI – International Competitions

1st European Tourist Plane Circuit – Orly – (5,942km) – Organiser: ACF

Date	Aviatrix	Plane	Reg.	No.	Posn.	Performance
4-18/8/1929	Winifred Spooner	D.H.60G Gipsy Moth	G-AAAL	H6	10th	121.50 pts
	Lady Mary Bailey	D.H.60G Gipsy Moth	G-AAEE	H7	-	-

2nd European Tourist Plane Circuit – Berlin – (7,560km) – Organiser: AC Germany

Date	Aviatrix	Plane	Reg.	No.	Posn.	Performance
16/7-8/8/1930	Winifred Spooner	D.H.60G Gipsy Moth	G-AALK	K8	4th	416 pts
	Lady Mary Bailey	D.H.60G Gipsy Moth	G-AAEE	K6	31st	235 pts

MacRobertson Race – England–Australia Race – (18,200km) – Organiser: Royal Aero Club

Date	Aviatrix	Plane	Reg.	No.	Posn.	Performance
October 1934	Jacqueline Cochran (USA)	Northrop Gamma 2G	NC13761	30	accident	-
	Ruth R. Nichols (USA)	Lockheed Altair	NC13W	49	withdrew	-
	Jessie Keith Miller (GB)	Airspeed Courrier A.S.5a	G-ACLF	52	withdrew	-
	Laura Ingalls (USA)	Lockheed Orion	NR14222	53	withdrew	-
	Louise Thaden (USA)	Beech A17FS	NR12567	57	withdrew	-
	Jim & Amy Mollison (GB)	D.H.88 Comet	G-ACSP	63	abandoned	-

International Oases Rally– Cairo–Luxor (2,096km) – Organiser: Royal Egyptian Aero Club

Date	Aviatrix	Plane	Reg.	No.	Posn.	Performance
22-26/2/1937	Lilly Dillon (Irl.)	Klemm L.25c-1a	EI-ABD	56	1st*	-
	Loftia Al-Nadi (Egypt)	D.H.87B Hornet Moth	SU-ABT	49	8th	-
	G. Le Pelley du M. (F)	Caudron C.600 Aiglon	F-ANSH	31	-	-
	M. & S. Glass (GB)	D.H.60G Gipsy Moth	G-ABOE	57	-	-
	Elly Beinhorn (Ger)	Bf.108 Taifun	-	17	withdrew	-
	Viviane Elder (F)	Farman 402	-	53 ?	withdrew	-

Position in women's category.

VII – American competitions

1928   National Air Tour (NAT) – Edsel B. Ford Trophy – (30 June–28 July)

Contest	Aviatrix	Plane	Reg.	No.	Posn.	Score
4th NAT	Phoebe F. Omlie	Monocoupe 70	N5878	26	24th	5'523.0 pts

1929   National Air Races (Cleveland, Ohio, 24 August–2 September)

Contest	Aviatrix	Plane	Reg.	No.	Posn.	Performance
'Powder Puff' Derby – Santa Monica-Cleveland						
Class CW (less than 510 cu.in.)	Phoebe Omlie	Monocoupe 113/70	NR8917	8	1st	25hr 10min 36sec
	Edith Foltz	Eaglerock Bullet	R705H	109	2nd	41hr 37min 41sec
	Keith Miller	Fleet	N	43	3rd	52hr 24min 24sec
	Thea Rasche	D.H.60G Gipsy Moth	NC372H	61	4th	-
	Claire Fahy	Travel Air	N	54	-	abandoned
	'Bobbi' Trout	Golden Eagle	N223M	100		outside time limit
Class DW (510-800 cu.in.)	Louise Thaden	Travel Air B-4000	R671H	4	1st	20hr 2min 2sec
	Gladys O'Donnell	Waco 10	NC9558	105	2nd	21hr 21min 43sec
	Amelia Earhart	Lockheed Vega	NC31E	6	3rd	22hr 12min 42sec
	Blanche Noyes	Travel Air	N	3	4th	-
	Ruth Elder	Swallow	NC8730	66	5th	-
	Neva Paris	Curtiss Robin	N	23	6th	-
	Mae Haizlip	American Eagle	N	76	7th	-
	Opal Kunz	Travel Air	N	18	8th	-
	Mary von Mack	Travel Air 2000	NC6045	5	9th	-
	Vera Dawn Walker	Curtiss Robin	N	113	10th	-
	Marvel Crosson	Travel Air Speedwing	R6473	1	-	accident
	'Pancho' Barnes	Travel Air 4000	NX4419	2	-	accident
	Ruth Nichols	Rearwin K-R	N... 44E	16	-	accident
	Margaret Perry	Spartan C-3	NC8058	11	-	abandoned
Ladies race, class CW (80 km)	Phoebe Omlie	Monocoupe 113/70	NR8917	8	1st	180.80 km/h
	Keith Miller	Fleet	N	43	2nd	158.86 km/h
	Mary Heath	Great Lakes	N		3rd	154.74 km/h
	Blanche Noyes	Great Lakes	N	3	4th	136.96 km/h
Ladies race, class DW (96 km)	Gladys O'Donnell	Waco 10	NC9558	105	1st	221.40 km/h
	Louise Thaden	Travel Air B-4000	R671H	4	2nd	211.47 km/h
	Blanche Noyes	Travel Air	N	3	3rd	205.58 km/h
Australian Pursuit Race for Women (1)	Gladys O'Donnell	Waco 10	NC9558	105	1st	222.38 km/h
	Thea Rasche	D.H.60G Gipsy Moth	NC372H	61	2nd	156.57 km/h
	Frances Harrell	D.H.60G Gipsy Moth	NC235K		3rd	180.59 km/h
Australian Pursuit Race for Women (2)	Thea Rasche	D.H.60G Gipsy Moth	NC372H	61	1st	160.45 km/h
	Louise Thaden	Travel Air B-4000	R671H	4	2nd	220.16 km/h
	Gladys O'Donnell	Waco 10	NC9558	105	3rd	221.45 km/h

1929   National Air Tour (NAT) – Edsel B. Ford Trophy – (5–21 October)

Contest	Aviatrix	Plane	Reg.	No.	Posn.	Score
5th NAT	Jessie Keith Miller	Fairchild KR-34C	NC289K	20	8th	28,504.18 pts
	Mae Haizlip	American Eagle	NC506H	18	23rd	17,408.80 pts
	Frances Harrell	D.H.60G Gipsy Moth	NC235K	19	28th	abandoned

1930   National Air Races (Chicago, Illinois, 23 August–1 September)

Contest	Aviatrix	Plane	Reg.	No.	Posn.	Performance
Transcontinental Handicap Air Derby	Phoebe Omlie	Monocoupe 110	NC518W		1st	
Santa Monica-Cleveland (23 August)	Martie Bowman	Inland W-500	NC252N		2nd	

Contest	Aviatrix	Plane	Reg.	No.	Posn.	Performance
	Mae Haizlip	Monocoupe	N		3rd	
	Edith Foltz	Bird	N		4th	
	Louise Thaden	Thaden T-4	NC502V		5th	
	Gladys O'Donnell	Waco CTO	NC21M			
	'Pancho' Barnes		N			
	Jean LaRene	Reawin 2000-C	NC592H			
	Debie Stanford		N			
	Ruth Stewart	Curtiss Robin	NC75H			
	Joan Fay Shankle	Stearman	N			
	Mildred Morgan	Travel Air 4000	NC8192			
	Clema Granger	Swallow	NC8730			
	Mary Charles	Travel Air	NC684K			
	Blanche Noyes		N			
	Winifred Spooner		N			
Women's Pacific Derby (class DW)	Gladys O'Donnell	Waco CTO	NC21M		1st	15hr 13min 16sec
	Mildred Morgan	Travel Air 4000	NC8192		2nd	21hr 8min 35sec
	Jean LaRene	American Eagle	N		3rd	21hr 45min 49sec
	Ruth Stewart	Curtiss Robin	NC75H		4th	26hr 38min 6sec
	Ruth Barron	Buhl Air Sedan	NC5860		5th	38hr 33min 41sec
	Margery Doig	Pitcairn	N		-	abandoned
Women's Dixie Derby (class CW)	Phoebe Omlie	Monocoupe 110	NC518W		1st	11hr 42min 21sec
	Martie Bowman	Fleet	N		2nd	14hr 48min 39sec
	Laura Ingalls	D.H.60 Moth	NC9720		3rd	16hr 47min 26sec
	Nancy Hopkins	Kittyhawk B-4	NC30V		4th	19hr 18min 18sec
	Charity Langdon	Whitworth Avian	N		5th	20hr 44min 47sec
	Vera D. Walker	Inland Sport	N		-	abandoned
Women's 500-cu.in. Open Ships	Mae Haizlip	Inland Sport	N		1st	12min 23.9sec
	Vera D. Walker	Inland Sport	N		2nd	12min 25.9sec
	Laura Ingalls	D.H.60G Gipsy Moth	NC9720		3rd	13min 16.8sec
	Betty Lund	Inland Sport	N		4th	14min 7.5sec
Women's 500-cu.in. Cabin Ships	Phoebe Omlie	Monocoupe 110	NC518W		1st	11min 5.7sec
	Marty Bowman	Monocoupe	N		2nd	11min 11.6sec
	Gladys O'Donnell	Monocoupe	N		3rd	11min 22.3sec
Women's Free-For-All	Gladys O'Donnell	Waco CTO	NC21M		1st	20min 0.8sec
	Mae Haizlip	Cessna	N		2nd	20min 12.8sec
	Opal Kunz	Travel Air	N		3rd	20min 34.9sec
	Margery Doig	Pitcairn	N		4th	21min 32.5sec
	Phoebe Omlie	Monocoupe 110	NC518W		5th	22min 17.6sec
	Ruth Nichols	Laird	N		-	disqualified
	Mildred Morgan	Travel Air 4000	NC8192		-	abandoned
Women's 800-cu.in. Open Ships	Gladys O'Donnell	Waco CTO	NC21M		1st	10min 45.4sec
	Margery Doig	Pitcairn	N		2nd	11min 5.4sec
	Mildred Morgan	Travel Air 4000	NC8192		3rd	13min 59.2sec
Women's 800-cu.in. Cabin Ships	Phoebe Omlie	Monocoupe 110	NC518W		1st	10min 43sec
	Gladys O'Donnell	Monocoupe	N		2nd	10min 43.6sec
	Mae Haizlip	Cessna	N		3rd	11min 8.1sec

1930 National Air Tour (NAT) – Edsel B. Ford Trophy – (11–27 September)

Contest	Aviatrix	Plane	Reg.	No.	Posn.	Score
6th NAT	Nancy Hopkins	Viking Kitty Hawk B-4	NC30V	22	14th	36,528.0 pts

1931 National Air Races (Cleveland, Ohio, 29 August-7 September)

Contest	Aviatrix	Plane	Reg.	No.	Posn.	Performance
Transcontinental Handicap Air Derby	Phoebe Omlie	Monocoupe 110	NC518W		1st	
	Mae Haizlip	Monocoupe	N		2nd	
	Marty Bowman	Inland Sport	N		3rd	
	Edith Foltz	Bird	N		4th	
	Louise Thaden	Thaden R-4	N		5th	
	Gladys O'Donnell	Waco 10T	N		6th	
	Clema Granger	Swallow	NC8730		7th	
	Mildred Morgan	Travel Air 4000	NC8192		8th	
	Joan Shankle	Stearman	N		9th	
	Ruth W. Stewart	Curtiss Robin	NC75H		10th	
Women's 350-cu.in. ATC Race	Mae Haizlip	Davis	N		1st	13min 56.40sec
	Florence Klingensmith	Monocoupe	N		2nd	14min 30.60sec
	Bettie Lund	Aeronca	N		3rd	21min 24.62sec
Women's 510-cu.in. Free-For-All	Phoebe Omlie	Monocoupe	N		1st	13min 51.50sec
	Mae Haizlip	Gee Bee D	N		2nd	13min 54.08sec
	Maud Tait	Gee Bee E	N		3rd	14min 1.56sec
Women's 650-cu.in. ATC Race	Phoebe Omlie	Monocoupe	N		1st	13min 35.21sec
	Mae Haizlip	Gee Bee D	N		2nd	13min 38.68sec
	Maud Tait	Gee Bee E	N		3rd	13min 43.33sec
	Jean LaRene	Rearwin 2000-C	NC592H		4th	15min 0sec
Women's 800-cu.in. Free-For-All	Gladys O'Donnell	Waco	N		1st	11min 9.87sec
	Mae Haizlip	Travel Air	N		2nd	11min 23.77sec
	Opal Kunz	Waco	N		3rd	11min 46.24sec
	Florence Klingensmith	Cessna	N		4th	12min 3.69sec
	Bettie Lund	Waco	N		5th	12min 27.48sec
	Margery Doig	Pitcairn	N		6th	12min 30.69sec
	Maud Tait	Gee Bee E	N		7th	13min 30.57sec
	Mildred Morgan	Travel Air 4000	NC8192		8th	14min 59.41sec
Women's 1000-cu.in. ATC Race	Gladys O'Donnell	Waco	N		1st	10min 49.17sec
	Mae Haizlip	Laird	N		2nd	10min 57.49sec
	Florence Klingensmith	Cessna	N		3rd	11min 14.88sec
	Mildred Morgan	Travel Air	N		4th	14min 21.08sec
Women's 1875-cu.in. ATC Race	Florence Klingensmith	Cessna	N		1st	10min 37.31sec
	Mae Haizlip	Laird	N		2nd	10min 41.99sec

Contest	Aviatrix	Plane	Reg.	No.	Posn.	Performance
	Gladys O'Donnell	Waco	N		3rd	11min 0.21sec
	Joan Shankle	Lockheed Sirius	NC13W		4th	11min 4.48sec
	Mildred Morgan	Travel Air	N		–	abandoned
Women's Free-For-All Aerol Trophy	Maud Tait	Gee Bee Y	N		1st	15min 59.62sec
	Mae Haizlip	Laird	N		2nd	18min 9.58sec
	Florence Klingensmith	Cessna	N		3rd	18min 42.70sec
	Joan Shankle	Lockheed Sirius	NC13W		4th	19min 35.54sec
	Phoebe Omlie	Monocoupe 110	N		5th	20min 7.65sec
	Bettie Lund	Waco TW	N		6th	20min 20.85sec
	Opal Kunz	Travel Air	N		7th	20min 34.75sec
	Gladys O'Donnell	Waco	N		8th	20min 47.64sec
Men's & Women's Mixed Race	Opal Kunz	Travel Air	N		4th	20min 52.47sec
	Bettie Lund	Waco TW	N		–	–

1932 National Air Races (Cleveland, Ohio, 27 August–5 September)

Contest	Aviatrix	Plane	Reg.	No.	Posn.	Performance
Cord Cup Race –	Gladys O'Donnell	Monocoupe	N		4th	
	Edith Foltz	Bird	N		15th	
	Clema Granger	Stinson	N		38th	
William B. Leeds Trophy Race	Jessamine Goddard	Monocoupe	N		5th	
	Blanche Noyes	Travel Air	N		15th	
510-cu.in. Handicap Race	Florence Klingensmith	Waco	N		2nd	13min 48.50sec
	Helen McCloskey	Monocoupe	N		5th	14min 7.71sec
Sohio Mystery Derby	Helen McCloskey	Pitcairn	N		8th	3hr 57min 0sec
Aerol Trophy Race – Free-For-All	Gladys O'Donnell	Howard Mike	N	38	1st	12min 56.38sec
	May Haizlip	Wedell-Williams 44	NR536V	92	2nd	13min 6.34sec
	Florence Klingensmith	Monocoupe	N	14	3rd	13min 47.78sec
	Bettie Lund	Waco	N	–	4th	23min 39.20sec
Amelia Earhart Trophy Race	Florence Klingensmith	Monocoupe	N		1st	15min 7.39sec
	Edith Foltz	Bird	N		2nd	15min 31.99sec
	Helen Richey	Bird	N		3rd	15min 36.78sec
	Mary Sansome	Fleet	N		4th	15min 47.88sec
	Helen McCloskey	Monocoupe	N		5th	16min 21.47sec
	Rae Trader	Trader Special	N		6th	17min 14.01sec
Shell Petroleum Corp. Speed Dashes	Mae Haizlip	Wedell-Williams 44	NR536V		1st	411.120 km/h
	Florence Klingensmith	Monocoupe	N		2nd	319.565 km/h
	Bettie Lund	Waco	N		3rd	289.290 km/h

1933 Floyd Bennett Field (New York, 4 June – Organiser: Annette Gibson)

Contest	Aviatrix	Plane	Reg.	No.	Posn.	Performance
Bendix Trophy Race	Amelia Earhart	Lockheed Vega	NC-965Y	88	–	withdrew
	Ruth Nichols	Lockheed Orion	NR-988Y	112	–	abandoned
Annette Gibson All-Women's Air Race	Henrietta Sumner	Travel Air Speedwing	NC5426		1st	17min 7sec
	Frances Marsalis	Waco	N		2nd	
	Jessamine Goddard	Monocoupe	N		3rd	
	Mary Samsoe	Fleet	N		4th	

1933 National Air Races (Los Angeles, California, 1–4 July)

Contest	Aviatrix	Plane	Reg.	No.	Posn.	Performance
Aerol Trophy Race – Free-For-All	Mae Haizlip	Wedell-Williams	N	92	1st	17min 50.04sec
	Martie Bowman	Gee Bee Y	N	54	2nd	18min 33.12sec
	Gladys O'Donnell	Waco	N	–	3rd	22min 23.24sec
	Henrietta Sumner	Travel Air Speedwing	NC5426	–	4th	23min 5.53sec

1933 International Air Races (Chicago, Illinois)

Contest	Aviatrix	Plane	Reg.	No.	Posn.	Performance
Women's International Free-For-All	Mae Haizlip	Wedell-Williams	N		1st	307.49 km/h
	Florence Klingensmith	Gee Bee Y	NR718Y	7	2nd	304.16 km/h
	Martie Bowman	Gee Bee	N		3rd	271.69 km/h
	Henrietta Lanz	Howard Special	N		4th	198.08 km/h

1934 First Women's National Air Meet (Dayton, Ohio, 4–5 August)

Contest	Aviatrix	Plane	Reg.	No.	Posn.	Performance
Bendix Trophy Race	Jackie Cochran	Gee Bee QED	N	77	–	abandoned
20-mile Free-For-All Handicap Race	Jeanette Lempke	Great Lakes	N		1st	
50-mile Free-For-All Handicap Race	Helen Richey	Eaglerock	N		1st	38min 53sec

1935 All American Air Maneuvers (Miami, Florida, 10–12 January)

Contest	Aviatrix	Plane	Reg.	Nº	Posn.	Performance
Women's Handicap Race	Edna Gardner Kidd	Aristocrat	N		1st	157.94 km/h

1935 National Air Races (Cleveland, Ohio, 30 August–2 September)

Contest	Aviatrix	Plane	Reg.	No.	Posn.	Performance
Bendix Trophy Race	Amelia Earhart	Lockheed Vega	NR-965Y	88	5th	13hr 47min 6sec
	Jackie Cochran	Northrop Gamma	NX-13761	55	withdrew	
Ruth Chatterton Trophy Race	Grace E. Prescott	Travel Air	N		1st	
	W. S. Woodson	Fleet	N		2nd	
	Leland Hayward	Waco	N		3rd	
	Cecile Hamilton	Aeronca	NC14693		4th	
	Ethel A. Sheeby	Great Lakes	N		5th	
Women's ATC Race – Free-For-All	Edith Berenson	Bird	N		1st	18min 18.78sec
	Melba Beard	Bird BW3003	NC724N		2nd	18min 31.60sec
	Edna Gardner	Porterfield	N		3rd	18min 38.94sec
	Genevieve Savage	Great Lakes	N		4th	18min 51.58sec
	Peggy Remey	Travel Air	N		5th	18min 52.48sec

1936 National Air Races (Los Angeles, California, 5–7 September)

Contest	Aviatrix	Plane	Reg.	No.	Posn.	Performance
Bendix Trophy Race	Louise Thaden	Beech C17R	NR15835	62	1st	14hr 55min 1sec
	Laura Ingalls	Lockheed Orion 9D	NR14222	53	2nd	15hr 39min 38sec
	Amelia Earhart	Lockheed Electra	NR16020	20	5th	16hr 34min
A. Earhart Trophy Race, ATC Race	Betty Browning	Cessna C-34	N	-	1st	15min 58.62sec
	Gladys O'Donnell	Ryan	N	-	2nd	16min 10.01sec
	Genevieve Savage	Ryan	N	-	3rd	16min 27.25sec
	Jeannette Lempke	Davis D1-W	N	-	4th	16min 30.94sec
	Nancy Love	Beech	N	-	5th	16min 44.06sec
	Henrietta Sumner	Cessna	N	-	6th	16min 44.58sec
	Edna Gardner	Porterfield	N	-	7th	16min 47.29sec
	Melba Beard	Porterfield	N	-	8th	16min 58.08sec

1937 National Air Races (Cleveland, Ohio, 3–6 September)

Contest	Aviatrix	Plane	Reg.	No.	Posn.	Performance
Bendix Trophy Race	Jacqueline Cochran	Beech D-17W	NR18562	13	3rd	10hr 29min 8sec
Amelia Earhart Memorial Trophy Race	Gladys O'Donnell	Ryan	N	-	1st	208.612 km/h
	Betty Browning	Cessna C-34	N	-	2nd	232.600 km/h
	Edna Gardner	Cessna	N	-	3rd	219.725 km/h
	Annette Gipson	Monocoupe	N	-	4th	181.112 km/h
	Dorothy Munro	Rearwin	N	-	5th	143.029 km/h

1938 National Air Races (Cleveland, Ohio, 3–5 September)

Contest	Aviatrix	Plane	Reg.	No.	Posn.	Performance
Bendix Trophy Race	Jacqueline Cochran	Seversky SEV-S2	NX1384	13	1st	401.838 km/h

1939 National Air Races (Cleveland, Ohio, 2–4 September)

Contest	Aviatrix	Plane	Reg.	No.	Posn.	Performance
Bendix Trophy Race	Arlene Davis	Spartan Executive 7W	X-17605	51	5th	316.719 km/h
	Jacqueline Cochran	Seversky AP-9	NX1384	13	-	abandoned

1946 National Air Races (Cleveland, Ohio, 30 August–2 September)

Contest	Aviatrix	Plane	Reg.	No.	Posn.	Performance
Bendix Trophy Race (3,295 km)	Jacqueline Cochran	NAA P-51B	NX28388	13	2nd	4hr 52min 0sec
Halle Trophy Race (120 km)	Marge Hurlburt	NAA AT-6	N	81	1st	322.746 km/h
	Jane Page	NAA AT-6	N	54	2nd	322.543 km/h
	Ruth Johnson	NAA AT-6	NX6377	41	3rd	315.719 km/h
	Arlene Davis	NAA SNJ-3	N	35	4th	307.477 km/h
	Dot Lemon	NAA AT-6	N	72	5th	175.392 km/h

1947 National Air Races (Cleveland, Ohio, 30 August–1 September)

Contest	Aviatrix	Plane	Reg.	No.	Posn.	Performance
Bendix Trophy Race (3,295 km)	Jane Page Hlavacek	Lockheed F-5G	NX21765	63	9th	398.73 km/h
	Diana Cyrus	Douglas A-26	NX67807	91	-	abandoned
Halle Trophy Race (120 km)	Ruth Johnson	NAA AT-6 special	NX63770	75	1st	359.434 km/h
	Grace Harris	NAA AT-6 special	N90641	44	2nd	346.080 km/h
	Edna Whyte	NAA SNJ-2 mod.	NX62382	42	3rd	339.159 km/h
	Jane Page	NAA AT-6 mod.	N	83	4th	336.854 km/h
	Anna Logan	NAA AT-6 mod.	NX51499	65	5th	300.643 km/h
	Dori Marland	NAA AT-6 mod.	NX61629	49	-	accident

1948 National Air Races (Cleveland, Ohio, 4–6 September)

Contest	Aviatrix	Plane	Reg.	No.	Posn.	Performance
Bendix Trophy Race (3,295 km)	Jacqueline Cochran	NAA P-51B	NX28388	13	3rd	4hr 35min 7.3sec
Kendall Trophy Race (120 km)	Grace Harris	NAA AT-6	N90641	44	1st	378.05 km/h
	Katherine Landry	NAA SNJ-3	N	31	2nd	351.97 km/h
	Dorothy Lemon	NAA AT-6	N	23	3rd	351.84 km/h
	Betty Clark	NAA AT-6	N	49	4th	346.88 km/h
	Nancy Corrigan	NAA AT-6	N	83	5th	344.74 km/h
	Ruth Johnson	NAA AT-6	NX63770	75	-	abandoned

1949 National Air Races (Cleveland, Ohio, 3–5 September)

Contest	Aviatrix	Plane	Reg.	No.	Posn.	Performance
Women's Trophy Race	Grace Harris	NAA AT-6	N90641	44	1st	348.627 km/h
	Katherine Landry	NAA SNJ-3	N	31	2nd	345.735 km/h
	Helen McBride	NAA SNJ-3	N	91	3rd	338.046 km/h
	Betty Skelton	NAA AT-6A	N	45	4th	335.628 km/h
	Jane Page	Curtiss CW-22B	N	28	-	withdrew

1967 4th National Championship Air Races (Reno, Nevada, 20–24 September)

Contest	Aviatrix	Plane	Reg.	No.	Posn.	Performance
Women's Stock Plane Race (28 May)	Judy Wagner	Beech Bonanza	N5395E	11	1st	313.30 km/h
	Elaine Loening	Aero Cdr 100	N670CE	26	2nd	300.56 km/h
	Mara Culp	Aero Cdr 100	N960D	5	3rd	302.12 km/h
	Edna Whyte	Aero Cdr 100	N2910T	1	4th	286.13 km/h
Women's Stock Plane Race (4 Sept.)	Pat Arnold	P. Comanche 250	N8548P	7	1st	292.103 km/h
	Edna Whyte	Aero Cdr 200	N2910T	1	2nd	284.569 km/h
	Elaine Loening	Aero Cdr 200	N670CE	26	3rd	274.067 km/h
	Mary Knapp	Mooney Super 21	N3389X	3	4th	264.795 km/h
	Dot Etheridge	Mooney Super 21	N2916L	8	5th	256.018 km/h
	Dorothy Julich	P. Comanche 180	N7400P	4	6th	240.299 km/h

1968   5th National Championship Air Races (Reno, Nevada, 22 September)

Contest	Aviatrix	Plane	Reg.	No.	Posn.	Performance
Women's Stock Plane Final	Dot Etheridge	Meyers 200	N1888E	8	1st	306.814 km/h
	Elaine Loening	Meyers 200	N357CE	26	2nd	304.728 km/h
	Mona Coons	P. Comanche 260	N9217P	2	3rd	294.897 km/h
	Pat Arnold	P. Comanche 260	N8548P	7	4th	294.334 km/h
	Judy G. Wagner	Beech E-33C	N775JW	11	5th	288.236 km/h

1969   Florida National Air Races (Fort Lauderdale, Florida, 13–16 February)

Contest	Aviatrix	Plane	Reg.	No.	Posn.	Performance
Women's Stock Plane Class	Berni Stevenson	Waco/Marchetti	N730	6	1st	396.20 km/h
	Judy Wagner	Beech E33C Bonanza	N775JW	11	2nd	387.63 km/h
	Dot Etheridge	Meyers 200	N1888E	8	3rd	383.28 km/h
	Pat Arnold	Piper Comanche 260	N8548P	7	4th	376.91 km/h
	Dorothy Julich	AeroCommander 200	N5501M	66	–	abandoned

1969   Cleveland National Air Races (Cleveland, Ohio, 29 August–1 September)

Contest	Aviatrix	Plane	Reg.	No.	Posn.	Performance
Stock Plane Class Race (10 4 km)	Judy Wagner	Beech E33C Bonanza	N775JW	11	1st	316.10 km/h
	Mary Knapp	Marchetti SF-260	N7895	3	2nd	311.55 km/h
	Elaine Loening	Meyers 200	N357CE	26	3rd	302.75 km/h
	Dot Etheridge	Meyers 200	N1888E	8	4th	300.05 km/h

1974   11th National Championship Air Races (Mojave, California, 13 October 1974)

Contest	Aviatrix	Plane	Reg.	No.	Posn.	Performance
Formula One Championship Race	Judy G. Wagner	Shoestring IV	N44JW	44	3rd	346.744 km/h

1976   13th National Championship Air Races (Reno, Nevada, 12 September 1976)

Contest	Aviatrix	Plane	Reg.	No.	Posn.	Performance
Formula One Championship Race	Judy G. Wagner	Shoestring IV	N44JW	44	4th	354.720 km/h

1977   14th National Championship Air Races (Reno, Nevada, 18 September 1977)

Contest	Aviatrix	Plane	Reg.	No.	Posn.	Performance
Formula One Championship Race	Judy G. Wagner	Shoestring IV	N44JW	44	2nd	349.989 km/h

1979   16th National Championship Air Races (Reno, Nevada, 16 September 1979)

Contest	Aviatrix	Plane	Reg.	No.	Posn.	Performance
Formula One Championship Race	Judy G. Wagner	Shoestring IV	N44JW	44	3rd	374.108 km/h

1980   17th National Championship Air Races (Reno, Nevada, 14 September 1980)

Contest	Aviatrix	Plane	Reg.	No.	Posn.	Performance
Formula One Championship Race	Judy G. Wagner	Shoestring IV	N44JW	44	3rd	384.213 km/h

1981   18th National Championship Air Races (Reno, Nevada, 20 September 1981)

Contest	Aviatrix	Plane	Reg.	No.	Posn.	Performance
Formula One Championship Race	Judy G. Wagner	Shoestring IV	N44JW	44	2nd	356.989 km/h

1987   24th National Championship Air Races (Reno, Nevada, 20 September 1987)

Contest	Aviatrix	Plane	Reg.	No.	Posn.	Performance
Biplane Gold Race	Peggy Penketh	Pitts	N	4	8th	254.877 km/h

1989   26th National Championship Air Races (Reno, Nevada, 17 September 1989)

Contest	Aviatrix	Plane	Reg.	No.	Posn.	Performance
Biplane Gold Race	Peggy Penketh	Pitts	N	4	8th	256.658 km/h

1990   27th National Championship Air Races (Reno, Nevada, 23 September 1990)

Contest	Aviatrix	Plane	Reg.	No.	Posn.	Performance
Unlimited Bronze	Erin Rheinschild	P-51D	N35FF	553	1st	623.846 km/h
Formula One Gold Race	Katharine Gray	Aero Magic	N43SJ	43	7th	350.406 km/h

1992   29th National Championship Air Races (Reno, Nevada, 20 September 1992)

Contest	Aviatrix	Plane	Reg.	No.	Posn.	Performance
Biplane Gold Race	Patti Johnson	Boland Mong	N32RJ	40	3rd	308.774 km/h
Formula One	Katharine Gray	Pogo		87	3rd	339.499 km/h

1993   30th National Championship Air Races (Reno, Nevada, 19 September 1993)

Contest	Aviatrix	Plane	Reg.	No.	Posn.	Performance
Biplane Gold Race	Patti Nelson	Boland Mong	N32RJ	40	1st	335.422 km/h

1994   31st National Championship Air Races (Reno, Nevada, 18 September 1994)

Contest	Aviatrix	Plane	Reg.	No.	Posn.	Performance
Formula One Gold Race	Katharine Gray	Riddle GR-7	N687RB	96	4th	364.331 km/h
	Lynn Getchell	Wagner	N	2	7th	342.413 km/h

1995   32nd National Championship Air Races (Reno, Nevada, 17 September 1995)

Contest	Aviatrix	Plane	Reg.	No.	Posn.	Performance
Formula Gold Race	Katharine Gray	Riddle GR-7	N687RB	96	5th	360.297 km/h
Biplane Gold Race	Patti Johnson	Boland Mong	N32RJ	40	1st	325.217 km/h

1996   33rd National Championship Air Races (Reno, Nevada, 15 September 1996)

Contest	Aviatrix	Plane	Reg.	No.	Posn.	Performance
Biplane Gold Race	Patti Johnson	Boland Mong	N32RJ	40	1st	342.413 km/h

1997 34th National Championship Air Races (Reno, Nevada, 14 September 1997)

Contest	Aviatrix	Plane	Reg.	No.	Posn.	Performance
T-6 Gold Race	Mary Dilda	T-6	N	21	1st	366.857 km/h

1998 35th National Championship Air Races (Reno, Nevada, 20 September 1998)

Contest	Aviatrix	Plane	Reg.	No.	Posn.	Performance
T-6 Gold Race	Mary Dilda	SNJ-6	N73RR	22	4th	357.002 km/h

1999 36th National Championship Air Races (Reno, Nevada, 19 September 1999)

Contest	Aviatrix	Plane	Reg.	No.	Posn.	Performance
T-6 Gold Race	Mary Dilda	SNJ-6	N73RR	22	3rd	361.317 km/h

2000 37th National Championship Air Races (Reno, Nevada, 14–17 September 2000)

Contest	Aviatrix	Plane	Reg.	No.	Posn.	Performance
T-6 Gold Race	Mary Dilda	SNJ-6	N73RR	22	5th	351.906 km/h

2002 39th National Championship Air Races (Reno, Nevada, 15 September 2002)

Contest	Aviatrix	Plane	Reg.	No.	Posn.	Performance
T-6 Gold Race	Mary Dilda	SNJ-6	N73RR	22	4th	356.070 km/h
Jet Gold Race	Mary Dilda	L-39 Albatros	N92NL	22	2nd	732.278 km/h

2003 40th National Championship Air Races (Reno, Nevada, 14 September 2003)

Contest	Aviatrix	Plane	Reg.	No.	Posn.	Performance
T-6 Gold Race	Mary Dilda	SNJ-6	N73RR	22	2nd	375.713 km/h
Jet Gold Race	Mary Dilda	L-39 Albatros	N92NL	22	1st	698.337 km/h

2004 41st National Championship Air Races (Reno, Nevada, 19 September 2004)

Contest	Aviatrix	Plane	Reg.	No.	Posn.	Performance
T-6 Gold Race	Mary Dilda	SNJ-6	N73RR	22	2nd	381.409 km/h

2005 42nd National Championship Air Races (Reno, Nevada, 18 September 2005)

Contest	Aviatrix	Plane	Reg.	No.	Posn.	Performance
T-6 Gold Race	Mary Dilda	SNJ-6	N73RR	22	1st	381.623 km/h
Sport Gold Race	Lynn Farnsworth	Lancair Legacy	N23LF	44	4th	547.773 km/h

2006 43rd National Championship Air Races (Reno, Nevada, 17 September 2006)

Contest	Aviatrix	Plane	Reg.	No.	Posn.	Performance
Sport Gold Race	Lynn Farnsworth	Lancair Legacy	N23LF	44	4th	542.868 km/h

2007 44th National Championship Air Races (Reno, Nevada, 12–16 September 2007)

Contest	Aviatrix	Plane	Reg.	No.	Posn.	Performance
T-6 Gold Race	Mary Dilda	SNJ-6	N73RR	22	4th	364.450 km/h
Sport Super Sport Gold Race	Lynn Farnsworth	Lancair Legacy	N23LF	44	4th	564.569 km/h

2008 45th National Championship Air Races (Reno, Nevada, 10–14 September 2008)

Contest	Aviatrix	Plane	Reg.	No.	Posn.	Performance
Sport Super Sport Gold Race	Lynn Farnsworth	Lancair Legacy	N23LF	44	3rd	553.829 km/h
Biplane Gold Race	Leah Sommer	Pitts S-1S	N11PJ	10	4th	303.539 km/h

2009 46th National Championship Air Races (Reno, Nevada, 16–20 September 2009)

Contest	Aviatrix	Plane	Reg.	No.	Posn.	Performance
Sport Super Sport Gold Race	Lynn Farnsworth	Lancair Legacy	N23LF	44	withdrew	–

Appendix 2

Characteristics and performance of the principal planes used by aviatrixes

Builder, model (year)	Engine	Power. (hp/kgp)	Wingspn. (m)	Length (m)	Wing area (m²)	Empty weight (kg)	Loaded weight (kg)	Max. speed (km/h)	Cruising speed (km/h)	Range (km)	Users
Aeronca C-2 (1929)	1 x Aeronca E-107A	30	10.98	6.10	13.2	180	305	128	104	380	H. Richey, I. Crum
Avro 594 Avian Mk.III (1926)	1 x ADC Cirrus III	95	8.53	7.39	22.8	424	651	164	140	645	Lady Heath
Beechcraft 17R Staggerwing (1932)	1 x Wright R-975-E2	420	10.46	7.39	30.0	1,223	2,038	323	273	1,220	L. Thaden, B. Noyes, J. Cochran
Bellanca CH-400 Skyrocket (1930)	1 x P & W Wasp C-1	420	14.10	8,50	25.4	1,176	2,085	249	215	1,080	E. Newcomer
Beriev MP-1bis (1937)	1 x M-34N	750	19.00	13.5	55.0	3,120	5,185	260	-	1,500	P. Ossipenko
Blackburn Bluebird IV (1929)	1 x DH Gipsy I	100	9.14	7.06	22.8	485	794	193	137	515	Mrs V. Bruce
Breguet 330 (1931)	1 x Hispano-Suiza 2Nb	650	17.01	9.85	47.9	1,866	2,598	250	-	900	M. Hilsz
Canadair F-86 Sabre 3 (1952)	1 x Avro Orenda 3	2,724	11.57	11.43	26.7	4,737	6,618	1,087	-	2,400	J. Cochran
Caudron G.3 (1914)	1 x Le Rhône	80	13.2	6.4	28.1	445	735	112	90	-	A. Bolland
Caudron C.109 (1925)	1 x Salmson 9Ad	40	11.50	6.44	19.1	345	532	122	-	350	M. Hilsz, L. Bernstein, M. Bastié
Caudron C.127 (1924)	1 x Le Rhône 9C	80	12.00	8,30	34.5	520	790	132	-	-	A. Bolland
Caudron C.450 (1934)	1 x Renault 456	300	6.74	7.12	6.9	520	900	500	-	-	H. Boucher
Caudron C.530 Rafale (1934)	1 x Renault 4Pei	140	9,20	7.50	12.0	545	880	300	265	1,300	H. Boucher, M. Charnaux
Caudron C.600 Aiglon (1937)	1 x Renault 4Pgi	100	11.38	7.64	14.5	619	1,160	210	-	5,000	E. Lion, A. Dupeyron
Caudron C.620 Simoun (1937)	1 x Renault 6Pfi	170	10.40	8.97	16.0	978	1,675	300	280	5,350	M. Hilsz
Caudron C.635 Simoun (1936)	1 x Renault 6Q-09	220	10.40	8.70	16.0	855	1,350	310	280	1,230	M. Bastié
Caudron C.684 (1936)	1 x Renault 6Pfi	170	7.70	7.07	9.0	640	1,000	307	-	1,550	M. Hilsz
Cessna 180 Skywagon (1953)	1 x Continental O-470-A	225	10.98	7.98	16.0	690	1,158	265	252	1,250	G.L. Mock
Cessna 206 (1964)	1 x Continental IO-520-F	300	11.15	8.53	16.3	776	1,633	280	264	1,335	G.L. Mock
Curtiss JN-4 Canuck (1916)	1 x Curtiss OX-5	90	13.29	8.29	33.5	631	872	120	96	-	N. Snook, A. Earhart
Curtiss 50C Robin C-1 (1928)	1 x Curtiss Challenger	185	12.49	7.64	20.7	771	1,107	193	164	480	E. Trout, E.M. Cooper, V.D. Walker
Dassault Mirage IIIC (1958)	1 x SNECMA ATAR 9B	6,000	8.22	14.75	34.8	5,922	11,700	2,300	-	1,200	J. Auriol
De Havilland D.H.60 Moth (1925)	1 x ADC Cirrus I	60	9.14	7.23	22.6	350	562	146	129	515	M. Bailey
De Havilland D.H.60G Gipsy Moth (1927)	1 x DH Gipsy I	100	9.14	7.29	22.6	417	748	164	137	515	L. Ingalls, A. Johnson, J. Batten
De Havilland D.H.80A Puss Moth (1929)	1 x DH Gipsy III	120	11.20	7.62	20.6	574	930	206	174	480	A. Johnson, M. Bailey, P. Salaman
De Havilland D.H.84 Dragon I (1932)	2 x DH Gipsy Major	130	14.43	10.52	34.9	1,043	1,905	206	175	740	A. Johnson
De Havilland D.H.88 Comet (1934)	2 x DH Gipsy Six R	230	13.41	8.84	64.8	1,288	2,414	381	354	4,700	B. Kirby-Green
Extra EA300S (1988)	1 x Lycoming AEIO-L1B5	300	8.00	6.90	10.7	672	950	407	-	2,960	C. Maunoury
Fairchild KR-125 (1930)	1 x Fairchild 6-390	125	8.23	6.73	17.9	587	857	180	153	610	L. Ingalls
Farman 192 (1930)	1 x Salmson 9Ab	230	14.38	10.38	40.2	1,007	1,800	200	160	800	L. Bernstein
Farman 230 (1930)	1 x Salmson 9Ad	40	8.10	5.56	10.8	275	443	150	-	450	L. Bernstein
Farman 291 (1931)	1 x Gnome Rhône 7Kb	300	14.38	10.42	40.2	1,122	1,900	193	-	840	M. Hilsz
Farman 357 (1933)	1 x Renault 4Pdi	120	9.35	6.40	15.8	487	885	252	-	1,300	M. Charnaux, G. Lallus
Gee Bee Y (1931)	1 x P & W Wasp Jr.	535	7.77	4.60	7.0	635	1,034	434	370	1,600	M. Tait, F. Klingensmith
Golden Eagle Chief (1929)	1 x LeBlond 7-D	90	9,30	6.40	15.3	438	671	193	158	600	E. Trout
Grumman F6F-5 Hellcat (1942)	1 x P & W R-2800-10W	2,000	13.06	10.24	31.0	4,190	5,779	611	270	1,755	T. Kenyon
Heinkel He 64 (1932)	1 x Argus As 8R	150	9.80	8.30	14.4	425	740	245	225	900	E. Beinhorn
Heinkel He 71b (1933)	1 x Hirth HM 4	78	9.50	6.97	12.9	335	670	212	-	2,500	E. Beinhorn
Junkers A50 (1929)	1 x AS Genet	80	10.02	7.12	13.7	360	600	172	145	600	M. von Etzdorf
Klemm L25al (1935)	1 x Salmson 9Ad	40	13.00	7.00	20.0	300	620	130	115	630	M. Fusbahn, M. Bastié, L. Bach
Klemm L.26eV (1930)	1 x Argus As.8	120	13.00	7.45	20.0	520	900	175	-	515	E. Beinhorn
Klemm L.32V (1932)	1 x Argus KRei	148	12.00	7.60	17.0	480	780	220	178	750	L. Bonney
Klemm L.35B (1937)	1 x Hirth HM 504 A2	105	10.40	7.50	15.2	460	750	212	190	665	L. Bach
Lockheed Vega 5C (1928)	1 x P & W Wasp C	420	12.49	8.38	25.5	1,163	2,041	298	265	1,165	A. Earhart, R. Nichols, E. Smith
Lockheed 3 Air Express (1928)	1 x P & W Wasp C	420	12,95	8.38	26.8	1,149	1,984	269	217	1,200	L. Ingalls
Lockheed 8 Sirius (1929)	1 x P & W Wasp C	420	13.03	8.64	27.2	1,468	2,220	333	282	935	A. Morrow-Lindbergh
Lockheed 9D Orion (1931)	1 x P & W Wasp S1D1	550	13.04	8.64	27.3	1,651	2,631	362	330	1,160	L. Ingalls
Lockheed 10-E Electra (1934)	2 x P & W Wasp S3H1	600	16.76	11.76	42.6	3,220	4,763	346	330	1,130	A. Earhart
Lockheed F-104G Starfighter (1960)	1 x J79-GE-11A	7,076	6.63	16.66	18.2	6,348	9,362	1,844	821	1,740	J. Cochran
Mauboussin M.122 Corsaire (1935)	1 x Salmson 9Aers	75	11.75	6.85	14.8	350	310	205	-	700	M. Hilsz
Messerschmitt Bf 108B-1 Taifun (1934)	1 x Hirth HM 8U	250	10.62	8.29	16.4	860	1,400	305	265	1,000	E. Beinhorn
Monocoupe 110 (1930)	1 x Warner Scarab	110	9.75	6.30	12.3	450	731	228	193	772	P. Omlie, M. Haizlip
Monocoupe 113 (1929)	1 x Velie M-5	65	9.75	6.02	13.3	385	612	158	137	800	F. Klingensmith
North American P-51C (1943)	1 x Packard V-1650-7	1,490	11.29	9.83	21.9	3,180	5,126	709	582	1,530	J. Cochran
Northrop T-38A Talon (1959)	2 x GE J85-GE-5A	1,744	7.70	14.13	15,8	3,475	5,465	1,295	930	1,770	J. Cochran
Percival Vega Gull (1935)	1 x DH Gipsy Six	200	12.04	7,77	17.1	714	1,247	274	257	1,000	J. Batten, B. Markham
Piper PA-24 Comanche 400 (1964)	1 x Lycoming IO-720	400	10.97	7.84	16.5	957	1,633	360	343	1,610	S. Scott
Piper PA-24 Comanche 260B (1965)	1 x Lycoming IO-540	260	10.97	7.71	16.5	784	1,406	312	293	1,160	S. Scott
Pitts S-1 Special (1966)	1 x Lycoming IO-360-B4A	180	5.28	4.71	9.15	326	521	283	227	500	M. Gaffaney, B. Stewart
Polikarpov U-2 (1930)	1 x M-11	100	11.40	8.17	33.1	635	890	150	100	400	Russian military aviatrixes
Potez 506 (1934)	1 x GR 14Kbrs	840	18.60	9.40	54.0	1,522	1,883	305	-	-	M. Hilsz
Raab Katzenstein RK 26a (1932)	1 x AS Lynx	215	8.40	6.55	20.2	-	1,100	190	-	-	L. Bach
Ryan B-3 (1929)	1 x Wright J6-9	300	12,90	8.61	26,0	1,021	1,814	222	180	1,200	M. Crosson
Seversky AP-7 (1937)	1 x P & W Twin Wasp	950	10.97	7.62	21.4	-	-	518	-	-	J. Cochran
SNCASE SE.535 Mistral (1952)	1 x HS Nene 104	2,270	11.60	9.37	25.9	3,480	6,100	925	-	1,800	E. Boselli
Sukhoï Su-26M3 (2003)	1 x M-9F	233	8.20	6.87	12.2	750	1,100	340	290	1,200	S. Kapanina, N. Sergeeva
Swallow F28W (1928)	1 x Wright J-5A	200	9.95	7.16	27.9	778	1,225	204	175	885	R. Elder, C. Granger
Travel Air 3000 (1926)	1 x Wright Hispano A	150	10.56	7.36	27.5	754	1,173	180	160	685	L. Thaden
Travel Air 4000 (1926)	1 x Wright J-5C	220	10.56	7.36	27.5	673	1,087	209	177	885	B. Noyes, L. Thaden
Travel Air Mystery Ship (1929)	1 x Wright J-6-9	425	8.89	6.15	11.6	672	883	370	297	-	F.L. Barnes
Udet Flamingo U-12a (1925)	1 x Siemens Sh 12	110	10.00	7.40	24.0	525	800	145	140	450	T. Rasche, L. Schröter, C. Schultes
Waco 10-T (1928)	1 x Wright J-5	220	9.22	6.86	21.1	810	1,179	217	177	1,290	G. O'Donnell
Wedell Williams 44 (1932)	1 x P & W Wasp Jr.	550	7.93	6.48	11.1	680	1,000	390	-	-	M. Haizlip
Wright-Bellanca WB-2 (1927)	1 x Wright J-5C	220	14.12	8.46	25.3	-	2,450	203	169	8,050	M. Boll
Yakovlev UT-1 (1936)	1 x Shvetsov M-11Ye	150	7.30	5.75	9.70	429	597	257	210	670	C. Mednikova
Yakovlev Yak-50 (1975)	1 x Ivchenko M-14P	360	9.50	7.46	15.0	740	875	320	-	495	L. Leonova, V. Yakova

Thea Rasche with her sponsor, Mrs Stillman, in front of the Bellanca named North Star. (H. Hazewinkel collection)

Names given by aviatrixes to their planes

Some aviatrixes personalised their aircraft by giving it a name that perhaps reflected one of its characteristics (eg *Trottinette* = scooter), someone close to them (eg *Mary Ann*) or the name of their birthplace (eg *Miss Cincinnati*), etc. The table below lists these nicknames, along with the full details of the plane and its pilot. The names of sponsors are not included.

Name	Type of plane	Prod. No.	Registration	Aviatrix
Akita*	Lockheed Vega 5 Special	619	NR496M	Ruth Nichols
American Girl	Stinson SM-1	M207	NX1384	Ruth Elder (passagère)
American Nurse	Bellanca CH-400	3004	NR796W	Edna Newcomer
Auto-da-fé	Lockheed Orion 9D	211	NR14222	Laura Ingalls
Baby Ruth	Monocoupe 110 Special	5W47	NC501W	Ruth Wells Baron
Bandeirante	Caudron G.3	-	-	Anesia Pinheiro Machado
Black Magic	D.H.88 Comet	1994	G-ACSP	Jim & Amy Mollison
Bluebird	Blackburn Bluebird IV	SB.245	G-ABDS	Mrs Victor Bruce
City of Long Beach	Piper Apache	-	N3251P	Joan Merriam Smith
City of Olympia	Travel Air 4000	203	NC1082	Glady's O'Donnell
Desert Cloud	D.H.80A Puss Moth	2247	G-ACAB	Amy Johnson
Gondolo	Arsenal Air 100	14	F-CBZF	Marcelle Choisnet
Good Hope	D.H.80A Puss Moth	2072	G-ABEH	Peggy Salaman
Harmony	Cessna 172			Vicki Van Meter
Jason	D.H.60G Gipsy Moth	804	G-AAAH	Amy Johnson
Jason II	D.H.80A Puss Moth	2077	G-AAZV	Amy Johnson & Mrs Humphreys
Jason III	D.H.60G Gipsy Moth	1868	G-ABOV	Amy Johnson
Jean	Percival Gull Six	D-55	G-APDR	Jean Batten
Jean Mermoz	Caudron 635 Simoun	7092.11	F-ANXO	Maryse Bastié
Joe I	Morane-Saulnier 60 Moth	1	F-AJOE	Maryse Hilsz
Joe II	Farman 291	7335.4	F-ALUI	Maryse Hilsz
Joe III	Breguet 330	02	F-AKFM	Maryse Hilsz
Kamerad	Klemm L.26 Va	341	D-2160	Elly Beinhorn
Kiek in die Welt	Junkers A50ce	3519	D-1811	Marga von Etzdorf
Ken-Royce	Rearwin 2000-C	103	NC592H	Jean LaRene
La Liberté	Caudron C.109/1	1	F-AHFE	Maryse Bastié & Maurice Drouhin
Lady Rolph	Curtiss Robin	-	-	Edna Mae Cooper & Bobbi Trout
Lest den Stürmer !	BFW M.23b	463	D-1671	Lisl Schwab
Lil' Stinker	Pitts Special S-1C	2	N22E	Betty Skelton
Lucky Thirteen	Blériot XI	-	-	Matilde Moisant
Mary Ann II	Travel Air 2000	574	NC6045	Mary E. von Mack
Maurice Finat	Caudron 600 Aiglon	7199.101	F-AOGT	Laurice Finat & Lt Raynaud
Mexico or bust	Travel Air 4000	379	NR4419	Florence 'Pancho' Barnes
Miss Chicago	American Eagle Phaeton	-	-	Jean LaRene
Miss Cincinnati	Lockheed Vega 5 Special	619	NR496M	Ruth Nichols
Miss Cleveland	Great Lakes 2T1A	189	NC302Y	Blanche W. Noyes
Miss Doran	Buhl CA-5 Air Sedan	10	NX2915	J. Pedlar, V. Knope & Mildred Doran
Miss Fargo	Monocoupe 113	277	7838	Florence Klingensmith
Miss Memphis	Monocoupe (Velie)	58	NC5878	Phoebe F. Omlie
Miss Moline	Monocoupe 113 Special	321	NR8917	Phoebe F. Omlie
Miss Tenneck	Lockheed Vega 1	14	NR7426	Ruth Nichols
Mrs ?	Lockheed Vega Special 5C	171	NR965Y	Elinor Smith
My Little Ship	D.H.60G Gipsy Moth	1812	VH-UPV	Maud Rose 'Lores' Bonney
My Little Ship II	Klemm KL.32V	402	VH-UVE	Maud Rose 'Lores' Bonney
Myth	Thruxton Jackaroo	N6850	G-APAM	Sheila Scott
Mythre	Piper Aztec E250	27-4568	G-AYTO	Sheila Scott
Myth Sunpip	Piper Comanche 400	26-52	N8515P	Sheila Scott
Myth Too	Piper Comanche 260B	24-4346	G-ATOY	Sheila Scott
North Star	Bellanca J	7085	NX3789	Thea Rasche
Offero	D.H.60G Gipsy Moth	1856	G-ABOE	Mabel & Sheila Glass
Outdoor Girl	Curtiss Thrush J	G-1	C-7568	Frances Marsalis & Helen Richey
Red Rose	Avro 594 Avian III	R3/AV/125	G-EBTU	J. Keith Miller & capt. Lancaster
Sauerland	Fieseler Fi 5R	-	D-ERIV	Ilse Fastenrath
Scarlett O'Hara	Lockheed Jetstar	5015	N172L	Jacqueline Cochran
Seafarer	D.H.84 Dragon I	6014	G-ACCV	Amy Johnson
Spatz	Raab-Katzenstein Kl Ic	70	D-1588	Luise Hoffmann
Spirit of Columbus	Cessna 180	30238	N1538C	Geraldine L. Mock
Taifun	Messerschmitt Bf 108B-1	825	D-IGNY	Elly Beinhorn
The American Girl	Stinson SM-1 Detroiter	M207	NX1384	George Haldeman & Ruth Elder
The Burberry	D.H.88 Comet	1996	G-ACSS	Betty Kirby-Green
The Dawn	Sikorsky S-36A	3	NX1282	Frances W. Grayson
The Flying Boudoir	Curtiss Thrush J	G-3	NR9142	Louise Thaden & Frances Marsalis
The Heart's Content	D.H.80A Puss Moth	2241	G-ABXY	Amy Johnson
The Huntress	Douglas A-26 Invader	44-34766	NX67807	Dianna Cyrus
The Messenger	Percival P.10 Vega Gull	K.34	VP-KCC	Beryl Markham
The New Cincinnati	Lockheed Vega 5 Special	619	NR496M	Ruth Nichols
The Tramp	Avro 594 Avian IV	320	G-AAHN	Andrée Peyre
Thursday's Child	Percival Proctor 4	NP353	G-AJMU	Mrs. R. Morrow-Tait
Tin Goslin	Thaden T-4	4	C502V	Louise Thaden
Tingmissartoq**	Lockheed Sirius	140	NR211	Anne & Charles Lindbergh
Trottinette	Klemm L.25al	179	D-1816	Maryse Bastié
Vincere	D.H.60G Gipsy Moth	1883	VH-UTN	Nancy Bird-Walton
Voyager	Rutan Modèle 76	001	N269VA	Jeana Yeager
Zanzi	Farman 230	10	F-ALGJ	Léna Bernstein

*In Indian: 'seek, discover'
**In Eskimo: 'one who flies like a bird'

Amy Johnson named her De Havilland biplane Jason after her father's fish business. (A. Pelletier)

Appendix 4

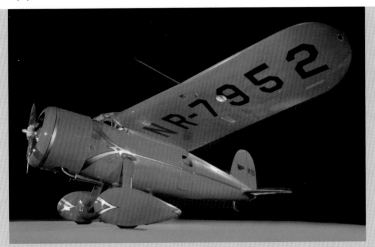

Amelia Earhart's Lockheed Vega 5B is one the jewels of the National Air & Space Museum's collection, in Washington D.C. (NASM)

Jean Batten's Percival Gull Six is suspended from the ceiling at Auckland International Airport in New Zealand. (Auckland IAP)

Liesel Bach's Klemm KI 35D on show at the Deutsches Technikmuseum in Berlin. (A. Pelletier)

The only extant Lockheed Sirius anywhere in the world is the one that belonged to the Lindberghs. It was named Tingmissartoq which, in Eskimo, means 'the one who flies like a great bird'. (NASM)

Amy Johnso first flew her De Havilland Gipsy Moth Jason on 5 May 1930. It can be seen today, suspended from the roof of the aviation gallery in the Science Museum, London. (A. Pelletier)

Preserved aircraft

Very few of the planes used by aviatrixes have survived to the present day. Some of the planes have been undergoing restoration for many years and at the time of writing are not on public display.

Plane (details)	Pilot	Present owner	Remarks
Avro 594 Avian III (G-EBUG/N7083)	Lady Heath, Amelia Earhart	Yellowstone Aviation Inc., Jackson, Wyoming, USA	Used on the first solo Cape Town-London on 5 January 1928, acquired in July 1928 by Amelia Earhart (NC541E)
Caudron G.3 no. 2551 (ex-F-AFDC)	Adrienne Bolland	Musée royal de l'Armée et d'Histoire militaire, Brussels, Belgium	Repainted in French Airforce colours
Caudron G.3 (identity unknown)	Anesia Pinheiro Machado	Museu Aerospacial, Rio de Janeiro, Brazil	
Cessna 180 (N1538C)	Geraldine Mock	National Air & Space Museum, Washington DC, USA	Used for round-the-world trip 19 March to 17 April 1964. Gift from Cessna
Curtis Pitts Special S1C (N22E)	Betty Skelton	National Air & Space Museum, Udvar-Hazy Center, Chantilly, Virginia, USA	Won the world international aerobatics championships in 1949 and 1950. Gift from Betty Skelton Frankman
De Havilland DH 60G Gipsy Moth (G-AAAH)	Amy Johnson	Science Museum, London, Great Britain	Used for the first solo flight from London to Australia from 5 to 24 May 1930
Extra 260 (N618PW)	Patty Wagstaff	National Air & Space Museum, Washington DC, USA	Won American aerobatics championships in 1991 & 1992. Gift from Katherine Hall Wagstaff
Farman 192 (F-AJJB)	Léna Bernstein	Musée de l'Air et de l'Espace, Le Bourget	Used in May 1930 to break the world women's endurance record
Klemm KI 35 (D-EDOD)	Liesel Bach	Deutsches Technikmuseum, Berlin, Germany	Used by L. Bach from 1955. Acquired by the museum in 1994
Lockheed Vega 5B (NR795)	Amelia Earhart	National Air & Space Museum, Udvar-Hazy Center, Chantilly, Virginia, USA	Used for the solo Atlantic crossing 20-21 May 1932 and for crossing of United States 24-25 August 1932. Gift from Franklin Institute
Lockheed Sirius (NR-211)	Anne Morrow-Lindbergh	National Air & Space Museum, Washington DC, USA	Transferred from USAF Museum in 1959
Monocoupe 113 Special (NR8917)	Phoebe Omlie	Ed Saurenman, Cheney, Kansas, USA (under restoration)	Won the first Powder Puff Derby August 1929
Percival Gull Six (G-ADPR)	Jean Batten	Auckland International Airport, New Zealand	Used to break the England-Brazil record, 11 to 13 Nov. 1933
Pilurs-Smith Miniplane DSA-1 (N1199)	Tracy Pilurs	International Women's Air & Space Museum, Burke Lakefront Airport, Cleveland, Ohio	Won the first women's national aerobatics championships 1962
Rearwin 2000-C (NC592H)	Jean LaRene	Pioneer Flight Museum, Old Kingsbury Airdrome, Texas, USA	Took part in Transcontinental Handicap Air Derby August 1931
Travel Air 4000 (NC4419)	Pancho Barnes	Harold Pinsky, Lucas County, Ohio, USA (under restoration)	Took part in first Powder Puff Derby August 1929
Travel Air 4000 (NR671H)	Louise Thaden	Air & Space Museum, Oklahoma City, USA	Took part in first Powder Puff Derby August 1929

Appendix 5

The Harmon Trophy

Awarded almost every year since 1926, the Harmon Trophy was established by Clifford B. Harmon to recognise the best pilots. There is one trophy for men and another for women, as well as a so-called 'National Trophy' which, until 1949, rewarded the best pilots. The table below lists all the aviatrixes to whom one of these trophies has been awarded.

Year	Harmon Aviatrix Trophy (1926-2006)	Harmon National Trophy (1926-1949)
1926	–	Shirley J. Short (USA)
1927	Mary Bailey (GB)	–
1928	Mary Bailey (GB)	–
1929	Winifred Spooner (GB)	–
1930	Amy Johnson Mollison (GB)	–
1931	Maryse Bastié (Fr.)	Ruth Nichols (USA)
		Amy Johnson (GB)
		Peggy Salaman (GB)
		Marta von Gronau (Ger.)
1932	Amelia Earhart (USA)	–
1933	Maryse Hilsz (Fr.)	Anne Morrow-Lindbergh (USA)
1934	Hélène Boucher (Fr.)	Laura Ingalls (USA)
		Maria Leloir de Udaondo (Arg.)
		S. Lippens (Bel.)
		Elly Beinhorn (Ger.)
1935	Jean Batten (NZ)	Bertha Alisch (Ger.)
	Amelia Earhart (USA), awarded posthumously	Elly Beinhorn (Ger.)
		Carina Negrone (It.)
1936	Jean Batten (NZ)	Louise Thaden (USA)
1937	Jean Batten (NZ)	Jacqueline Cochran (USA)
1938	Jacqueline Cochran (USA)	Élisabeth Lion (Fr.)
		Hanna Reitsch (Ger.)
1939	Jacqueline Cochran (USA)	–
1940/1949	Jacqueline Cochran (USA)	–
	Pauline Gower (USA), awarded posthumously	
1951	Jacqueline Auriol (Fr.)	
1952	Jacqueline Auriol (Fr.)	
1953	Jacqueline Cochran (USA)	
1955	Jacqueline Auriol (Fr.)	
1956	Jacqueline Auriol (Fr.)	
1961	Jacqueline Cochran (USA)	
1963	Betty Miller (USA)	
1964	Joan Merriam Smith (USA)	
1966	Sheila Scott (GB)	
1969	Turi Widerøe (Nor.)	
1970	Sheila Scott (GB)	
1971	Geraldyn Cobb (USA)	
1975	Marion Rice Hart (USA)	
1981	Janice Lee Brown (USA)	
1983	Sally Ride (USA)	
1984	Brooke Knapp (USA)	
1986	Jeana Yeager (USA)	
1987	Lois McCallin (USA)	
1988	Anne Baddour (USA)	
1989	Gaby Kennard (Aus.)	
1995	Eileen M. Collins (USA)	
2001	Jennifer Murray (USA)	

The Harmon Trophy. (DR)

In 1953, Jacqueline Cochran received the Harmon Trophy for the fourth time, on this occasion from the President of the United States himself. Standing between J. Cochran and Eisenhower is the test pilot, Charles Yeager. (USAF/FTCHO)

Appendix 6
The 'Powder Puff Derbies', 1947–1977

After the Second World War, one of the objectives of the '99' club was to revive the women's competitions. 1947 witnessed the first All-Woman Air Race, between Palm Springs, California, and Tampa, Florida. That year, the race had only two contestants, but the following year there were seven. In 1948 and 1949, the Jacqueline Cochran All-Woman Transcontinental Air Races (AWTAR) marked the official start of the competition that went under the name of the 'Powder Puff Derby' in memory of the Women's Air Derby of 1929 (see p. 51). During the 1960s, the 99s also organised the All-Woman's International Air Race, known as the 'Angel Derby'. The last AWTAR took place in 1977, a victim of rising costs, a lack of sponsors and increasingly dense air traffic.

Year	Course	km	Plane	Crew
1947	Palm Springs – Tampa	3,607	Ercoupe	Carolyn West/Beatrice Medes
1948	Palm Springs – Miami	4,087	Navion	Frances Nolde
1949	San Diego – Miami	4,093	Piper Clipper	Laurette Foy/Sue Kindred
1950	San Diego – Greenville	3,990	Taylorcraft	Jean Parker/Boots Seymour
1951	Santa Ana – Detroit	3,778	Cessna 140	Claire McMillan/Frances Bera
1952	Santa Ana – Teterboro	3,789	Cessna 140	Shirley Blocki/Martha Baechle
1953	Lawrence – Long Beach	4,309	Stinson 165	Frances Bera/Marcella Duke
1954	Long Beach – Knoxville	3,199	Cessna 140A	Ruth Deerman/Ruby Hayes
1955	Long Beach – Springfield	4,484	Cessna 180	Frances Bera/Edna Bower
1956	San Mateo – Flint	3,807	Beech Bonanza	Frances Bera/Edna Bower
1957	San Mateo – Philadelphia	4,130	Beech Bonanza	Alice Roberts/Iris Critchell
1958	San Diego – Charleston	3,503	Beech Bonanza	Frances Bera/Evelyn Kelly
1959	Lawrence – Spokane	3,974	Cessna 172	Aileen Saunders/Jerelyn Cassell
1960	Torrance – Wilmington	4,037	Cessna 172	Aileen Saunders/June Douglas
1961	San Diego – Atlantic City	4,359	Beech Bonanza	Frances Bera
1962	Oakland – Wilmington	4,097	Beech Bonanza	Frances Bera/Edna Bower
1963	Bakersfield – Atlantic City	3,990	Piper Cherokee	Virginia Britt/Lee Winfield
1964	Fresno – Atlantic City	4,140	Piper Cherokee	Mary Ann Noah/Mary Aikins
1965	El Cajon – Chattanooga	3,873	Piper Cherokee	Mary Ann Noah/Mary Aikins
1966	Seattle – Clearwater	4,626	Piper Cherokee	Bernice Steadman/Mary E. Clark
1967	Atlantic City – Torrance	4,018	Beech Bonanza	Judy Wagner
1968	Van Nuys – Savannah	3,973	Bellanca CM	Margaret Mead/Billie Herrin
1969	San Diego – Washington DC	4,047	Piper Comanche	Mara Culp
1970	Monterey – Bristol	4,441	Piper Comanche	Margaret Mead/Susan Oliver
1971	Calgary – Baton Rouge	3,929	Cessna 210J	Gini Richardson
1972	San Carlos – Toms River	4,209	Piper Comanche	Marian Banks/Dottie Sanders
1973	Carlsbad – Elmira	4,090	Cessna 182	Marian Burke/Ruth Hildebrand
1974	*No competition held in this year*			
1975	Riverside – Boyne Falls	4,169	Beech Bonanza	Trina Jarish
1976	Sacramento – Wilmington	4,714	Beech Bonanza	Trina Jarish
1977	Palm Springs – Tampa	3,525	Cessna RG177	Patricia Udall/Nanette Gaylord

Appendix 7
Women in space

Here is a list of female astronauts and cosmonauts in chronological order of their first flight into space. The gaps mark the interruptions in the shuttle programme following the *Challenger* (28 January 1986) and *Columbia* (1 February 2003) disasters.

Number	First space flight	First name, surname (country)	Remarks; flight nos	No. of flts
1	16 June 1963	Valentina V. Tereshkova (USSR)	1st woman in space; Vostok 6	1
2	19 August 1982	Svetlana Y. Savitskaya (USSR)	1st woman to do a spacewalk; Soyuz T7 & T12	2
3	18 June 1983	Sally K. Ride (USA)	1st American woman in space; STS-7 & -41G	2
4	30 August 1984	Judith A. Resnik (USA)	Died in Challenger disaster, 28 January 1986; STS-41D, -51L	2
5	5 October 1984	Kathryn D. Sullivan (USA)	1st American woman to do spacewalk; STS-31, -41G & -45	3
6	8 November 1984	Anna L. Fisher (USA)	STS-51A	1
7	12 April 1985	Margaret R. Seddon (USA)	STS-40, -51D & -58	3
8	17 June 1985	Shannon W. Lucid (USA)	1st Asian in space; STS-34, -43, -51G, -58 & -76	5
9	30 October 1985	Bonnie J. Dunbar (USA)	STS-32, -50, -61A, -71 & -89	5
10	26 November 1985	Mary L. Cleave (USA)	STS-61B & -30	2
11	18 October 1989	Ellen L. Schulman-Baker (USA)	STS-34, -50 & -71	3
12	22 November 1989	Kathryn C. Thornton (USA)	STS-33, -49, -61 & -73	4
13	9 January 1990	Marsha S. Ivins (USA)	STS-32, -46, -62, -81, -98	5
14	5 April 1991	Linda M. Godwin (USA)	STS-37, -59, -76 & -108	4
15	18 May 1991	Helen P. Sharman (GB)	1st Brit. woman in space; Soyuz TM-12/-11	1
16	5 June 1991	Tamara E. Jernigan (USA)	STS-40, -52, -67, -80 & -96	5
17	5 June 1991	Millie E. Hughes-Fulford (USA)	STS-40	1
18	22 January 1992	Roberta L. Bondar (Canada)	1st Canadian woman in space; STS-42	1
19	12 September 1992	Nancy Jan Davis (USA)	STS-47, -60 & -85	3
20	12 September 1992	Mae C. Jemison (USA)	1st Afro-American woman in space; STS-47	1
21	13 January 1993	Susan J. Helms (USA)	STS-54, -64, -78, -101 & -102	5
22	8 April 1993	Ellen L. Ochoa (USA)	1st Hispanic woman in space; STS-56, -66, -96 & -110	4
23	21 June 1993	Janice E. Voss (USA)	STS-57, -63, -83, -94 & -99	5
24	21 June 1993	Nancy J. Sherlock-Currie (USA)	STS-57, -70, -88 & -109	4
25	8 July 1994	Chiaki Mukai (Japan)	1st Japanese woman in space; STS-65 & -95	2
26	3 October 1994	Elena V. Kondakova (Russia)	1st Russian woman on space shuttle; TS-17 & STS-84	2
27	3 February 1995	Eileen M. Collins (USA)	1st fem. pilot and mission cdr.; STS-63, -84, -93 & -114	4
28	2 March 1995	Wendy B. Lawrence (USA)	STS-67, -86, -91 & -114	4
29	13 July 1995	Mary E. Weber (USA)	STS-70 & -101	2
30	20 October 1995	Catherine G. Coleman (USA)	STS-73 & -93	2
31	17 August 1996	Claudie Haigneré (France)	1st French woman in space; Soyuz TM-24/-23, TM-33/-32	2
32	4 April 1997	Susan L. Still-Kilrain (USA)	Pilot; STS-83 & 94	2
33	19 November 1997	Kalpana Chawla (USA/India)	1st Indo-American woman in space. Died in Columbia disaster, 1 February 2003; STS-87 & -107	2
34	17 April 1998	Kathryn P. Hire (USA)	STS-90 & -130	2
35	2 June 1998	Janet L. Kavandi (USA)	STS-91, -99 & -104	3
36	27 May 1999	Julie Payette (Canada)	STS-96 & -127	2
37	11 October 2000	Pamela A. Melroy (USA)	STS-92, -112 & -120	3
38	5 June 2002	Peggy A. Whitson (USA)	1st female cdr. of the ISS; STS-111/113 & TMA-11	2

Number	First space flight	First name, surname (country)	Remarks; flight nos	No. of flts
39	7 October 2002	Sandra H. Magnus (USA)	STS-112 & -126	2
40	1 February 2003	Laurel B. Clark (USA)	Died in Columbia disaster, 1st February 2003; STS-107	1
41	4 July 2006	Stephanie D. Wilson (USA)	STS-120, -121 & -131	3
42	4 July 2006	Lisa M. Nowak (USA)	STS-121	1
43	9 September 2006	Heidemarie M. Stefanyshyn-Piper (USA)	STS-115 & -126	2
44	18 September 2006	Anousheh Ansari (USA/Iran)	1st space tourist; TMA-9/-8	1
45	1 December 2006	Sunita L. Williams (USA)	Longest flight by a woman (195 days); STS-116/117	1
46	1 December 2006	Joan E. Higginbotham (USA)	STS-116	1
47	8 August 2007	Tracy E. Caldwell (USA)	STS-118	1
48	8 August 2007	Barbara Radding Morgan (USA)	1st teacher in space; STS-118	1
49	8 April 2008	Yi So-yeon (South Korea)	1st Korean in space; Soyuz TMA-12	1
50	31 May 2008	Karen L. Nyberg (USA)	STS-124	1
51	11 May 2009	K. Megan McArthur (USA)	STS-125	1
52	28 August 2009	Nicole P. Stott (USA)	STS-128, -129 & -133	3
53	5 April 2010	Dorothy M. Metcalf-Lindenburger (USA)	STS-131	1
54	5 April 2010	Naoko Yamazaki (Japan)	STS-131	1
55	15 June 2010	Shannon Walker (USA)	Soyuz TMA-19	1

Helen Patricia 'Lenochka' Sharman is, at the time of writing, the only British woman astronaut. She took part in Soyuz mission TM-12/TM-11, between 18 and 28 May 1991. (DR)

Tracy N. Caldwell was selected by NASA in June 1998. She took part in shuttle mission STS-118 on board Endeavour from 8 to 21 August 2007. (NASA/JSC)

The Quebecoise Julie Payette took part in two shuttle missions: STS-96 (27 May to 6 June 1999) and STS-127 (18 to 31 July 2009). (NASA/JSC)

Acronyms

ACF	Aéro-Club de France
ACdF	Aéronautique Club de France
ACFC	Air Corps Ferrying Command
ACI	Aero Club d'Italia
AFB	Air Force Base
ATA	Air Transport Auxiliary
ATC	Air Transport Command
CAG	Civil Air Guard
CAP	Civil Air Patrol
CEV	Centre d'Essai en Vol
DLH	Deutsche Lufthansa
DFS	Deutsches Forschungsinstitut für Segelflug
DLV	Deutschen Luftsportverband
FAI	Fédération aéronautique internationale
FLAT	First Lady Astronaut Trainees
GLAM	Groupe de liaisons aériennes ministérielles
IAP	Istrebitelny Aviatsionny Polk (Fighter Aviation Regiment)
NACA	National Advisory Committee for Aeronautics
NASA	National Aeronautics and Space Administration
NASM	National Air and Space Museum
NSDAP	National-Sozialiste Deutsche Arbeiter Partei (National Socialist German Workers' Party - Nazis)
NSFK	Nationalsozialistisches Fliegerkorps (National Socialist Flying Corps)
RAC	Royal Aero Club
RUNA	Reale Unione Nazionale Aeronautica
UPCF	Union des pilotes civils de France
USAAF	United States Army Air Force
WAAC	Women's Auxiliary Army Corps
WAFS	Women's Auxiliary Ferrying Squadron
WAFT	Women's Auxiliary Ferrying Troop
WASP	Women Airforce Service Pilot
WFTD	Women's Flying Training Detachment
WRAF	Women's Royal Air Force

Bibliography

1. General works on Aviatrixes

Beauregard, Marie Josèphe de, *Femmes de l'air* (France Empire, Paris, 1993).
Boase, Wendy, *The Sky is the Limit: Women Pioneers in Aviation* (MacMillan, London, 1979).
Brooks-Pazmany, Kathleen, *United States Women in Aviation, 1919-1929* (Smithsonian Institution Press, Washington, 1983).
Cadogan, Mary, *Woman with Wings* (MacMillan, London, 1992).
Cheeseman, E. C., *Brief Glory* (ATA Association, 2001).
Douglas, Deborah G., *United States Women in Aviation, 1940-1985* (Smithsonian Institution Press, Washington, 1991).
Du Cros, Rosemary, *ATA Girl* (Frederick Muller, 1983).
Escott, Beryl (Sqn Ldr), *Women in Air Force Blue* (Patrick Stephens Ltd., Somerset, 1989).
Gower, Pauline, *Women with Wings* (John Long, 1988).
Haynsworth, Leslie and Toomey, David, *Amelia Earhart's Daughters* (William Morrow, New York, USA, 1998).
Heath, Lady Sophie Mary and Murray-Wolfe, Stella, *Women and Flying* (John Long, London, 1929).
Holden, Henry M. and Griffith, L., *Ladybirds: The Untold Story of Women Pilots in America* (Blackhawk Pub. Co., 1991).
Hollander, Lu, Jessen, Gene N. and West, Vera, *The Ninety-nines, Yesterday-Today-Tomorrow* (Turner Publishing Co., Paducah, Kentucky, 1996).
Hormann, Jörg-M., and Zegenhagen, Evelyn, *Deutsche Luftfahrtpionere* (Delius Klasing Verlag, Bielefeld, 2008).
Italiaander, Rolf, *Drei deutsche Fliegerinnen: Elly Beinhorn, Thea Rasche, Hanna Reitsch* (G. Weise, Berlin, 1940).
Jablonski, Edward, *Ladybirds: Women in Aviation* (Hawthorn Books, Westerleigh, 1968).
Jessen, Gene Nora, *The Powder Puff Derby of 1929* (Sourcebooks Inc., Naperville, Illinois, 2002).
Kazimiera, Cottam, J., *Women in Air War* (New Military Publishing, Nepean, Ontario, Canada, 1997).
Lauwick, Hervé, *Conquérantes du ciel* (Presses de la Cité, Paris, 1958).
Lebow, Eileen F., *Before Amelia* (Brassey's Inc., Washington, D.C., 2002).
Lomax, Judy, *Women of the Air* (Dodd, Mead & Company, New York, 1986).
Marck, Bernard, *Les Aviatrixes* (L'Archipel, Paris, 1993).
– *Elles ont conquis le ciel* (Arthaud, Paris, 2009).
May, Charles Paul, *Women in Aeronautics* (Thomas Nelson & Sons, New York, 1962).
Merryman, Molly, *Clipped Wings: The Rise and Fall of the WASP in World War Two* (New York University Press, New York, 1998).
Millard, Liz, *Women in British Imperial Airspace, 1922-1937* (McGill-Queen's University Press, Montreal, 2007).
Mitchell, Charles R. and House, Kirk W., *Flying High: Pioneer Women in American Aviation* (Arcadia Publishing, Charleston, SC, 2002).
Moggridge, Jackie, *Woman Pilot* (Pan, 1959).
Moolman, Valerie, *Women Aloft* (Time-Life Books Inc., Chicago, 1981).
Myles, Myles, *Night Witches, The Untold Story of Soviet Women in Combat* (Presidio Press, Novato, California, 1981).
Nicolaou, Stephane, Mismes-Thomas, Elisabeth and Haignere, Claudie, *Aviatrices, un siècle d'aviation féminine française* (Altipresse, Levallois-Perret, 2004).
Noggle, Anne, *A Dance with Death, Soviet airwomen in World War Two* (Texas A & M University Press, 1994).
Oakes, Claudia M., *United States women in aviation through World War I* (Smithsonian Institution Press, Washington, 1978).
– *United States Women in Aviation 1930-1939* (Smithsonian Institution Press, Washington, 1991).
Paluel-Marmont, *Princesses de l'air, d'Adrienne Bolland à Jacqueline Auriol* (G. P., Paris, 1954).
Pennington, Reina and Erickson, John, *Wings, Women and War: Soviet Airwomen in World War Two Combat* (University Press of Kansas, Lawrence, Kansas, 2002).
Probst, Ernst, *Königinnen des Lüfte in Deutschland* (Grin Verlag, 2010).
Romeyer, Jean, *Aviatrices aux destins tragiques et glorieux* (Le Cercle d'Or, Paris, 1946).
Sakaida, Henry, *Heroines of the Soviet Union, 1941-1945* (Osprey Publishing Ltd, Oxford, 2003).
Schmitt, Günter, *Die Ladys in den fliegenden Kisten* (Brandenbrugisches Verlagqshaus, Berlin, 1993).
Tessier, Roland, *Femmes de ciel* (Correa and Cie, Paris, 1941; Flammarion, Paris, 1948).
Van Wagenen Keil, Sally, *Those Wonderful Women in their Flying Machines: The Unkown Heroines of World War Two* (Four Directions Press, New York, 1994).
Vogel, Heike, and Waibel, Barbara, *Die Schwestern des Ikarus* (Jonas Verlag, 2004).
Walker, Diana Bernato, *Spreading my Wings* (Patrick Stephens Limited, Somerset, 1994).
Walker, Mike, *Powder Puff Derby, Petticoat Pilots and Flying Flappers* (John Wiley and Sons Ltd., Chichester, Great Britain, 2004).
Whittel, Giles, *Spitfire Women of World War II* (Harper Perennial, London, 2008).
Zegenhagen, Evelyn, *Schneidige deutsche Mädel: Fliegerinnen zwischen 1918 und 1945* (Wallstein Verlag, Göttingen, 2007).

2. Autobiographies and biographies

Aigle, Caroline:
– Merchet, Jean-Dominique, *Caroline Aigle, vol brisé* (Jacob Duvernet, Paris, 2007).
André, Valérie:
– André, Valérie, *Ici ventilateur* (Calmann-Lévy, Paris, 1954).
Auriol, Jacqueline:
– Auriol, Jacqueline, *Vivre et voler* (Flammarion, Paris, 1968).
Bach, Liesel:
– Bach, Liesel, *Bordbuch D-2495* (Zeitgeschichte Verlag and Vertr. Gesell., Berlin,1937); *Den alten Göttern zu. Eine deutsche Fliegerin in Indien* (Greven Verlag, Cologne, 1954).
Bailey, Mary:
– Falloon, Jane, *Throttle Full Open* (The Lilliput Press Ltd, GB, 1999).
Barnes, Pancho:
– Grover, Ted, *The Lady who Tamed Pegasus* (Aviation Book Co., Glendale, California, 1984; Maverick, 1986).
– Hunter-Schultz, Barbara, *Pancho: The Biography of Florence Lowe Barnes* (Little Butes Pub, Lancaster, Calif., 1996; Little House, Lancaster, Calif., 2000).
– Kessler, Lauren, *The Happy Bottom Riding Club: The Life and Times of Pancho Barnes* (Random House, New York, 2000).
Bastié, Maryse:
– Amanrich, vice-amiral, *Une Française, Maryse Bastié* (Bardinière, Paris, 1953).
– Bastié, Maryse, *Ailes ouvertes, Carnets d'une Aviatrice* (Fasquelle, Paris, 1937).

– Clément, Virginia, *Maryse Bastié* (Les Flots Bleus, Monaco, 1956).
– Migeo, Marcel, *La Vie de Maryse Bastié* (Le Seuil, Paris, 1952).
Batten, Jean:
– Batten, Jean, *Solo Flight* (Jackson and O'Sullivan, London, 1934); *My Life* (Harrap, London, 1938); *Alone in the Sky* (Airlife, Shrewsbury, 1979).
– Mackersey, Ian, *Jean Batten, the Garbo of the Skies* (Macdonald, London, 1980).
– Baumgartner-Carl, Ann B., *Wasp Among Eagles* (Smithsonian Institute Press, Washington, 1999).
Bedford, Duchess of:
– Bedford, John, Duke of, *The Flying Duchess* (MacDonald, London, 1968).
– Curtis, Lettice, *Winged Odyssey, the Flying Career of Mary du Caurroy Duchess of Bedford* (Air Research Publications, Surrey, 1993).
– Gore, J., *Mary, Duchess of Bedford* (John Murray, 1938).
Beese, Melli:
– Probst, Ernst, *Melli Beese, die erste deutsche Fliegerin* (GRIN Verlag, 2010).
Beinhorn, Elly:
– Beinhorn, Elly, *Flying Girl* (Geoffrey Bles, London, 1935 – Original title: *Ein Mädchen fliegt um die Welt*); *Alleinflug mein Leben* (Langen-Müller, Munich, 1977); *Premieren am Himmel* (Langen Müller, Munich, 1991).
Bird, Nancy:
– Bird, Nancy, *Born to Fly* (Angus and Robertson, London, 1962).
Bonney, Lores:
– Gwynn-Jones, Terry, *Pioneer Airwoman; The Story of Mrs Bonney* (Rigby, Adelaide, 1979).
Boucher, Hélène:
– Caillava, Raymond, *Horizons sans fin* (André Martel, Paris, 1953).
– Chambe, René, *Hélène Boucher, pilote de France* (France Empire, Paris, 1964).
– Marck, Bernard, *Hélène Boucher, la fiancée de l'air* (l'Archipel, Paris, 2003).
– Mortane, Jacques, *Hélène Boucher, Aviatrice* (Plon, Paris, 1936).
– Rodier, Antoine, *Hélène Boucher, jeune fille française* (Flammarion, Paris, 1935).
– Tessier, Roland, *Hélène Boucher* (Flammarion, Paris, 1943).
Charnaux, Madeleine:
– Charnaux, Madeleine, *La Passion du ciel. Souvenirs d'une Aviatrice* (Hachette, Paris, 1942).
Cochran, Jacqueline:
– Cochran, Jacqueline, *Les étoiles de midi*; Original title: *The Stars at Noon* (France Empire, Paris, 1955); in collaboration with Marryann B. Brinley, *Jackie Cochran* (Bantam Books, New York, 1987).
Coleman, Bessie:
– Beal, Jacques, *Bessie Coleman, l'ange noir* (Michalon, Paris, 2008).
– Fisher, Lillian M., *Brave Bessie, Flying Free* (Hendrick-Long Pub. Co., Dallas, Texas, 1995).
– Hart, Philip S. and O'Connor, Barbara, *Up in the Air: The Story of Bessie Coleman* (Carolrhoda Books, Minneapolis, 1996).
– Johnson, Dolores, *She Dared to Fly: Bessie Coleman* (Benchmark Books, 1997).
– Plantz, Connie, *Bessie Coleman, First Black Woman Pilot* (Enslow Pub. Inc., Berkeley Heights, New Jersey, 2001).
– Rich, Doris L., *Queen Bess, Daredevil Aviator* (Smithsonian Institute Press, Washington, 1993).
Curtis, Lettice:
– Curtis, Lettice, *The Forgotten Pilots* (G.T. Foulis, London, 1971); *Lettice Curtis* (Red Kite, 2004).
Earhart, Amelia:
– Briand, Paul L., *Amelia Earhart, fille du ciel* (France Empire, Paris, 1960 – Original title: *Daughter of the sky*).
– Brink, Randall, *Lost Star, the Search for Amelia Earhart* (Norton, New York, 1994).
– Burke, John, *Winged Legend. The Story of Amelia Earhart* (Arthur Barker, London, 1971).
– Carrington, G., *Amelia Earhart, What Really Happened at Howland, Report II* (Britnav, Canada, 1989).
– Davis, Burke, *Amelia Earhart* (G. P. Putnam and Sons, New York, 1972).
– Earhart, Amelia, *20 hrs, 40 mins* (G. P. Putnam and Sons, New York, 1929); *Plaisir des ailes* (Gallimard, Paris, 1932); *Dernier vol* (Gallimard, Paris, 1938 – Original title: *Last Flight*).
– Earhart-Morrisset, Muriel, *Courage is the Price* (McCormick-Armstrong, Wichita, Texas, 1963); in collaboration with Osborne, Carol L., *Amelia, My Courageous Sister* (Osborne Publisher, Santa Clara, California, 1983).
– Goerner, F., *The Search for Amelia Earhart* (The Bodley Head, London, 1966).
– Goldstein, Donald M. & Dillon, Katherine V., *Amelia, a life of the aviation legend* (Brassey's, Washington, DC, 1997).
– Lesieur, Jennifer, *Amelia Earhart* (Grasset, Paris, 2010).
– Loomis, Vincent and Ethell, Jeffrey L., *Amelia Earhart, the Final Story* (Random House, New York, 1985).
– Lowell, Mary S., *The Sound of Wings, the Biography of Amelia Earhart* (Hutchinson, London, 1989).
– Marck, Bernard, *Amelia* (Arthaud, Paris, 2010).
– Putnam, George Palmer, *Soaring Wings: A Biography of Amelia Earhart* (Harcourt Brace, New York, 1939).
– Rich, Doris L., *Amelia Earhart, a Biography* (Smithsonian Institute Press, Washington, 1989).
– Snook-Southern, Neta, *I Taught Amelia to Fly* (Vantage Press, New York, 1974).
– Strippel, Dick, *Amelia Earhart: The Myth and the Reality* (Exposition Press, New York, 1972).
Gentry, Viola:
– Gentry, Viola, *Hangar Flying* (V. Gentry, Chelmsford, Massachusetts, 1975).
Hilsz, Maryse:
– De Chazeaux, Olivier, *Maryse Hilsz, la femme qui aimait tant le ciel* (Jean-Claude Lattès, Paris, 1999).
Johnson, Amy:
– Babington-Smith, Constance, *Amy Johnson* (Collins, London, 1967).
– Gillies, Midge, *Amy Johnson, Queen of the Air* (Weidenfeld and Nicolson, London, 2003).
– Johnson, Amy, *Skyroads of the World* (W. and R. Chambers, London, 1939).
– Smell, G., *Amy Johnson, Queen of the Air* (Hodder and Stoughton, London, 1980).
Markham, Beryl:
– Gourley, Catherine, *Beryl Markham: Never Turn Back* (Conari Press, San Francisco, California, 1997).
– Lovell, Mary S., *Straight on Till Morning: The Biography of Beryl Markham* (Century Hutchinson Ltd, Londres, 1987).
– Markham, Beryl, *West with the Night* (first edition, 1942 – North Point Press, New York, 1983).
– Trzebinski, Errol, *The Lives of Berryl Markham* (W.W. Norton and Co., New York, 1993).

Marvingt, Marie:
– Maggio, Rosalie and Cordier, Marcel, *Marie Marvingt: la femme d'un siècle* (Pierron, Sarreguemines, 1991).
Moisant, Matilde:
– Rich, Doris L, *The Magnificent Moisants: Champions of Early Flight* (Smithsonian Institute Press, Washington, 1998).
Morrow-Lindbergh, Anne:
– Hertog, Susan, *Anne Morrow-Lindbergh: Her Life* (Nan A. Talese, New York, 1999).
– Morrow-Lindbergh, Anne: *North to the Orient* (Harcourt Brace, New York, 1935).
– Winters, Kathleen C., *Anne Morrow-Lindbergh: First Lady of the Air* (Palgrave Macmillian, 2008).
Nichols, Ruth:
– Nichols, Ruth, *Wings for Life* (Lippincott, Philadelphia, 1957).
O'Donnell, Gladys:
– O'Donnell Doyle, Lorraine, *Second to None* (LSDS Publishing, Rancho Santa Fe, California, 2003).
Quimby, Harriet:
– Brown, Sterling A., *First Lady of the Air: the Harriet Quimby Story* (Tudor Pub., Greensboro, North Carolina, 1999).
– Davis, Anita P., *Harriet Quimby, America's First Lady of the Air* (Honoribus Press, 1993).
– Koontz, Giacinta B., *Birdwoman, the Incredible Life of Harriet Quimby* (Little Looper Press, Los Angeles, California, 2003).
Raskova, Marina:
– Raskova, Marina, *Fliegerinnen. Erlebnisse einer russischen Pilotin* (Paul-List Verlag, Leipzig, 1949).
Reitsch, Hanna:
– Jochim, Bertold K., *Hanna Reitsch, die erste Testpiloten der Welt* (Pabel, Rastatt in Baden, 1960).
– Lomax, Judy, *Flying for the Fatherland* (Trafalgar Square, London, 1990).
– Piskiewicz, Dennis, *From Nazi Test Pilot to Hitler's Bunker. The Fantastic Flights of Hanna Reitsch* (Praeger, London, 1997).
– Reitsch, Hanna, *The Sky my Kingdom* (The Bodley Head, London, 1955; Greenhill Military Paperback, Mechanicsburg, Pennsylvania, 1997 – Original title: *Fliegen, mein Leben); Aventures en plein ciel: du planeur à l'avion-fusée* (La Palatine, Paris–Genève, 1952; Éditions de la Table Ronde, Paris, 1973).
Scott, Blanche:
– Cumings, Julie, *Tomboy of the Air, Daredevil Pilot Blanche Stuart Scott* (Harper Collins, New York, 2001).

Scott, Sheila:
– Lomax, Judy, *Sheila Scott* (Hutchinson, London, 1990).
– Scott, Sheila, *On Top of the World* (Hodder and Stoughton, Londres, 1973); *Barefoot in the sky* (Macmillan, Basingstoke, Hants, 1974).
Sharp, Evelyn:
– Armour, Dian Ruth, *The Life Story of Evelyn Sharp, Nebraska's Aviatrix* (Dageforde Publishing, Lincoln, Nebraska, 1996).
Smith, Elinor:
– Smith, Elinor, *Aviatrix* (Harcourt, Brace Jovanovich, London and New York, 1981).
Stinson, Katherine and Marjorie:
– Underwood, John W., *The Stinsons, a Pictorial History* (Heritage Press, Glendale, Calif., 1976).
Thaden, Louise:
– Thaden, Louise, *High, Wide and Frightened* (Stackpole and Sons, New York, 1928; Air Facts Press, 1973).
Trout, Bobbi:
– Veca, Donna and Mazzio, Skip, *Just Plane Crazy, Biography of Bobbi Trout* (Osborne Publisher, Santa Clara, 1987).
Von Etzdorf, Marga:
– Von Etzdorf, Marga, *Kiek in die Welt* (Union Deutsche Verlagesell., Berlin, 1931).

3. Periodicals and magazines consulted:

French specialist press:
– *L'Aérophile, Les Ailes, L'Air, Aviation Magazine, Pionniers, Le Fana de l'aviation.*
– *Icare*: no 127, "Les IPSA et les convoyeuses de l'air"; no 196, "Les pionnières de l'aviation"; no 205, "Les conquérantes de l'air".
French periodicals:
– *L'Illustration, L'Excelsior.*
English-language press:
– *Flight, Aeroplane, AAHS-Journal, Airport Journal.*

Index of women referred to

For all the help and support they have given me throughout the lengthy preparation of this book, I particularly wish to thank: Shlomo Aloni, Giorgio Apostolo, Gerald Balzer, Michel Bénichou, André Bréand, Juan Arraez Cerdà, Hans-Peter Dabrowski, Trafford Doherty, Jim Dunn, Vital Ferry, René J. Francillon, Pierre Gaillard, Georges Grod, Harm J. Hazewinkel, Kevin Holcomb, Kirk W. House, Phillip Jarrett, Svetlana Kapanina, Volker Ross, Herbert Léonard, Michel Liebert, Chuck Mitchell, Jacques Moulin, Christian Ravel, Claude Salaün, Peter Selinger, John Underwood, Michelle Wardle and Alexander Zablotski.

I am also indebted to the following institutions and organisations:
AAHS, Audi AG, Auckland IAP, Beate Uhse AG, Boeing Company, Breitling, Curtiss Museum, DoD, EPAA (Stéphane Azou), GPPA, Grumman Historical Center, Imperial War Museum, Library of Congress (LoC), McKeesport Heritage Center, NASA/JFK, NASA/LaRC, National Museum of USAF, Segelflug Museum, Royal Australian Air Force, Canadian Forces, US Air Force, US Army, US Coast Guard, US Department of Defense, US Navy.

I especially wish to thank my wife, Maryse, for her patience, for proofreading the text and her assistance in translating numerous documents.

Acknowledgements